Rossanna Mensah

MURDER
IN ITALY

The Shocking Slaying
of a British Student,
the Accused American Girl,
and an International Scandal

Candace Dempsey

Name: Rossanna
Mensah

B

BERKLEY BOOKS, NEW YORK

THE BERKLEY PUBLISHING GROUP
Published by the Penguin Group
Penguin Group (USA) Inc.
375 Hudson Street, New York, New York 10014, USA

Penguin Group (Canada), 90 Eglinton Avenue East, Suite 700, Toronto, Ontario M4P 2Y3, Canada (a division of Pearson Penguin Canada Inc.)
Penguin Books Ltd., 80 Strand, London WC2R 0RL, England
Penguin Group Ireland, 25 St. Stephen's Green, Dublin 2, Ireland
(a division of Penguin Books Ltd.)
Penguin Group (Australia), 250 Camberwell Road, Camberwell, Victoria 3124, Australia
(a division of Pearson Australia Group Pty. Ltd.)
Penguin Books India Pvt. Ltd., 11 Community Centre, Panchsheel Park, New Delhi—110 017, India
Penguin Group (NZ), 67 Apollo Drive, Rosedale, North Shore 0632, New Zealand
(a division of Pearson New Zealand Ltd.)
Penguin Books (South Africa) (Pty.) Ltd., 24 Sturdee Avenue, Rosebank, Johannesburg 2196, South Africa

Penguin Books Ltd., Registered Offices: 80 Strand, London WC2R 0RL, England

The publisher does not have any control over and does not assume any responsibility for author or third-party websites or their content.

MURDER IN ITALY

A Berkley Book / published by arrangement with the author

PRINTING HISTORY
Berkley mass-market edition / May 2010

Copyright © 2010 Candace Dempsey
Cover design by Elaine Groh
Cover photos of Meredith Kercher and Amanda Knox © Franco Origlia / Stringer / Getty Images; othe photos: Jupiter Images.
Book design by Kristin del Rosario

ISBN: 978-0-425-23083-1

BERKLEY®
Berkley Books are published by The Berkley Publishing Group,
a division of Penguin Group (USA) Inc.,
375 Hudson Street, New York, New York 10014.
BERKLEY is a registered trademark of Penguin Group (USA) Inc.
The "B" design is a trademark belonging to Penguin Group (USA) Inc.

PRINTED IN THE UNITED STATES OF AMERICA

10 9 8 7 6 5

To my mother, Carmela Scarcello Dempsey. And to the dearly departed: my father, Curran Dempsey; sister, Carole Dempsey; uncles, Henry, Sam, and Arthur Scarcello; aunts, Amelia Scarcello Garcea, Ann Scarcello, and Esther Scarcello Travis; and cousins, Kevin Scarcello, Effie Leonetti, and Virginia Mantese. Thank you for the stories and the love. And to my irreplaceable grandparents, Josephina Esposito Scarcello and Antonio Scarcello, and my great-aunt Angelina DeLuca Scarcello and great-uncle Francesco Scarcello, for bringing your songs, tasty dishes, quick wit, strength, and gaiety from Calabria to America all those years ago.

Che noi possiamo ancora una volta incontrarci per il pranzo domenicale in Idaho!

May we all meet again for Sunday dinner in Idaho!

NOTABLE PEOPLE

THE VICTIM

Meredith Kercher: a British Erasmus scholar from Coulsdon, South London, UK

THE ACCUSED

Amanda Knox: Meredith's roommate, an honor student from Seattle, Washington, United States

Raffaele Sollecito: Amanda's wealthy Italian boyfriend, from Bari, Italy

Rudy Guede: a young drifter and Perugia resident originally from the Ivory Coast

Patrick Lumumba: Amanda's boss at the Le Chic bar, a Perugia resident originally from the Congo

THE FRIENDS AND NEIGHBORS

Filomena Romanelli and Laura Mezzetti: Meredith and Amanda's Italian roommates

Giacomo Silenzi, Stefano Bonassi, Marco Marzan, and Riccardo Luciano: their downstairs neighbors

Marco Zaroli: Filomena's boyfriend

Paola Grande and Luca Altieri: Filomena's best friend and her boyfriend

Robyn Butterworth, Amy Frost, Sophie Purton, Jade Bidwell, Helen Powell, Samantha Rodenhurst, and Natalie Hayward: Meredith's British friends in Perugia

Spyros Gatsios and Louerguioui (Juve) Juba: Amanda's friends in Perugia

David Johnsrud (DJ) and Madison Paxton: Amanda's friends in Seattle

Jovanna Popovic: Serbian medical student and friend of Raffaele's

Alexander Caudo, Giacomo Benedetti, and Gabriele Mancini: Rudy's friends

Hicham Khiri, aka Shaky: Tunisian pizza chef and friend of the British girls

Pasquale (Pisco) Alessi and Pietro Campolongo: co-owner and bartender respectively of Merlin's, a popular Perugia pub, and friends of the British girls

Esteban Garcia Pascual and Lucy Rigby: owners of La Tana Dell'Orso, a wine bar popular with the British girls

Elisabetta Lana, Alessandro Biscarini, and Fiametta Biscarini: the family that found Meredith's cell phones

THE FAMILIES

Arline and John Kercher: Meredith's parents

Stephanie, Lyle, and John Jr. Kercher: Meredith's siblings

Edda and Chris Mellas: Amanda's mother and stepfather

Curt and Cassandra Knox: Amanda's father and stepmother

Deanna, Ashley, and Delaney Knox: Amanda's siblings

Janet Huff and Christina Hagge: Amanda's aunts

Dorothy Craft Najir: Amanda's German cousin

Francesco and Marta Sollecito: Raffaele's father and stepmother

Vanessa Sollecito: Raffaele's sister

Giuseppe, Sara, and Annamaria Sollecito: Raffaele's uncle, aunt, and cousin

Roger Guede: Rudy's father, a resident of the Ivory Coast

Paolo Caporali: Rudy's adoptive father in Perugia

Aleksandra Kania and Davide: Patrick's common-law Polish wife and infant son

THE POLICE

Arturo De Felice: police chief, and commander of the Perugia police force

Domenico Giacinto Profazio: director of the Flying Squad in Perugia

Marco Chiacchiera: vice director of the Flying Squad

Monica Napoleoni: homicide chief, Flying Squad

Lorena Zugarini, Rita Ficarra, Oreste Volturno, Mauro Bigini, Stefano Gubbiotti, Stefano Buratti, Mauro Barbidori, and Armando Finzi: Flying Squad officers

Anna Donnino, Aida Colantone, and Assistant Fabio D'Astolto: Flying Squad interpreters

Edgardo Giobbi: head of SCO (Rome's Central Service Organization)

Daniele Moscatelli and Ivano Ruffo: SCO officers

Michele Battistelli, Fabio Marzi: Postal Police

THE SCIENTISTS

Patrizia Stefanoni and Renato Biondi: DNA analysts, Forensic Genetics Section, Forensic Police Service, Rome

Carlo Torre and Dr. Sarah Gino: DNA analysts for the defense

Professor Stefano Conti and Professor Carla Vecchiotti: neutral experts appointed by Appeal Court Judge Hellmann, from University of Rome–La Sapienza

Luca Lalli: coroner and pathologist who performed Meredith's autopsy

THE LAWYERS

Claudia Matteini, Paolo Micheli, Giancarlo Massei, Beatrice Cristiani, Claudio Pratillo Hellmann, and Massimo Zanetti: judges

Giuliano Mignini, Manuela Comodi, and Giancarlo Costagliola: Perugia prosecutors

Francesco Paolo Maresca and Serena Perna: Kercher family lawyers

Luciano Ghirga, Carlo Dalla Vedova, and Maria del Grosso: Amanda's lawyers

Giulia Bongiorno, Marco Brusco, Luca Maori, Delfo Berretti, Daniela Rocchi, and Donatella Donati: Raffaele's lawyers

Nicodemo Gentile and Valter Biscotti: Rudy's lawyers

Carlo Pacelli and Giuseppe Sereni: Patrick's lawyers

THE INTERNATIONAL MEDIA

Francesco "Frank Sfarzo" Sforza: Perugia-based investigative journalist and creator of the Perugia Shock blog

Zach Nowak: expat American writer, translator, and author of *Peril in Perugia*, a detective novel

Douglas Preston and Mario Spezi: American and Italian coauthors of the nonfiction bestseller *The Monster of Florence*

Meo Ponte: Italian crime reporter for *La Repubblica*

Elio Bertoldi: crime reporter for *Corriere dell'Umbria*

Richard Owen: reporter for the *Times* of London

Alessandro Capponi: crime reporter for *Corriere della Sera*

Fiorenza Sarzanini: reporter for *Corriere della Sera* and author of *Amanda e Gli Altri: Vite Perdute Intorno al Delitto di Perugia* ("Amanda and the Others: Lives Lost Around the Murder in Perugia")

Garfield Kennedy: director of Eye Films' *The Trials of Amanda Knox*

CONTENTS

PART ONE

THE MEREDITH
MYSTERY BEGINS

CHAPTER ONE

AN ITALIAN HALLOWEEN

Wednesday, October 31, 2007

"You may have the universe if I may have Italy."

—Giuseppe Verdi

NIGHT fell over the thick stone walls of Perugia, an Italian college town balanced atop one of Umbria's celebrated hills. Students wrapped in thick winter coats and blue jeans snapped up the last Count Dracula capes and Spider-Man masks left in the shops; soon the students would gather on the cobblestones along elegant Corso Vannucci, ready for a long night of Halloween costume parties and pub crawls. Too sophisticated for *dolcetto o scherzetto*, "trick or treat," they would instead descend steep staircases to underground bars and discos carved into medieval buildings as atmospheric as those from an Edgar Allan Poe horror tale.

On this chilly Italian night, twenty-one-year-old British exchange student Meredith Kercher was happy and excited. Called "Mez" by her friends and family, she planned to disguise herself as a vampire and celebrate with classmates in the *centro storico*, the walled "old town." A lovely girl with olive skin, big brown eyes, and long black hair, Meredith was a Londoner known for her intelligence, sense of humor, and dazzling smile. She looked charming in her Facebook photos, always beautifully turned out in smart little dresses or pastel sweaters over jeans, posing with friends in her favorite local bars, Merlin's Pub or La Tana Dell'Orso ("The Bear's Den").

> What are you doing tonight? Want to meet up later?
> Got a costume?

Meredith received a couple of text messages on Halloween night from Amanda Knox, her twenty-year-old American roommate, a third-year honor student from the University of Washington in Seattle. Amanda was a striking girl, momentarily blond, with startlingly blue eyes and an Ivory Soap complexion. Friends described her as energetic, athletic, and kind. She was a "pacifist hippie," they said, a maker of cakes and jam, a lover of soccer, yoga, rock climbing, bicycling, and guitar playing.

Perugia had nearly 40,000 college students, making up a quarter of its 160,000 residents. Over a long, rocky history, the old town had survived Romans, Goths, papal overlords, Napoleon's troops, and other intruders. By 2007 an ever-changing army of young people had turned the acropolis into a sort of college campus, a place to meet up, strum guitars, shop, drink beer, and act like university students anywhere. Many of the old families now lived in apartment towers outside the Etruscan walls, preferring modernity to the costly, cramped, and noisy lodgings in the silvery center where church bells rang all day and karaoke blasted all night. Students could find whatever they needed to keep the fun—and learning— going on Corso Vannucci, the grand pedestrian boulevard that offered everything from gelato shops, bars, boutiques, and movie theaters to bookstores, restaurants, and art museums. The Corso ran from the chic hotels on Piazza Italia to Piazza IV Novembre, Perugia's "living room," where many-tiered Fontana Maggiore sprayed steely water into the sky.

Italian scholars ruled the hilltop, vastly outnumbering the foreign invaders. In the fall of 2007, Italians accounted for nearly all of the 34,000 scholars enrolled in the *Università degli Studi di Perugia*, the University of Perugia, a public institution created before the discovery of the New World and housed in frescoed brick buildings located just behind and slightly downhill from Piazza Grimana, where 5,300 exchange students of innumerable nationalities studied at the *Università per Stranieri di Perugia*, the University for Foreigners.

While outwardly friendly, the Italian students tended to shun the here-today, gone-tomorrow foreigners when handing out party invitations. In places where people are just passing through, Italians lose their legendary affability, noted Tim Parks, author of *Italian Neighbors*: "A person they will never see again is not a person but a chore."

Created after World War I to showcase Italian language and culture, the *Stranieri* was a Tower of Babel occupying the gloriously weathered eighteenth-century Palazzo Gallenga, once home to the exiled House of Stuart, pretenders to the English throne. *Stranieri* scholars recited Italian grammar in the Baroque, frescoed rooms of the original palazzo, learned to roll their Rs in the unadorned fascist-era addition, and took classes on a modern campus of lemon-colored buildings set among pines outside the city walls.

Unlike the many foreigners who flitted in and out of Perugia like migrating butterflies, Meredith had signed on for a full school year in the prestigious Erasmus Project, an exchange program open only to Europeans. A love of Italy had brought her from Coulsdon, South London, to the Umbrian capital in late August. Like other Erasmus scholars, Meredith initially buffed up her Italian at the *Stranieri*, but then took courses at the University of Perugia. As she told friends on Facebook:

> I have been trying to go to uni. am taking modern history, modern political theories and cinema history. It's all mostly about the French revolution which i know nothing about, would say it's going well!! Miss u, especially dancing xx.

The British girl was one of a handful of exchange students in Perugia from the University of Leeds, a state-run university in Yorkshire with about thirty thousand scholars. Enrolled in the third year of a four-year European studies program, Meredith planned either to be a journalist like her father, John Kercher, or to work for the European Parliament in Brussels.

When Meredith first arrived in Perugia, she'd boarded in a hotel, but confided to her mother, Arline Kercher, that she felt lonely there and so looked about for shared lodgings. Now, two months into her Italian adventure, she had three roommates—Amanda and two Italian girls, Laura Mezzetti and Filomena Romanelli. They rented the upper story of a whitewashed *villetta*, a converted farmhouse cottage with a wild garden a few steps outside the city walls and close to the *Stranieri*.

Meredith was a serious student who burned the midnight oil, but she also loved to dance and read detective novels. Her newfound British friends, mainly from Leeds or the University of Manchester, said she was warmhearted and witty, but also cautious and a little reserved. They traveled around in a happy group, doing what foreign students have done in Perugia for generations: they threw dinner parties in tiny flats, shared fixed-price meals in restaurants, and went out for espresso, pizza, drinks, and dancing.

Meredith was never without a tiny British cell phone, because her mother had been hospitalized with kidney disease and might need to reach her. Yet she never seemed troubled, her friends said; she was always smiling and serene.

If she had any worries on her last Halloween, then she kept them to herself.

AMANDA Knox had dreamed of living in Italy since 2001, when she visited the country briefly on a family trip. Like so many other Americans, she'd fallen in love with the people, the food, and the culture. She planned to be a writer, translator, or a combination of the two. At the University of Washington (UW, pronounced "U-Dub"), she majored in Italian and German and minored in creative writing. Her mother, Edda Mellas, had been born in Germany, to a German mother who'd fallen in love with and married an American soldier. The family had moved to the United States when Edda was a young girl.

Amanda's family had encouraged her to study abroad in Germany, where relatives could help out if anything went wrong, but her Italian needed more work than her German, and so she chose Perugia. "I got advice that instead of going to Rome, where there are so many tourists, it would be better for me to go to a smaller place where I would be surrounded by Italians instead of other Americans."

Italians called Perugia, a sister city to Seattle, "the city of chocolate and jazz," famed for Perugina chocolates called *baci* (kisses) and the Umbrian Jazz Festival hosted each spring. Perugini were a "mountain people," liberal in politics but conservative in dress and behavior. Their windswept fortress near the sacred shrine of Assisi had always been a world apart from sunnier, more sensual Rome, about a hundred miles southwest, or arty Florence, the glamour choice for many exchange students, about a hundred miles northwest.

Month after month foreign students entered *il cuore verde d'Italia*, "the green heart of Italy," to hit the books, hang out in the old town, smoke hashish, quaff the local wines, sample the draft beer, taste the shaved-truffle pasta, try out their bad Italian in the kebab shops, and just as importantly, get on a first-name basis with the pub owners. If these newcomers did not achieve fluency in Italian, then they could at least impress visiting friends by ordering gelato flavors, pizza toppings, and espresso in the language of Dante.

Just being American made Amanda Knox unusual in the hilltop town. Of the 40,000 students, only a tiny percentage came from the United States. Not only did American exchange students typically prefer Rome or Florence, but the few who chose Perugia usually enrolled in the American-run Umbra Institute, where a few hundred scholars lived, studied, and socialized together. Instead, Amanda chose the *Stranieri* and looked around for her own lodgings. Amanda had moved into the cottage in mid-September and told her friends on MySpace that "I'm in one of the happiest places in my life."

If she had wanted a clean break from UW and its 43,000 students, then Perugia was the perfect choice. The giant university had placed three hundred scholars in Italy that fall, but nearly all chose the University of Washington Rome Center, housed in a palazzo on ultra-trendy Campo dei Fiori. Only three other UW students picked Perugia, but that was fine with Amanda. She told friends that she wanted a real adventure and total immersion in Italian culture. She liked the fact that *Stranieri* students had to speak Italian even to buy groceries, see a movie, or mail a package.

Away from home for the first time, she might also have been seeking the things many twenty-year-olds secretly desire. Freedom, change, and a roll of the dice.

"Ignorance is a pet peeve," she wrote on Facebook. "I love new situations and I love to meet new people. The bigger and scarier the roller coaster the better."

Amanda was also determined to spend as much time with Italians as she could. She wanted to *feel* Italian, she told friends, not realizing that she faced a cultural divide as broad as nearby Lago Trasimeno, Italy's fourth largest lake.

Amanda saw herself as a free spirit, a trait perfect for the West Coast of America but jarring in the deeply Catholic *Bel Paese*, where rules about how to cut a *bella figura* (how to look and act properly) were drummed into *bambini* at birth. In Perugia, Amanda dressed just as she did in Seattle, where tech billionaires showed up for work in fleece jackets and hiking boots, looking like they'd just scaled Mount Rainier. Her wardrobe also reflected her fondness for Beatles music and the flower-child look of the sixties. MySpace photos from Perugia showed her decked out in athletic sweats or girlish flowered tops over light-colored jeans or shorts. She looked neat and clean, but seldom wore makeup or fussed with her hair. If she had to dress up, then she wore a bright yellow sundress over sneakers or sandals.

"Amanda doesn't really care about clothes," said Madison Paxton, a serious-looking, brown-haired UW student and one of Amanda's college friends back in Seattle. Most of their "crew" of friends had met in the dorms freshman year or at the UW climbing wall, where students practiced the moves needed to scale the nearby mountains.

"Clothes are just things to wear," Madison continued. "A blouse. Pants. Shoes. That's how Amanda thinks. She just gets up in the morning and puts things on. She gave away lots of clothes and other things before she left Seattle. She wanted to save room in her luggage for her hiking and mountain-climbing gear. She thought she was going to take all these great side-trips in Italy. She wanted to get out into the countryside. She was excited about that."

In her diary, Amanda listed her Toshiba laptop computer, musical equipment, and hiking gear as her most important possessions, noting that she'd worked very hard to pay for them.

She always carried a big patterned bag, inside of which she stored brightly colored notebooks, the covers stamped with cartoon characters. She scribbled down her every thought, even her sexual fantasies.

A habit she would soon regret.

AMANDA and Meredith shared the picturesque cottage with two Italian girls, Laura Mezzetti and Filomena Romanelli. It hung over the Fossa del Bulagaio, a steep ravine tangled with shrubs and vines. An unruly garden, flush with pear and chestnut trees, flowed down into the wilderness without fencing at the bottom. Tenants could see the upper reaches of the Tiber River Valley and the Umbrian hills, spiked with church steeples, terra-cotta-roofed houses, vineyards, olive trees, chipped stone structures, flowering shrubs, and pines. The rolling hills turned to purple as they rose up to the snow-dusted peaks of the Apennine Mountains, offering what American novelist Henry James called Perugia's "infinite view."

When the flatmates were home, the cottage was a cheerful, bustling place. The side balcony had a white plastic table where Amanda liked to sit, enjoying the sun and strumming a guitar. Often, Meredith would pull up a chair next to her and read mystery novels.

Meredith and Amanda's bedrooms were in the back end of the apartment, side by side, in a modern addition that faced the ravine. The two Italian roommates had chosen bedrooms nearer to the street and next to each other. Laura and Filomena were in their late twenties, close friends, and trainee lawyers in the same local law firm. They'd found the cottage through a leasing agent in August 2007 and then run newspaper ads and posted flyers in search of additional tenants.

Amanda had responded first. She'd breezed into Perugia at the tail end of August on a two-day trip with Deanna, her much taller and blonder nineteen-year-old sister. The Seattle girls got lost their first day and wandered up and down the steep slopes of town, becoming hot and cranky, until finally locating their hotel. The next day they'd explored the old town, charmed by the chic shops on the Corso.

In a video Deanna shot around that time, Amanda fidgeted with her hair and fretted about finding lodgings for the semester, saying she could think of nothing else. So on September 2, the sisters spent a stressful day searching for a place Amanda could rent. Their search took them downhill from the center, through the much-photographed Etruscan Arch and into gritty Piazza Grimana, which had a drugstore, coffee shop, bookstore, and newsstand. Right outside the University for Foreigners, Deanna spotted a brown-haired girl putting up a flyer that advertised two rooms for rent. Deanna ran back to tell her sister.

On MySpace, Amanda described this first encounter with Laura (the skinny girl) and Molly (Filomena):

Deanna wants to shop some more, but I need to find a place to live, so I search desperately through Italian classifieds. I also buy a phone. Then when we walk down a steep road to my university, we run into a very skinny girl who looks a little older than me putting up a page with her number on the outer wall of the university. I chat it up with her, she speaks English really well, and we go immediately to her place, literally two minutes from my university. It's a cute house that is right in the middle of this random garden in the middle of Perugia.

Around us are apartment buildings, but we enter through a gate and there it is. I'm in love. I meet her roommate Molly. The house has a kitchen, two bathrooms, and four bedrooms. Not to mention a washing machine . . . Not to mention, she owns two guitars and wants to play with me. Not to mention the view is amazing. Not to mention I have a terrace that looks over the Perugian city/countryside. Not to mention she wants me to teach her yoga. Not to mention they both smoke like chimneys and she offers me one of the open rooms after we hang out for a bit. We exchange

numbers. I put down a down payment. I'm feeling sky
high. These girls are awesome. Really sweet, really
down to earth, funny as hell. Neither are students . . .
they are desperate for roommates because the two
they wanted disappeared all of a sudden. They
are relieved to meet me believe it or not, because
apparently everyone else they have met have been
really not cool.

After Amanda signed on the dotted line, she and Deanna
departed for Germany to stay with their mother's relatives.

Not long after, Meredith Kercher also heard about the
room for rent, and contacted Filomena. She showed up at the
cottage to take a quick tour. She, too, liked the mesmerizing
view and easy access to the universities. Indeed, the cottage
was a find in a country where stand-alone houses lay outside
the reach of many paychecks. The remodeled kitchen even
had a tacked-on "living room"—a luxury item in Perugia,
where builders chop student flats out of ancient buildings.
Thus a flat may consist of little more than a long hallway with
doors opening onto tiny bedrooms, plus cooking facilities and
a bathroom or two.

Meredith moved in on September 10, 2007; Amanda, after
returning from Germany, on September 20, 2007. Each girl
put down 300 euro a month (about $450) to live in the flat.

"So Amanda actually saw the house first, but Meredith
moved in before her," said Filomena, a vivacious girl with
long brown hair and little round spectacles. "I remember
that, because Meredith was able to give Amanda some advice
about getting around in the center and things like that."

The friendship between the two foreign students blos-
somed at first, Filomena added, because both girls were students, English-speaking, and new in town. Amanda had less
time to hang out at home after she started classes in early
October, taking Italian grammar, culture, conversation, and
pronunciation. A few weeks later, she found a part-time job
at Le Chic, a local pub. Meredith was also busy, but the two
girls continued to explore bookstores, run errands, go out for
dinner, and hang out together in the center. When the popular,

weeklong Eurochocolate Festival began in late October, they attended it together, exploring the white tents pitched on the Corso, where vendors offered everything from chocolate pop-corn to *Perugina* chocolates. Afterward, Amanda told her parents that she'd had a great time, and described her British roommate as fun, beautiful, and smart.

"They had interests in common, at the beginning they surely had a good relationship, there was no reason not to get along," Filomena said, noting that both were pretty girls who made friends easily. "Along the way, they didn't really go separate ways, but they developed personal interests that they pursued individually."

Like Meredith, Filomena found the high-spirited Ameri-can girl eccentric. "She had quite a lot of interests. She liked music, sports, yoga, and languages. Sometimes she had unusual attitudes, like she would start doing yoga while we were speaking, or she would play guitar while we were watch-ing TV."

For Amanda, everything was perfect. She missed loved ones in Seattle, she said on her last MySpace blog post, on October 15, 2007, but had made plenty of friends and was having lots of fun:

Everything is going great. . . . My house is awesome.

ALTHOUGH the little cottage offered many charms, few par-ents would have chosen it for a daughter. Mapped at Via Per-gola 7, it actually stood on busy Sant'Angelo, an arterial that spiraled upward from the valley floor. Locals called the area a *brutta zona*, "bad neighborhood." Developers had built a solid wall of modern apartments right across the noisy street, plus a large beige garage. Drug dealers hung out in the parking area and on the nearby basketball court.

Isolated on the ravine, the cottage lacked the solid encir-cling walls, grilled windows, burglary systems, protective lighting, and BEWARE OF DOG signs that protected monied estates on the same slope (and even there, break-ins were a problem). Any athletic person could clamber over the cottage's metal fence or simply stroll in through the never-bolted gate. Leafy trees and shrubs shrouded the cottage's exterior walls on three sides, providing cover for intruders. Once, the tenants had found a drunk sleeping in the garden.

The house was also very dark at night, Filomena complained.

After seeing a photo of the cottage, one of Amanda's aunts had told her to be careful and always lock her doors. And that was even before the aunt discovered that the front door had a defective lock.

"If you didn't close the door with the key, it opened by itself," Amanda later explained. "You couldn't just shut it; the wind would blow it open."

Meredith's friend Pietro Campolongo, a Merlin's bartender, had warned her never to spend a night alone in the cottage. "I warned her a thousand times," he said to London's *Daily Telegraph*. "Girls should never stay at home alone."

Still, the girls felt safe most nights, because the cottage came with their "protectors," four Italian male students who lived in the downstairs flat. Giacomo Silenzi, Stefano Bonassi, Marco Marzan, and Riccardo Luciani. The girls enjoyed going out for pizza or a beer with these neighbors, and for nearly three weeks, the British girl had been seeing Giacomo, a good-looking, muscular twenty-two-year-old with a shaved head and gold-studded ears, who was in the second year of an international communications program.

"Meredith moved into the flat above mine at the end of the summer and we would pop into each other's places just to say hello or have a cup of coffee, the things that neighbors do," he told the UK's *Daily Mail*. "She was very pretty and I was also impressed with her Italian. We would share CDs and play music together."

THE bartenders kicked off "Crawloween" each year in Perugia's center, the perfect place to observe the town's day/night split, its willingness to serve the sacred and the profane. In the daytime, students and tourists alike perched on the steps of the Duomo, a thirteen-century cathedral on Piazza Novembre, directly across from Fontana Maggiore. The church steps were the place to meet friends, people-watch, search for romance, or be on the lookout for a casual hookup. Students showed up with sketch pads, trying to capture the stunning Palazzo dei Priori, the Gothic town hall honeycombed with staircases, porticos, balconies, and a bell tower. Adorned with a lion and a griffin, the city symbols, the palazzo also offered a vaulted entrance into the Galleria Nazionale dell'Umbria, one of Central Italy's best collections of provincial art.

Come nightfall, bats circled the old stone towers and the scent of burning marijuana replaced that of baking bread. The cobblestones reeked of spilled beer. Darkly clad students flowed out of the crooked alleyways and onto the white-lit Corso. They settled on the church steps in Piazza Novembre like the crows in Alfred Hitchcock's *The Birds*. Near a set of columns in the shadows of the Duomo, drug dealers peddled their wares. A student could get high for less than $20.

"The dealers are there for the students," said a prominent Perugia official. "They know what their customers like and they give it to them." He raised his arms and spread them apart to demonstrate the enormity of Perugia's drug problem. Indeed, a lawless mix of Mafiosi and foreign gangs was feeding the town's growing reputation as the hashish capital of central Italy, conveniently located on the drug highway between North African suppliers and Northern Italian customers. Heroin was also a concern, flowing into Italy from Afghanistan, while marijuana came in from Albania and other places. Students could also get cocaine and amphetamines.

The same drug-peddling scenes played out in university districts around the globe, because dealers followed the money and students had the cash. But only a shrewd observer could tell if Perugia's students were drunk on life or illegal substances. Their names seldom appeared in the felony reports. They may never have noticed the large and up-to-date *questura* (police station) at the bottom of the hill. They were more likely to have their pockets picked or hearts broken than to be shoved into a cop car.

Meanwhile, it was good to be young in the old town. Hip tunes blasted from the neon-lit pubs, pumping up the energy level on the twisting streets. Students who couldn't get into U.S. bars, where the legal drinking age was twenty-one, made merry in the clubs, many of which featured all-you-can-drink specials during Happy Hour. Students also huddled outside Merlin's, Joyce's Pub, the Shamrock, and other favorites at night, smoking cigarettes and chugging beer from plastic cups, even when the air was so cold that they could see their breath. They thought nothing of hanging out until 3 A.M., talking and laughing, oblivious to the drifters and petty thieves, the heroin addicts and derelicts who stumbled past them, bent on one grim errand or another.

YES, Meredith texted to Amanda on Halloween, she did have a costume. She and her friend Sophie Purton, another Erasmus scholar from Britain, were going as vampires. Many older people in Perugia cast suspicious eyes on the "night of the witches," seeing it as a pagan American ritual with occult undertones. But the holiday had a long history in the United Kingdom, where it began as All Hallows' Eve, a night when the dead mingled with the living, when fairies, witches, and demons played their most mischievous pranks.

Meredith adored Halloween. Her father remembered her as a little girl, constructing a costume out of garbage sacks. Then she put a lighted candle inside a carved pumpkin, mounted on a stick, and went out to call on the neighbors.

Halloween was also starting to catch on in Italy's larger cities, fueled by the Italian fondness for dressing up, the *Nightmare on Elm Street* movies, and "vampire chic"—a look inspired by American television shows such as *Buffy the Vampire Slayer* and best-selling books like Stephenie Meyer's *Twilight* series of vampire romance novels.

On Halloween night Meredith came out of her bedroom to show off her newly bought Count Dracula cape, black choker, and fake teeth to Filomena, one of her Italian roommates. The two girls happily discussed the difficulty of achieving vampire chic through makeup. Meredith was a careful girl, who liked to get things just right. She spoke to Filomena in the Perugia patois, a confusing mix of English, Italian, and abundant hand gestures.

Then the British girl went into the white-tiled bathroom she shared with Amanda. The builder had barely managed to squeeze a bidet, sink, and shower stall into the closet-size space.

On the tiled floor, the girls had spread a very ordinary-looking blue bath mat.

Meredith brushed her thick black hair, letting it fall straight down around her shoulders. Then she changed into her costume. Before she left the house, she texted her American roommate to let her know that she couldn't join her because she had already been invited to a dinner party. As girlfriends do, she signed off with a little "x," a kiss.

When Amanda received the text, she was at the nearby flat of Raffaele Sollecito, her wealthy Italian boyfriend, whom she'd been seeing less than a week. He was a tall, awkward Harry Potter look-alike with light brown hair and green eyes, who wore rimless glasses and a wardrobe of thick scarves, designer shirts, wool sweaters, blazers, and trench coats. His mother had died of natural causes (not by suicide, as the press would later claim) when he was in his teens, and he got along fine with Mara, his father's second wife, a striking blonde who wore oversize black sunglasses and couture wool coats with fur collars, like an Italian movie star. Raffaele had many loyal friends and a close relationship with his father, Francesco Sollecito, a well-known urologist, and with his sister, Vanessa.

Amanda had bought Halloween makeup for Raffaele and suggested they go to a disco, but he told her that he hadn't celebrated the holiday since he was fifteen and preferred a quiet evening at home. Besides, he had many things on his plate, including a thesis to write and a hovering father who kept asking when it would be done.

At 8:30 P.M., Amanda replied to Meredith's text, saying she was headed for Le Chic, where she worked two days a week:

Maybe we'll see each other. Call me.

MEREDITH turned up the collar on her Count Dracula cape and said good-bye to Filomena for the last time. Then she left the cottage. She climbed the stone stairs on Via della Pergola and kept going up until she got to the flat of Robyn Butterworth and Amy Frost on Via Bontempi, about a fifteen-minute walk. There she joined Sophie Purton and other British guests for a dinner-and-drinks party.

According to Robyn, a tall, black-haired Leeds student from Northampton, Amanda was most certainly not invited to share in their fun. She said that Meredith felt bad about refusing Amanda's invitations because "she was trying to work on the friendship," which Robyn characterized as "at times a bit awkward. It wasn't always smooth."

The breezy American had never been Robyn's cup of tea. She found Amanda "strange," her actions "inappropriate." On Amanda's first night in the cottage, Meredith had invited her to meet Robyn and several other British friends in Il Bacio, an underground pizzeria in the center. The Seattle girl had managed to scandalize the entire table.

"She burst into song loudly during the meal—it was very out of place and very odd," Robyn complained.

Asked about this singing incident a year later, Il Bacio's manager shrugged, fingered the cash register keys wearily, and said he didn't remember the American girl with the loud voice. How could he?

"Yes, yes, the students, they like to sing. Why do you want to know this?"

Indeed, large groups of Italian students singing loudly in unison, and even banging on the tables, are as typical of Perugia as truffles in the fall. Perhaps Amanda thought she was back in the States, where strolling troubadours of varying talent warble "O Sole Mio" in Italian cafés. In countercultural Seattle, she sang while driving, on the street, wherever she felt like it. She was especially fond of Broadway show tunes and anything by the Beatles: "Oh! Darling," "Here Comes the Sun," "Let It Be."

"If she felt like singing in a restaurant, then she would," said Amanda's friend Madison. "Maybe she felt really happy that night because she was in Italy. Amanda is one of the least judgmental people I've met, so sometimes it's hard for her to understand that even if she doesn't overanalyze every little thing, like others do, people will still do that to her. It wouldn't cross her mind that her singing would bother people, because it would never bother her if others did that."

Only a few members of Meredith's British social set had actually met Amanda, but they all knew about the singing. At their dinner parties, they often dished about the brash UW student. Meredith shared a laundry list of grievances, saying Amanda skimped out on the cleaning, neglected to flush the toilet, annoyed her by speaking Italian at every opportunity, and strummed the same chord on the guitar over and over again. Meredith also considered Amanda overly admiring of Laura, one of their Italian roommates. Not only did Amanda have too many ear piercings, according to Meredith, but she'd only gotten them because she wanted to imitate Laura, who had at least four in each ear.

"Meredith would tell us about things Amanda did that got on her nerves, but she didn't necessarily think these things were bad. Just strange," said Amy, Meredith's best friend in Perugia, a blond student from Derby with blue eyes and a small upturned nose.

Indeed, differences between roommates about noise, cleanliness, and visitors are the stuff of which college handbooks are made. Communication is said to be the key to resolving differences, but Meredith couldn't quite bring herself to talk to Amanda about the issues. Friends blamed her reluctance on British reserve. Criticizing somebody else's bathroom habits was bound to make one feel uncomfortable.

"It was a bit awkward," Robyn said. "Meredith didn't know quite how to proceed. She talked to us about the best way to go about it."

Meredith also expressed surprise at how quickly Amanda had found romance, mentioning to her father, "Amanda arrived only a week ago and she already has a boyfriend."

Amanda *did* have a boyfriend, but not from her first week in Perugia. She'd met Raffaele Sollecito on October 25 during a classical music concert at the *Stranieri*. She'd gone there with Meredith, but the British girl went home during the intermission.

"Then Raffaele came and sat near me," Amanda said later, noting that she'd already picked him out of the crowd, because he looked like "an Italian Harry Potter." He was just Amanda's type, said her friends: quiet, shy, intelligent, geeky.

"You have weird taste in men," a Seattle friend had once told her.

"Tell me about it," she said.

After the concert Amanda told Raffaele that she had to wait tables at Le Chic that night and suggested he drop by for a chat. Then she went back to her flat to prepare for work.

"I told Meredith that I had met someone and we had talked," she said later. "Then after talking to her, I went to work and he came, and I also told her that."

Raffaele wrote to his father:

> *My first impression was that this was an interesting girl, she looked at me over and over again and seemed to be searching for something in my eyes, like a particular interest. Then I sat near her to talk and I noticed that her opinions on the music were odd because she didn't concentrate on the emotions it provoked but on only the rhythm—slow, fast, slow.*

Raffaele and a few friends did show up at Le Chic that night. He had a beer, waited until the bar closed, and then took Amanda back to his *monolocale* (studio apartment) at Corso Garibaldi 110, only about a ten-minute walk from the girls' house. Few students could afford to live alone in the expensive old town, but Raffaele not only had his own place but also weekly maid service. He kept a black Audi parked outside, a major status symbol.

Amanda slept with him that night and every night after that, Raffaele later said in his diary. In fact, they were all but inseparable. The American girl did, however, return to the cottage each morning to shower, change clothes, and catch up with her roommates.

In addition to her new boyfriend and her classes at the *Stranieri*, Amanda had the job at Le Chic, a pub in the center owned by Diya Patrick Lumumba, a popular local who'd emigrated to Italy from the Congo decades earlier. He'd hired Amanda to hand out flyers in the daytime and bring customers their drinks at night. She'd worked every day at first, but by late October, they had "organized" (as she put it) a two-day schedule, Tuesday and Thursdays, from 10:30 P.M. to 1:30 A.M. She called those days "pretty full" and felt lucky to have Monday, Wednesday, and Friday afternoons to play her guitar, walk around, hang out with friends, and study.

As she wrote in her MySpace blog, on October 15, 2007, in her idiosyncratic syntax, complete with typical typos and misspellings:

> I really like the italian lifestyle. everything shuts down in the middle of the day so everyone can have a 3 hour lunch break. i love it. i wish we had that in america. i think americans work to much and dont live. Having that time in the middle of the day reminds you that life really isnt all about going to work and making money. its about who you are and what you choose to do and who you choose to spend your time with.

Living *la dolce vita* is, of course, a popular American fantasy, fed by such delicious books as *Eat, Pray, Love* and *Under the Tuscan Sun*. In these bestsellers, readers enter a fabulous world where the most enchanting dreams come true. British literature offers a similar Eden. Is a trip to Italy promised at the beginning of an English romance novel? Then a happy ending hovers on the horizon.

And why not? A vacation in Italy promises—and might actually deliver—Latin lovers, succulent food, splendid ruins, a colorful history, spirituality, healing, fresh starts, and a slowed-down lifestyle. Snow never falls in this Italy, cars don't break down, and the euro never drops. Four-course meals magically appear. Graffiti never stains ancient monuments, nor does traffic choke potholed roads. Prisons, hospitals, police stations, and cemeteries hardly seem necessary. Italians are seldom fat, wrinkled, or stressed.

Authors were far more jaded in the Gilded Age of the late nineteenth century, when Italy was a must-do on the Grand Tour. American heiresses saw the Bel Paese through rose-colored lenses at their peril in Edith Wharton's short story "Roman Fever" and Henry James's novel *Daisy Miller*. The writers pitted their heroines' openness and optimism against the unfamiliar restraints of an antique Catholic culture. They used "Roman fever" to refer not only to influenza, but also to a sort of willful blindness about the dangers of the world.

The flirtatious Daisy Miller, for instance, makes an ill-advised nighttime visit to the Roman Colosseum, notoriously germ-ridden during that era. Later, she tells Winterbourne, one of many suitors, that she never saw anything so pretty as Rome after dark.

"I am afraid that you would not think Roman fever very pretty," he replies. "This is the way people catch it."

THE cottage's Italian tenants had a far different take on the two foreign girls and their relationship than did Meredith's friends. None of the lodgers, upstairs or downstairs, reported any tension between the two girls. Nobody ever heard Amanda criticize Meredith or raise her voice to anyone at any time. In fact, Marco Marzan, one of the boys downstairs, said the relationship was "idyllic." Laura called it *normale.*

Giacomo, Meredith's boyfriend, used the word *tranquilla* (tranquil). "Of all the people in the house, they got on best together," he said, calling the girls natural allies and good friends. "Amanda was always outgoing. She started coming down to our flat almost from the start when we hardly knew each other. Sometimes she brought us cakes she had made. Other times she asked me to play music with her. I play bass and she had just begun playing the guitar. She loved music, especially the Beatles."

Neither girl enjoyed confrontations. According to Amanda's friends and family, she fell apart when people yelled at her, losing her self-confident façade. She turned red and burst into tears. When someone made her angry, she left the room and wrote them a letter, outlining her grievances, trying to understand them herself.

Another habit Amanda would regret.

As for housework, according to the boys downstairs Filomena and Laura complained that they did more scrubbing than the two foreign girls combined. Meredith did a bit, the Italian roommates said, Amanda did none. For that reason, Filomena had installed a cleaning chart only days before Halloween.

Amanda had already missed a cleaning session. If she kept up that pattern, Filomena could not imagine how many infractions she would tally up by year's end. Laura believed in vigorous bathroom scouring and floor mopping, but wondered if she herself was perhaps too meticulous.

Cleaning aside, the foreign girls caused few problems. They had cash. They paid the rent. They were studious. Neither of them made scenes or even threw a single party.

"The way Amanda described it, the two Italian roommates hung out together," said Amanda's friend Madison. "They were older. They had the same job. Then there was Meredith, who already had a group of friends. Amanda was running in and out, saying, 'Hi.' She would kind of scoot by them and try to get along with everybody."

"I felt very comfortable with Meredith," Amanda said later. "I trusted her, I often asked her for advice." In fact, she found the Londoner glamorously European, admiring the multicultural good looks that Meredith shared with her sister, Stephanie, and two brothers, Lyle and John Jr. (courtesy of their mother, who was of Indian descent, and their Caucasian father).

No doubt Amanda and Meredith had wildly different personalities, yet on paper they made a good match. Amanda also had three siblings: her sister Deanna and two half sisters, Ashley and Delaney. Both Meredith and Amanda were English-speaking, book smart, and middle-class. They had gone to pricey prep schools—Amanda to the Jesuit-run Seattle Preparatory Academy; Meredith, to the all-girls Old Palace School of John Whitgift. They were both enrolled in giant public universities. Their parents were divorced, but the families were close and loving. The girls adored their mothers, loved Italy, longed to master the language, and had worked hard to make their Italian dreams come true. Meredith was on scholarship in Perugia. While carrying a full load of classes at the UW, Amanda had managed to simultaneously hold down two part-time jobs, including a barista gig at World Cup, a coffee shop in Seattle's raffish University District.

Later, when Amanda became infamous around the world, a former customer would leave a rare compliment on the Web site of the *University of Washington Daily*:

I don't really know Amanda Knox personally, but I met/talked to her a few times when she worked at the espresso place. . . . She took my orders a few times and made my sandwiches and got my soup. She seemed really nice, bubbly. Sometimes I would walk in there and she would be at the table studying Italian.

I hope she didn't do it.

CHAPTER TWO

HALLOWEEN NIGHT

Wednesday, October 31, 2007

"It was a joyous night, that Halloween. The last peaceful night for
the London student, although she could not know it, Meredith and
her English friends, all in disguise."

— *Corriere dell'Umbria*

ON Halloween night, Meredith and her friends lingered at
the supper table, talking and drinking punch until about 10:30
P.M. At some point Meredith worked on her vampire look with
Sophie Purton, a twenty-one-year-old Leeds student with a
pert face, blue eyes, and long brown hair. They dabbed white
makeup on their cheeks to create a ghostly pallor, brushed
on smoky eye shadow, and rubbed fake blood around their
mouths.

Then the happy group climbed uphill toward the nightspots in the center, a perfect backdrop for "Crawloween."
They followed the steep passageways that writers over the ages
have compared to caves, because of the arches that sometimes
ran their entire length, darkening the route. Shafts of garish
light played off the medieval façades at the top of the hill,
barely penetrating the dusky alleyways. The eerie white city-
scape looked impossibly old. A Villanovan tribe had first
settled on the hilltop in the ninth century B.C. Three centuries
later, the mysterious Etruscans began crafting the impregnable walls and stone acropolis. Even London, Meredith's

hometown, was young compared to Perugia, and the first European settlers didn't drop anchor in the area that is now Seattle until the 1850s. The land was so wild and the forests so thick that the women sobbed as they left the safety of the boats.

On Halloween, Meredith, Robyn, Amy, Sophie, and other friends headed straight for Merlin's, a popular pub for British students, where they could order drinks in English, eat pizza, dance, and, of course, drink beer.

The bartenders at Merlin's knew just how to pull in Erasmus scholars. Orientation parties upon arrival. Flyers handed out on the Corso and at the universities between classes. Theme parties, birthday shindigs, two-for-one-beer specials, and drinks with sexy names like "Blo-Job" shots. Happy Hour from 8:30 to 11:30 every night.

In fact, Merlin's was a rite of passage for foreign students, so essential to Perugia's study-abroad experience that it formed the backdrop for Zachary Nowak's *Peril in Perugia*, a detective novel in which nobody dies. An American author, translator, and tour guide, Zach had come to the hilltop town as a student and even bartended a few times at Merlin's, where he observed the club dynamics.

Groups of eye-catching girls got red-carpet treatment in all the nightspots, Zach said, because of their drawing power. The bartenders courted them and memorized their names. As he wrote in his detective novel:

Merlin's, like a lot of Perugia's pubs, was subterranean. The entrance was all but hidden in this back alley just off the main street, and you walked down steep steps to get to the bar. To your right was the largish dance floor and DJ console, while off to the left was the dining area where locals ate pizzas and then started their pub crawls with a few beers. . . . The one disadvantage of this layout was that, coming down the stairs at the entrance, you could see instantly how full the place was. As with every bar, Merlin's needed a certain number of people out there grooving, or at least at the bar, to be critical mass, to be a magnet for others coming in the door. If it looked empty, the gaggle of Belgians or what have you might move on to another bar in search of a better party.

On Halloween night, thirty-seven-year-old Pasquale (aka "Pisco") Alessi, the pub's co-owner, greeted the English girls from behind the bar. One of Perugia's most recognizable citizens, Pisco was slim and charismatic, of medium height, and dressed perennially in black. He wore his long black hair tied back and sported a neatly clipped goatee. Raised in Reggio di Calabria, far south in the boot of Italy, Pisco had come to Perugia as a student and never looked back. His understanding of the club culture was second to none. To the English girls, he was a confidant and what Amy called "a friend, a very good friend, and nothing more."

Pisco worked the bar that night in a big black vampire cape. Earlier that day, he and Meredith had been thrilled to score the last set of vampire fangs in the shops. Pisco said it was typical of the English student to work out a sharing arrangement. He flaunted the upper choppers, the better part of the deal, while she made do with the lower.

"Meredith was tiny," Pisco recalled. "Just a really nice girl. She liked to go out with her friends, but I never see her with problems, never see her drunk. She liked to dance, and those girls sometimes they would get up and dance on the tables." He laughed. "I have a picture of Meredith up on a table like that. . . . She always liked to go out with Sophie and Robyn and have fun, but she would watch out for them. She was the careful one. 'Now we have to go home,' she would say. 'We have to get up tomorrow and go to class.'"

The DJ at Merlin's kept the Halloween party running far into the night with top-of-the-charts tunes mixed in with the occasional Madonna hit from the 1980s. Amid the crush of masked students, Meredith posed with two buddies for a striking photo: she leaned in from the left, her lips outlined with fake blood, the collar on her Count Dracula coat covering her neck. In the center stood her friend Pietro Campolongo, a Merlin's bartender in a garish white mask from the movie *Scream*. To the right, another friend was disguised in a *polizia* uniform, wearing a shiny helmet with the visor pulled down and pointing a plastic assault rifle in Meredith's direction.

She looked happy, self-confident, fun. "A lover of life," as her aunt called her.

"We were having a great time," said Pietro later to a British tabloid reporter, "but there were lots of people we didn't know, especially because they were masked."

A few evenings later, police would come into Merlin's and other bars, trying to match names to the masks, wondering if Meredith could have met someone on Halloween who showed up on her doorstep the next night.

INDEED, a gregarious young man named Rudy Guede would make that very claim. An Italian resident from the Ivory Coast, he was a music lover of uncertain occupation, a fantastic dancer, a skinny twenty-year-old black man in a white country, estranged from his family in a culture where family is everything. He often shot hoops on the court in Piazza Grimana, a five-minute walk from the girls' cottage, and had played for a while on a local team. He dressed like a basketball star, too, in team jerseys and baggy shorts even in chilly weather, or in a T-shirt over athletic pants.

Rudy had a tiny *monolocale* just around the corner from Raffaele's, but unlike the wealthy students' place, Rudy's didn't offer much; just a bed, a hot plate, and a bathroom. Rudy didn't mind, because he was a boulevardier, always out on the streets, looking for fun. Indeed, he was in constant motion, drinking in the bars, hanging out on the church steps, chatting with friends on the Corso. Rudy lived for the disco and the *festa* (party). He was a fixture at the Domus, a late-night disco club in the center where foreign students rocked to loud music until dawn.

Rudy knew many people. He fit in everywhere without really fitting in anywhere. Although he would later be characterized as a drifter, he'd lived in Perugia since he was five years old and wasn't completely rootless. In fact, he palled around with quite respectable friends from his school days and also with newly met college students. He would often engage in afternoon chats with the two Spanish Erasmus scholars, Marta Fernandez and Carolina Espinilla, who shared the flat above him.

Rudy knew the boys from the cottage, because they shot hoops with him on the basketball court. He'd even been over to their place and met the two pretty foreign girls in mid-October. He'd been hanging out by the church steps in the center that

day, talking to the boys, when Amanda came up to them, just
to say hello. The boys introduced her to Rudy. As she described
this meeting:

"They said, 'Amanda this is Rudy. Rudy, this is Amanda.'
That's all."

Then the whole group walked back to the cottage together.
Rudy went into the downstairs flat to hang around with the
boys. Amanda joined them eventually and then Meredith
showed up. Rudy stayed on after the girls returned to their
apartment. He socialized with the boys, drinking and/or
smoking a *spinello*, a hand-rolled joint commonly made with
hashish or marijuana mixed with tobacco.

At some point he became too wasted to leave, so he went
into the bathroom, forgetting even to close the door, sat on the
toilet, and fell asleep. Stefano found him there later that night
and let him sack out on the couch.

Not long before Halloween, Rudy came over, uninvited,
to watch the Grand Prix on TV with the boys. He'd asked
whether Amanda was single the first time he came over, but
now he didn't mention her all night. He wasn't a pest, just a
guy who liked to drink and be sociable, the boys said. Laura
Mezzetti, from the upstairs flat, happened to drop by, and she
also met Rudy; so only Filomena did not.

Even though he'd once pretended to be Count Dracula in
a homemade video he'd posted on Facebook, on this Halloween he didn't slip into a disguise. He hung out with the Spanish girls all night, the two who lived upstairs from him, and
would later claim that he'd encountered Meredith at a party.
He said he hadn't recognized her right way because she was
dressed like a vampire. "When I recognized her, I said, 'Do
you want to suck my blood because you lost the Cup?' "

Meredith had laughed, Rudy claimed, because South
Africa had recently defeated Britain in a rugby final.

He also said they flirted and he stole a kiss, whereupon
she asked him to stop by the next night at 8:30, the idea being
only to talk.

ON Halloween night Amanda painted cat whiskers on her
face and left Raffaele to his quiet evening.

"Amanda is American," he said later. "For her Halloween is a very important night."

The truth was that he'd already had a very full day. First he'd gone to a graduation party for his friend Francesco, then he'd hung out at his buddy Paolo's place, and finally he'd whiled away the afternoon with Amanda and shared supper with her. They were suspended blissfully in that honeymoon phase so annoying to outsiders, when lovers make up pet names, find each other perfect, and indulge in public displays of affection.

All of Amanda's flatmates had met her new boyfriend, to mixed reviews. On October 26, Amanda had introduced him to Filomena, who thought he treated her "sweetly." Laura met him on the 30th, also at the cottage. She found the courtship a bit much. Cloying, in fact.

"*Piccioncini*," she called them. Little lovebirds.

"He followed her every footstep," she said. "He was very affectionate with her, almost obsessive."

The British roommate had also met him, because he stopped by in the afternoons to make lunch for his new girlfriend.

"Meredith was complaining that they spent quite a lot of time in the kitchen," said Robyn.

For his part, Raffaele found Meredith a nice, intelligent girl, but his lack of English prevented them from having a true conversation. When the foreign girls had moved into the cottage, they'd tried speaking only in Italian, just to get in some practice, but they were unable to voice deeper thoughts than "Would you like mozzarella on that panini?" So now Amanda and Meredith spoke exclusively in rapid English.

Raffaele didn't try to keep up. He was content to eat lunch at the table, basking in Amanda's presence, while she enjoyed the gossip.

In any case, the lovers were usually over at his little flat, which offered a tiny kitchen and bathroom, plus a main room with a bed and desk. Only a half block up from the *Stranieri*, the flat was on twisting Corso Garibaldi, a colorful street with several good bars and restaurants, plus a church, kebab shop, and pocket park. Besides an Internet Point, a shop where customers could surf the Web and make international phone calls, Garibaldi also boasted a Laundromat and two Conad grocery stores.

"Raffaele, sure, we all remember," said a barber whose shop was across the street from Raffaele's flat. A short, good-natured man with bushy gray hair and a round face, he wore a black V-necked sweater over red cotton pants. He'd never seen the American girl, but the Italian boy, yes, of course. He rubbed his fingers together to show that Raffaele had *soldi* (money). This was obvious to everyone, because of the Audi parked on the narrow street.

"Every day we see the car. One time it was sticking out and I had to ask him to move it."

The barber laughed as he clipped a client's hair. He explained that Perugia was a quiet place. People were cautious, observant. They recalled these little incidents, seen through windows on the street.

"Yes, Raffaele was very polite. He moved the car right away. And he was always quiet. Never a problem over there."

The barber gestured with his scissors at the nondescript terra-cotta building where Raffaele had his flat.

"Erasmus scholars are very nice boys and girls, but also very loud," he said, explaining that they often begin the school year with admirable intentions, planning to hit the books, but then they discover the *festa* concept of life. Pretty soon they are spending most of their time and money in the clubs. They don't clean their rooms. The books gather dust.

"Fun. Erasmus. Fun. Erasmus." The barber put down his scissors to demonstrate this balancing act. He pretended to put fun on the palm of one hand, Erasmus on the other. In the end, fun tipped the scales. It wasn't even a contest.

"What can you do?" he laughed.

Although Raffaele was three years older than Amanda, the age difference wasn't overly apparent. In fact, both students seemed young for their ages, in looks and naïveté. Although he was a serious boy for the most part, Raffaele had a playful side. He was very fond of video games and dreamed of being a "gamer," creating the games himself, in a high-tech center like Seattle. He liked to download Manga cartoons on his computer, even when Amanda was over. He was the product of a sheltered life, having spent his prep school years at the Onaosi, a very strict boarding school in Perugia reserved for doctors' sons. During his first two years at the University of Perugia, he'd lived in a dorm, and then had escaped to Germany for his Erasmus year. Theoretically, the German connection could've been a bond between him and Amanda, except that Raffaele had found the experience depressing, apart from the partying. He was, by his own admission, a nervous person who used hashish to calm his nerves. He admitted to having experimented with cocaine at seventeen, but told Amanda that he avoided harder drugs.

Before meeting Amanda, Raffaele had written on his blog that he was "tired of the usual evenings" and longed for "extreme experiences"—two phrases that surely would come back to haunt him.

One local understood Raffaele's longing for the new only too well. Frank Sfarzo (creator of the Perugia Shock blog) was a personable, black-haired investigative journalist with intense brown eyes.

Like Raffaele, Frank Sfarzo was a doctor's son and a former Onaosi student. After getting a philosophy degree from the University of Perugia, he had done many things, from working in the film industry to being a part-time professor.

"My original name was Francesco Sforza," he explained. "But I moved to the U.S. and in a couple of weeks they translated that into Frank, and I just felt comfortable with a shorter name that I didn't have to repeat twice. I got used to it and I slightly changed my last name, too, because I felt the change had to be complete."

He was back in Italy, living in Florence, when he read about the Meredith mystery. He decided to move back to the hilltop town, because he felt he understood the types of people caught in the crosswinds, from the foreign girl handing out flyers for Le Chic, to the bar owner, the upper-class Italian boy, and, later, the drifter known as the Fourth Man.

"These were my people," he said. "I had to write about them." So he started a blog he called Perugia Shock, to follow the case and its players. After studying Raffaele's blog, he told readers on Perugia Shock:

What emerges is a very childish figure who at the age of 23 still lives like an adolescent starting to discover life away from home, wasting his time chatting with friends, rolling joints every now and then. . . . Nothing for days or weeks and then suddenly a flow of words lacking any intelligence or creative content and annoying to be read even by an Italian speaking person.

NATURALLY, the talkative Amanda had already told the world about Raffaele, even discussing him with her American ex-boyfriend David Johnsrud, whom everybody called "DJ." He was a tall boy with a long-legged, athletic build and brown hair, which he usually wore long, parted down the middle. He often tucked a red bandana into the back pocket of his khakis.

DJ and Amanda had met when they were UW freshman, through mountain-climbing activities, and dated throughout their sophomore year. "We immediately became friends," DJ said, adding that he'd been attracted to her "positive, friendly attitude. Most everyone likes Amanda when they first meet her, although some people don't like her for having so much energy. I think they're just bitter though."

When junior year rolled around, they both chose to study abroad, Amanda in Italy, DJ in China. For that reason, they decided to break up. "Neither of us wanted to hold the other back," said DJ. "However, we continued to be close friends and stayed in close touch."

When Amanda left for Italy, DJ drove her to the airport. He also bought her special headphones so that she could talk to him on Skype, a computer program that allows users to hear and see each other over the Internet.

"She looked so cute with the headphones on," he said. "Twice a week we talked over Skype. I can't even imagine how much money she must have spent in Internet cafés."

Soon, the Italian press would accuse Amanda of being a femme fatale, but before she met Raffaele, she had complained to DJ and other friends about the rudeness of Italian men. She hated the catcalls on the street. She said she'd never been around males who were that blunt about their sexual interest.

"Your place for me?" was the pickup line that Italian men yelled at foreign girls on the Corso.

"Amanda dislikes it when people focus on her beauty," DJ said. "She doesn't think of herself as beautiful. That's for starters. And she doesn't like it when people are superficial and go on and on about her looks."

"She's always been attracted to nerds," said Amanda's stepfather, Chris Mellas, a computer-network manager at a real-estate development company in Seattle. "Amanda's kind of a nerd herself. When she was in college, she'd come over to our house and the first thing she'd do is get down on the rug and play with her dog. That's who she is. Very down-to-earth. Not trying to put on airs."

A round-faced, brown-haired man with a sardonic sense of humor, Chris had married Amanda's mother, Edda, in 2002, when Amanda was fifteen. She had been divorced from Curt Knox since Amanda was three years old, and had raised their two girls in a tiny house within a ten-minute drive from the home of Curt and Cassandra Knox, Curt's second wife, the mother of Amanda's two half sisters. After Edda married Chris, thirteen years her junior, they remodeled and enlarged their West Seattle dwelling.

Edda, a brunette schoolteacher with the huge blue eyes characteristic of her family, described her daughter as the type of girl who "told you everything. Even things you didn't want to know. You'd say, 'Amanda, enough, I don't need to hear every single thing.'"

When Amanda told her mother about Raffaele, though, it came as a relief, because Edda had worried about her daughter heading home in the dark after work.

"Don't worry, Mom, there's this really nice boy and he walks me home every night," Amanda had assured her.

"We just knew Raffaele from the phone," Chris said. "Amanda put him on one night. She said, 'Here, say hello to someone.'" Raffaele's English was "functional, certainly better than Amanda's Italian."

Since Amanda was determined to learn Italian, however, she tried to speak to Raffaele in his language. He was happy to function as her translator, speaking first in Italian and then repeating the same thought in English as best he could.

"They were literally at the phase where you would point to a chair and say 'chair' in another language so you could pick up that word," said Christina Hagge, Edda's sister. She also lived in Seattle, part of a large extended family that socialized frequently together.

"During that time when we were together she was elusive," Raffaele would write later to his father. "I thought that she was out of this world. She lived her life like a dream, she was detached from reality, she could not distinguish dream from reality. Her life seemed to be pure pleasure, she had a contact with reality that was almost nonexistent."

Given Raffaele's reliance on video games, hashish, and Manga comic books for his own entertainment, that description seemed sweet, poignant, and almost comical. For not only was Amanda, the UW honor student, unable to express a deep thought in Italian, but she was also far from her hometown, family, and normal life. Clearly, she had a dreamy personality, but she was hardly the first American to see only the pretty side of Italy.

Euphoria, according to experts, is the first stage of culture shock, similar to the start of a love affair. Everything is perfect until something goes wrong. Real life will inevitably enter the dreamscape, whether in Italy or in Cleveland.

Despite their evident bliss, Raffaele and Amanda made something of an odd couple. He was tall and skinny; she was short and athletic. He wore beautiful custom shirts that had to be laundered by hand. Like a true Seattleite, she blanched at anything that needed ironing. He was Catholic; she was a "practicing agnostic." He was wealthy; she'd been raised in pleasant but not opulent circumstances.

There was also a class difference peculiar to Italian society.

"For an American girl to go around in public with an upscale Italian guy, that's really quite a coup," said Zach Nowak, who worked part-time at the Umbria Institute. "Raffaele was telling people that she was his girlfriend, he was taking her around, talking about introducing her to his dad. She was meeting his friends. You don't see Italian guys do that for foreign girls. So, hey, good for her."

The relationship ran on accelerated time, even by Perugia

standards. Raffaele was scheduled to receive his degree in computer science on November 16, 2007. His father was already scouting around, looking for just the right restaurant for the graduation party. Raffaele envisioned a merry celebration, a banquet with friends and relatives, plus "at night a romantic restaurant for me and Amanda only."

Once the festivities were over, his father planned to travel with him to Milan, where Raffaele was to register for a master's degree at Bocconi University.

Meanwhile, Amanda studied. Raffaele worked on his thesis. Two nights a week she worked at Le Chic, and he showed up after hours to walk her home. He enjoyed cooking meals for her. She called herself his "sous chef." One night Raffaele had even dialed his father and asked for a recipe, because he wanted to make Amanda a risotto, a deliciously creamy, time-consuming rice dish.

"I liked to cuddle her, give her security," he would say later, when the press portrayed him as Amanda's pawn. "It made me feel important."

AFTER Amanda left him on Halloween, she strolled uphill from Piazza Grimana to Le Chic, to enjoy some off-work moments. The cozy bar had walls sponged in bright colors, white futuristic-looking bar stools, and ethnic paintings. Patrick Lumumba, Amanda's boss and the owner, was a well-known and respected local who wore his hair in short braids. He lived quietly with his common-law Polish wife, Aleksandra Beata Konia, and Davide, their nineteen-month-old son. Amanda described Le Chic on MySpace:

> Its a really small place owned by this man from the congo. his name is patrick. my other fellow employee is a guy from algeria who is a crazy good dancer and yet still really likes dancing with me. havent quite figured that one out.

The Algerian guy was Louerguioui Juba, known as Juve. In one degree of separation in Perugia, Laura had introduced Juve to Amanda, and Juve had introduced Amanda to Patrick.

"Juve was my personal contact at work," Amanda said. "At least, he was the one who often had to translate for me, to tell me what I was supposed to do. Also, because since my Italian wasn't great, I would listen to Patrick, and then turn to Juve to ask him what I was really supposed to do. He spoke to me in English."

"Amanda was the first American we met and we decided to hire her because of that," Patrick later said.

In some ways, Amanda was well suited for the work—she was outgoing, attractive, and talkative. But she was also somewhat absentminded, the kind of person who never checked the time. Patrick found her sweet but complained that he had to remind her to wait on customers and stop chattering with her friends.

At first Amanda had worked every night, but then they "organized," as Amanda put it, the two-nights-a-week gig. Patrick's bar was only about a month old, not terribly busy; so it wasn't clear if he'd scaled back her hours because he didn't need the help, or if he was unhappy with her performance.

For her part, Amanda said Patrick was a good boss, though she disliked being used as "eye candy." While conceding that he did tell her to stop chatting with her friends, she also believed it was enough to bring customers their beer and peanuts, smiling while she did it.

"I went out of my way NOT to flirt with customers," she would write in her diary.

In any case, working while going to school was tiring. She was beginning to question why she bothered when she had more than $4,400 stashed away in her U.S. bank account. It might be better to quit and just enjoy her semester in Italy.

After leaving Le Chic on Halloween night, Amanda went to meet Spyros Gatsios, a big, well-liked Greek student with black hair that formed a widow's peak. He'd become a friend because he supervised the Internet Point near the cottage, where she went to talk to DJ on Skype. Spyros was just coming out of Merlin's when she met up with him. They went to a few other places, and then Amanda said she was tired. She asked him to drop her off by the fountain, saying she had a date with a new guy—somebody she really liked because he was so shy.

"She added that she didn't feel great about it," Spyros

would later tell the *Telegraph*, "because she was having a simultaneous relationship with an American boy whom she kept in touch with . . . but she was smiling about it."

In Raffaele's diary, he described drawing an "abstract figure" on his face and going to meet his new American girlfriend by the fountain.

"I took a stroll downtown and after that I met Amanda. From there we returned home immediately and passed the night watching a film."

WHEN closing time hit Merlin's at 2 A.M., the British girls weren't ready to call it a night. The shutters went down on every club in the center at that time except for the Domus on Via Priori. There, the action didn't even get started until midnight and continued until dawn.

"The music is pretty funny," said Iagora.com, a Web site aimed at Perugia college students. "It's very much a pick-up joint for the *Italiano* boys in the area to prey on the foreign girls, but if you go with a bunch of friends, it is very harmless and great fun! I wouldn't go every night, but it is a place where everyone inside is having a great time."

Pisco often moved his customers over to the Domus at closing time. On Halloween night Meredith and her friends left Merlin's and headed out over the Corso. They turned left at the fountain and walked through Piazza Morlacchi, its lively espresso bars closed for the night. The streets twisted and narrowed at that point, until they came to the red door of the Domus, a small, packed club built underground in the Perugian fashion.

Rudy Guede was on the dance floor, accompanied by the two Spanish Erasmus scholars who lived upstairs from him, Carolina and Marta. Later, he would claim that he flirted with Meredith there, forgetting that the first time he said he saw her at a party. On Perugia Shock, Frank Sfarzo sketched out the verifiable facts:

> On the evening of the 31st the Spanish girls go to a party and they find Rudy there. Then they all moved to the second Spanish party. Then they all go to the Domus and

Rudy is there, in a two-room discotheque packed with Halloween party people. Probably more than the 140 allowed by law. He's there, where Meredith also is, but as we know, nobody saw him talking to her. Marta goes home but Carolina stays until 5:30 A.M. and says she saw Rudy dancing with a blond girl with long straight hair.

Later Rudy would put out a SOS for this mystery blonde, pleading for her to come forward and confirm that she saw him talking to Meredith, the British girl in the vampire cape.

AT 5:30 A.M., the British girls had finally had enough of Halloween. Robyn and Amy walked Meredith almost all the way home.

"We wanted to make sure of doing that," Robyn stressed. "We always did that for her. She walked down the stairs and across the street and into her house."

It was quiet all across Perugia, quiet on the Corso, in Piazza Grimana, even on Meredith's busy street. Too early even for the church bells that rang every hour across the old town. At that time, the plump gray sparrows called *passeri* twittered in the pear trees around the cottage, in the brief envelope of time before traffic started up again.

Nobody was home to greet Meredith. She walked down the hall to her room, just past the kitchen area. Her room was small and cold, with a slanted roof, polished terra-cotta tiles, and exposed beams. She had only enough space for a single bed, a white desk, a one-drawer nightstand, a flower-stamped wardrobe, and a few shelves. But her room was quiet, away from the busy street, a good place for studying. And Meredith was the only roommate who could throw back her shutters and see the beautiful valley, filling up with mist in the mornings, the leaves on the trees turning orange in the fall light.

Under the bed, Meredith had stashed a suitcase filled with the Perugian chocolates that she planned to share with her family. On November 9, only eight days away, she intended to fly to London. Her Facebook page was full of happy anticipation:

Hey, I'm back for a bit in nov for my mum's bday,
9th til the 14th. then back again for xmas around the
15th·I am having a good time thanks, it's starting to
get really cold now tho but choc festival is on at the
moment so just a good excuse to drink a lot of hot
chocolate. How's stuff at home?? xxx.

Now, on the morning of November 1, Meredith slept for
the last time on this earth.

CHAPTER THREE

ALL SAINTS' DAY: FINAL GOOD-BYES

Thursday, November 1, 2007

"Before I left town, Meredith said, 'Go. I will be waiting for you here.' Those were the last words she said to me."
— Giacomo Silenzi to the *Sunday Mirror*

"There were always junkies and drug dealers around, especially in the garden and in our car park. We would come out and find syringes everywhere. I never felt safe."
— "Valentina," a former tenant, to the *Telegraph*

ALL Saints' Day was November 1, followed by All Souls' Day, November 2, known to Christians as the Day of the Dead. The two religious holidays ushered in a solemn time for Italians, who, as they had since pagan times, gathered in cemeteries and in their homes to honor saints and mourn the dead. Many also attended Mass and shared multi-course meals, topped off with finger-shaped *ossi dei morti*, "bones of the dead," tasty almond cookies crafted in local bakeries.

Two things were predictable about November 1, 2007, as anybody familiar with the local culture would know. First, rent fell due on the first of the month for everyone in town, Rudy and Raffaele as well as Amanda and Meredith. Since Perugia landlords didn't accept checks, Amanda and Meredith were cash-rich, each having withdrawn 300 euro (about $450) from bank machines to pay their rent.

The second predictable thing: most Italian students would be out of town.

"All Souls' Day is an official holiday; so it's a day off from school and many (not all) businesses are closed," explained

Zach Nowak. "When a holiday falls on a Thursday [as it did in 2007], the Friday after is called *ponte*, or "bridge," because it forms a bridge between the day off and Saturday. That long weekend was an opportunity for Italian students to go back to their home regions. Ergo, anyone watching that house for the wrong reasons could be certain that the four boys downstairs would not be there."

In fact, all six Italian tenants had already departed by November 1, taking advantage of the long holiday weekend to visit their families or wedge in a getaway. Giacomo, Stefano, and Marco had all gone home to Porto San Giorgio in The Marche, a lovely mountainous region on the Adriatic coast about two hundred miles south. Riccardo was in Bologna. Laura had gone to Montesfasciono and then to Viterbo near Rome. Filomena, as she did every weekend, was staying with her boyfriend, Marco Zaroli, in his Perugia flat—only about a ten-minute drive from the cottage—and she popped in only occasionally. Likewise, since October 25, Amanda had bunked at Raffaele's.

That meant only Meredith would be spending Thursday night in the cottage.

TAKING on a managerial role, Filomena had addressed two security issues with the landlord. She'd complained about the faulty lock on the front door, saying it had worked fine when the girls had first moved in, but by October the door had begun to open on its own unless locked. The ancient shutters in her room also needed fixing. One was warped, preventing her from locking the set. Worse, the wind blew the shutters open. Since Filomena's window was near the street and just to the left of the front door, any passerby could spot the conveniently opened shutters, in a burglary-prone neighborhood.

Only the week before, at 9:30 P.M. (a significant hour, it would turn out), Stefano's friend Giorgio Cocciaretto had seen an intruder standing in the cottage garden, but he couldn't pick out a face because it was too dark. A few days later, Meredith told Giacomo that she'd been frightened when she saw a shadow in the garden. On both occasions, the boys had searched the grounds but found nothing.

The muscular Giacomo boasted that he'd never felt afraid

in the cottage. No, he was not the worrying type. At midday on October 29, he came upstairs to say good-bye to Meredith, accompanied by the soft-spoken, much smaller Stefano. Giacomo handed his keys over to Meredith and asked her a favor. One of his cats had a cut ear. Could she look after it while he was gone?

She said yes. He kissed her and waved good-bye. Then he and Stefano caught a train for The Marche.

Meredith must have had mixed feelings.

Certainly, the popular Giacomo had never pretended to be a Romeo. Or a Casanova, really. He hung out at the Red Zone, an exciting disco with a rowdy reputation, where dealers peddled hashish, cocaine, ketamine, and other drugs in the parking lot. In addition to looking in on the cat, he'd asked Meredith to water the seven luxuriant marijuana plants he was growing in the downstairs flat.

This request made Meredith so nervous that she sought out her friend Amy's advice on what to do, but in the end she agreed to do the watering.

Giacomo never called Meredith from his parents' home.

She texted him once, just to say hello.

He texted back, but not to say how much he missed her. Instead he made a simple request:

Hey, can you take my sheets off the line?

IN her diary Amanda painted a rosy picture of life in the cottage, with four girls of three different nationalities living together as harmoniously as the March sisters in *Little Women*. They didn't keep a party house, she proudly told her Seattle friends. The girls were clean and neat and quiet. They crammed their refrigerator with fruit juice, mineral water, cheeses, and yogurt.

Each girl had her own shelf. Meredith stocked mainly fresh vegetables: mushrooms, carrots, onions. Amanda stored mozzarella cheese, tomatoes, mushrooms, lettuce, French cheese, and lots of pesto. She kept to a simple, mainly vegetarian diet, partly through choice and partly because she suffered from stomach problems that often resulted in painful spasms.

Despite their busy lives, the four girls found time to hang out together in the kitchen, a cheerful room with modern appliances, wooden cabinets, purple flowered window seats, and a rectangular wooden table with a green top. The girls liked to watch TV together at night. They would sometimes roll a joint and pass it around, but in Perugia this was apparently no more remarkable than serving espresso.

Now this peaceful life was about to come to an abrupt halt.

THE following reconstruction of events comes from witness reports, court testimony, diaries, and, in particular, a long e-mail that American student Amanda Knox sent to everyone on her online address book on November 4, 2007.

On November 1, All Saints' Day, Amanda returned home while Raffaele was still sleeping. She had the American habit of daily showers and the American impatience with faulty European bathroom fixtures. She hated her boyfriend's shower stall, which was cramped and leaky. So, as usual, she headed for the cottage, where she kept her shampoo, beauty supplies, and clean clothes. She arrived at around 10:30 A.M.

Meredith's door was still closed. Amanda assumed that she was sleeping.

After showering, the American student changed into clothes that she'd hung on a drying rack. Then she went into the kitchen and started getting the pans out for lunch.

Filomena dropped by with her boyfriend, Marco, around 12:30 P.M. "I went to Via della Pergola with my boyfriend to change clothes because we were going to lunch at Luca Altieri's house, a friend of Marco's," she said later.

Filomena asked Amanda to help her wrap a present for Luca's birthday, not wanting to ask Marco because evidently he was all thumbs. Luca was dating her best friend, Paola Grande, and the couples planned to spend the evening together at an amusement park.

Amanda helped her wrap the package, after which Filomena rushed off with her boyfriend.

A bit later, Meredith came out of her room. In the e-mail, Amanda said:

> The last time I saw Meredith, beautiful, funny, was when I came home. After I had taken a shower and was fumbling around in the kitchen she emerged from her room with the blood of her costume (vampire) still dripping down her chin. We talked for a while in the kitchen, how the night went, what our plans were for the day. Nothing out of the ordinary. Then she went to take a shower and I began to start eating.

In a later document, Amanda would elaborate, adding that Meredith mentioned that she couldn't wash off the vampire makeup. She said the British girl also described a pink fruit juice drink that her friends had concocted for Halloween, into which they had inserted with great creativity a wraithlike "hand" made out of ice.

According to Amanda, she then told Meredith that she wanted to confide in her, saying she'd had an upsetting talk with Juve, her coworker at Le Chic, about her relationship with Raffaele. Juve didn't approve of Raffaele because Amanda had previously told him how wonderful DJ was. Amanda also felt like she was cheating on DJ, even though they'd split up. She said Meredith advised her to do what was right in her heart and not worry about Juve.

This was an encore presentation. On October 30, the four flatmates had gathered around the kitchen at lunchtime for the very last time. Amanda told them that she was depressed, because she felt conflicted about her relationship with Raffaele.

According to Filomena, "Amanda said she liked Raffaele and he was nice but she felt a little guilty about her American boyfriend, DJ, among other things, who at that time was in China or Japan, I do not remember."

Was this cheating? Amanda had wondered aloud.

Laura and Filomena shrugged, not feeling the need to weigh in on the love lives of unmarried twenty-year-olds. The latter did manage a tactful remark about the difficulty of long-distance relationships and the many miles between Amanda and DJ.

Meredith, on the other hand, said she'd never cheat under any conditions. She had never cheated in her life. She hated cheating.

Although Laura took this as a slam on Amanda, DJ later said that she had never cheated on him. "She never betrayed my trust. First off, we weren't together. She could make her own choices. Even so, when she first started becoming interested in Raffaele, she told me about him. She asked me if it was okay to date him. She didn't want to hurt me. I told her, 'We're not together. Do what makes you happy. That'll make me happy.' "

In any case, Meredith was most likely talking about her own boyfriend. The week before she had told Jade Bidwell, another British friend, that she suspected Giacomo of unfaithfulness.

"We sat drinking at the same table and chatting in general about relationships and relationships with boys and Meredith said her boyfriend wasn't very reliable in the sense that he seemed not to be the type who would be faithful," Jade later told police. "She happened to call during an evening in which he said he would be at home, but she had the feeling that he was not home. From the manner in which she spoke of this boy, I don't think she considered him as 'boyfriend' but as a person she saw sometimes but not as a serious attachment."

On October 30, Meredith stressed to her flatmates that "fidelity was important in a relationship," but she couldn't have been terribly upset with anyone at the table. Soon Raffaele showed up and made pasta for the girls. Laura did not participate, having already eaten, but the British student joined the others at what Filomena called a "very nice" lunch.

That was the last time Laura ever saw Meredith.

ON November 1, Meredith and Amanda wrapped up their talk, and Meredith headed for the shower to wash off the vampire makeup. Around 2 P.M., Raffaele showed up and made pasta once again. "As we were eating together Meredith came out of the shower and grabbed some laundry or put some laundry in, one or the other," Amanda wrote in the e-mail.

Around the same time, Meredith called her mother, Arline, telling her that she was going to watch a film with friends that afternoon and then come home early to finish an essay. They also discussed Meredith's upcoming trip to London.

The British girl usually called her parents at night, because money was tight, and rates were slightly cheaper then. But on November 1, she dialed her father at 2:15 P.M., just to touch base. He was at a bank counter in Croydon when his phone rang. Meredith explained that she didn't have classes that day, because of the holiday. They chatted for two minutes. She said she was about to go out. He told her that he loved her and would call her later that night.

That was the last time John ever spoke to his daughter.

In her e-mail, Amanda said she was playing guitar with Raffaele when Meredith emerged from her room around 4 P.M., but that the British girl "said bye and left for the day," without mentioning where she was going. Meredith wore a white T-shirt tucked under a white knitted top, a bright blue Adidas jacket, and Puma athletic shoes. Raffaele later mentioned that he'd thought it was "cute" that Meredith was also wearing frayed jeans that had belonged to her ex-boyfriend back in London.

The couple hung around the cottage while Amanda strummed the guitar, and they shared a *spinello*, a popular pastime on both floors of the cottage. Then they went back to Raffaele's flat.

They never saw Meredith again, the lovers would tell police.

LATER, they would tell confusing accounts about how they spent the rest of the evening. They never claimed to have amnesia, a popular accusation; instead they agreed upon what they did, for the most part, but couldn't remember exactly what time they did what. A confusion they blamed on the marijuana, and the fact that Amanda didn't wear a watch.

They either did or did not clean Amanda's ears or take a long shower together. They either did or did not have sex.

Both remembered Raffaele made a fish dinner, rather late, and that afterward they had problems with a broken pipe under the sink. Amanda was sure she'd read a *Harry Potter* book in German. They remembered watching the film *Amélie* on Raffaele's computer. The popular French movie had a childish flair that seemed ideal for this particular couple.

In the e-mail, Amanda said they went to his place to watch a movie, eat dinner, and spend the evening indoors.

"We didn't go out," she stressed.

For certain, they were at Raffaele's place at 5:45 P.M., because Jovanna Popovic, a Serbian medical student, rang the doorbell and saw both of them. She told Raffaele that she needed to retrieve a suitcase that her mother was sending by bus that evening, and could he drive her to the station at midnight?

When questioned later by police, Jovanna said Raffaele acted, oh, maybe a bit differently than usual, but only in contrast to his normal "warm and fun-loving nature." He readily agreed to meet her on Garibaldi Street when she needed him.

At 8:18 P.M., Patrick Lumumba, Amanda's boss at Le Chic, texted her to say that it was slow at work, just like a Sunday, and she didn't need to come in. As Meredith had complained, Amanda used Italian at every opportunity. With Patrick, she had no choice, because his English was practically nonexistent. At 8:35 P.M., she texted a simple message in schoolgirl Italian.

Certo ci vediamo più tardi buona serata! "Okay see you later good evening!" (as Amanda translated it).

"I didn't really want to go to work that night, I preferred to stay home with Raffaele," she later said. "I was very pleased. In fact I actually jumped on Raffaele and went 'Woo! I don't have to go to work.'"

Shortly afterward Amanda turned off her cell phone, both to save the battery, she said, and to avoid getting another call from Patrick asking her to come in after all. Raffaele also turned off his phone sometime later, perhaps to get some privacy.

"My father bombarded me with telephone calls, even four per day," Raffaele later said. "He wanted me to study, to prepare my thesis, but I had written only a draft."

At 8:42 P.M., Raffaele received a three-minute, forty-one-second phone call from his father.

Around 8:45 P.M., Jovanna Popovic again rang Raffaele's doorbell to let him know that his services wouldn't be needed after all. Her mother, it turned out, had called to say that the suitcase never made it to the station.

Amanda answered the buzzer and invited the girl in, but Jovanna said no thanks, she needed to get home. Later, she told police the American girl had not acted strangely and that she was always cheerful and outgoing.

At 9:10 P.M., records show that *Amélie* ended on Raffaele's computer. Freed from any social obligations, the lovers simply lazed around for the rest of the evening, doing this and that in no particular order, they would later tell police.

MEREDITH had been in one place all this time, Robyn Butterworth and Amy Frost's flat, the same place where she'd dined on Halloween. Sophie Purton was also there, as were a few other British friends. They were all squeezed together on a bed, watching *The Notebook*, a hit American film about a couple who fall madly in love, break up, and find each other again after many years.

Everyone was still tired from Halloween, they said later, but Meredith was perfectly calm and quiet. They didn't gossip about Amanda that night, but instead talked about boys they knew back home. The girls kept pausing the movie to look at photos taken on Crawloween. Meredith had captioned her Facebook shots "Halloween Perugia Styliieeeeee!"

When they got hungry around 6 P.M., they stopped the movie to eat a pizza they'd baked, followed by coffee-flavored gelato and an apple crumble. Nobody drank anything alcoholic. Meredith wasn't very hungry, Sophie remembered, and ate only part of her pizza.

A little before 9 P.M., Meredith said she was tired and wanted an early evening. That surprised no one, given their jam-packed Halloween. She never mentioned anything about a date that night. That would have surprised them.

"She would have told us," Amy said.

Before Meredith left that night, she borrowed a history

book from Robyn. They had an exam coming up, and both girls mistakenly thought they had class the next day, not knowing that the university would be closed on All Souls' Day. Meredith promised to return the book to Robyn before the 10 A.M. class.

Then Sophie and Meredith left the flat together, zipping up their jackets against the chill. They headed downhill on Via Bontempi, talking about how they needed to catch some sleep. Soon they turned into Via del Roscetto and kept going until they got to Via del Lupo ("Street of the Wolf"), where they parted at 8:55 P.M. Sophie was sure of the time, because she had a TV show she wanted to watch, and she got home in time to see it.

If Meredith took her usual path, then she continued on seedy Via Roscetto, past a Chinese restaurant, and then took the stairs down Via della Pergola, past the dicey basketball court, and then crossed the street in front of the parking garage.

Near 9 P.M., Meredith must have reached the cottage, her final destination. Around that time, she tried to place a call to her mother, but it was cut off.

At 10 P.M., somebody tried to use Meredith's British cell phone to reach her London bank, but couldn't get through, apparently because the caller had neglected to punch in the London area code. At 10:13 P.M., her bank sent an automated message to that same phone, but nobody answered. Both calls appeared to originate from somewhere on Via della Pergola, according to police.

At 10:30 P.M., an Italian couple returning from a romantic dinner in the center came down the stairs on Via della Pergola to get their car. A "colored man" running in the opposite direction nearly ran into them.

At about the same time, a car driven by Pasqualino Coletta, a tourist visiting Perugia, broke down right outside the parking garage. He waited for a tow truck from 10:30 P.M. to 11 P.M. He saw nothing strange, nor did he hear any screams.

Elderly Nara Capezzali, who lived in an apartment across the street from the cottage, had gone to bed around 9 or 9:30 P.M., but slept fitfully. She got up, about two hours later, she thought, to use the bathroom. Then she heard a "long, prolonged scream."

"At one point I heard the cry of a woman," she later said. "It was not a normal cry. My hair stood on end." Her apartment had double-glazed windows and faced away from the cottage, but she did have a bathroom window that looked out in that direction. She looked through it, but didn't see anything unusual. Then she thought she heard two people running, in opposite directions, away from that area. Or, as she put it, "the sound of dry leaves and gravel along the path of the house of the crime and, almost simultaneously, the steps of someone hurrying along the metal steps of the car park."

Nara didn't look at her watch, nor did she call the police.

Shortly after midnight, Meredith's father, John, called his daughter as he'd promised. She did not pick up the phone.

Around 1 A.M. a young Tunisian man named Hicham Khiri (aka Shaky), who knew the British girls from the clubs, accompanied a friend to the parking garage on Sant'Angelo, right across the street from the cottage. They stopped to chat. Before they said good-bye, they looked over at the cottage. Everything seemed calm and peaceful.

At 2:30 A.M., Rudy Guede was spotted at the Domus disco, dancing with his Spanish friends.

CHAPTER FOUR

ALL SOULS' DAY

WHERE IS MEREDITH KERCHER?

Friday, November 2, 2007

"She was at home, locked up inside, how could she have protected herself any better? It is horrible."

—Perugia resident to the Associated Press

ON All Souls' Day, the sun shone in the slanted trees around the cottage. The front door with the bad lock stood wide open. Someone had thrown a rock through Filomena's window, the one with the shutters that wouldn't stay shut. At first glance, everything inside the apartment looked pristine. The dishes had been put away in the spick-and-span kitchen. The hallways looked swept. But someone had left odd traces in each bathroom.

Nothing stirred in Meredith's room, crammed with notebooks, calendars, Italian dictionaries, pretty dresses, purses, schoolbooks, family photos, jewelry, writing paper—all the necessities of student life. Behind her bedroom door, locked now from the outside, the second act of the Meredith mystery was about to unfold.

THE first person to step into an alternate reality was a complete stranger, twenty-six-year-old Alessandro Biscarini. Around 8:30 A.M. on that clear autumn day, the boyish Perugia resident was having breakfast with his mother, Elisabetta Lana, and his sister, Fiametta, in their posh *villa indipendente*, a beautiful private house set in an enormous well-maintained garden. About a half mile uphill from the cottage, it appeared on the map on Via Sperandio, but was actually on Via Andrea da Perugia, near an early Christian church built on a former pagan temple. Towering trees and thick bushes concealed the property from the road. In fact even many Perugini didn't know there was a house behind all that shrubbery.

Elisabetta was recovering from a disturbing night. She had received a menacing phone call around 10 P.M. A male voice had warned: "*C'é una bomba nel vostro water—non fate pipi, non tirate l'acqua, e uscite di casa perché puo esplodere!*" There is a bomb in your toilet—do not piss, do not flush, and get out of the house because it may explode!

At first Elisabetta thought she was the butt of a practical joke. She simply put down the phone. But then she became uneasy. This caller appeared to be a mind reader. She had been on the verge of using the toilet.

Worse, even on this enviable street, she had reason to worry.

"My family had suffered in the past," Elisabetta said later, "a burglary in 2003, one in 2004 of particular importance, and an attempted robbery in December 2006."

She also felt rattled because she'd been receiving crank calls in the middle of the night. When she answered the phone, the caller either hung up or breathed into the phone.

Elisabetta didn't share the typical Italian reluctance about calling the police. She dialed 113, a simple act that would drastically alter the lives of several strangers. There were many different kinds of police officers in Italy, as well as units within units, each with specialized skills. A foreigner could go crazy trying to figure whom to dial, but Elisabetta chose the *Polizia Postale* (the Postal Police), the division that handled telephones and other communication devices.

The cops took her call right way and promised to send over a squad car.

Next, Elisabetta dialed her son's cell phone and asked him to hurry over. She reached him at 10:30 P.M., at a friend's house. Alessandro jumped into his car and rushed to the villa. When he reached the house, the Postal Police had already pulled into the drive. Under his mother's watchful eye, they made a sweep of house and garden—albeit in the dark—and found no bombs.

Elisabetta calmed down. The officers told her to call again if she received more threats.

Now a phone call from Alessandro's girlfriend interrupted his breakfast. Feeling the need for *un po' di privacy*, "a little privacy," Alessandro went outside. He strolled around the half-acre garden, enjoying the crisp morning air and talking on the phone.

Around 9 A.M. an object caught his eye. He stopped to look. He saw a light-colored Motorola, flipped over, its keyboard resting on the ground. It was in the middle of the lawn, less than sixty feet from the wooded Via Andrea da Perugia, which wound uphill from the cottage.

Alessandro scooped up the phone, went into the house, and showed it to his mother, who thought one of the officers might have lost it during the previous night's search. Again, she called the Postal Police. They ask her to bring the phone to their office. So Elisabetta dropped it into a plastic bag and took the phone to the station. She signed a statement at 11:31 A.M., left matters in the hands of the cops, and headed for a nearby market to pick up groceries.

Neither she nor anyone in her family ever heard that phone ring.

At 11:50 A.M., the Postal Police called Elisabetta from the station. "Do you know a Filomena?" they asked, because police had removed the Vodafone SIM card from the phone and traced it back to its buyer, Filomena Romanelli, on Via della Pergola. Filomena, it turned out later, had loaned an extra phone of hers to Meredith to make local calls.

No, Elisabetta said, neither she nor her family members knew anyone called Filomena. Elisabetta then wondered if it might belong to their maid, but when the latter was questioned, she also drew a blank.

Around 12 P.M. at the villa, Alessandro went into the kitchen to make himself a panino. Fiametta and the maid decided to search the garden for signs of an intruder from night before.

Suddenly the two women heard a ringing noise

from somewhere off in the shrubbery. Fiametta followed the sound and started poking around in the bushes with a spade. Incredibly, she found *another* cell phone under dead leaves and brambles, less than twenty feet from Via Andrea da Perugia.

Fiametta stared at the tiny phone, a gray and black Sony Ericsson, later determined to be British. By the time she reached it, it had stopped ringing. She brought it into the house and asked Alessandro to take a look.

It rang again. He checked the display.

"AMANDA," it said.

WHY didn't Meredith answer her phone?

That was the question her friends and family would be asking all day.

For Robyn Butterworth, the worrying had begun at 10 A.M. Meredith had not shown up for their class. Even though it turned out to have been canceled, Robyn still waited around for her friend to appear. She didn't want to nag her about the book, but it was new and expensive and she needed it back so that she could study for the exam.

"I didn't worry too much at first because, to be honest, Meredith was always late," she said. "We texted each other, never called. But after a while I started getting nervous. I called. Then I called again. I kept calling."

Meredith never did pick up.

MEANWHILE Amanda and Raffaele were in holiday mode, as they said later. They planned to ditch their schoolbooks that day and drive to Gubbio, a beautiful medieval mountain town. But first, Amanda wanted to take her customary shower at the cottage while Raffaele wanted to catch up on his sleep. Amanda said she put on her gray-striped sweater and jeans from the night before and set off for the cottage, carrying an empty sack to pick up her dirty laundry and planning to grab a mop from home because Raffaele's floor was still damp from the busted pipe under the sink. Since Raffaele had maid service, he'd never purchased a mop.

When Amanda reached the cottage, around 10:30 A.M., she said that she saw the open door but wasn't surprised because of the bad lock; as she later told her mother, "I didn't go from seeing an open door to thinking, oh, there's been a murder."

Amanda described that first look at the cottage in the long e-mail:

> The door was wide open. strange, yes, but not so strange that i really thought anything about it. i assumed someone in the house was doing exactly what i just said, taking out the trash or talking really quickly to the neighbors downstairs. so i closed the door behind me but i didnt lock it, assuming that the person who left the door open would like to come back in. when i entered i called out if anyone was there, but no one responded and i assumed that if anyone was there, they were still asleep. lauras door was open which meant she wasn't home, and filomenas door was also closed.

Meredith's door was closed, but the American girl assumed that she was sleeping in, just as she had the previous day. Then Amanda went into the bathroom to take a "quick" shower.

> It was after i stepped out of the shower and onto the mat that i noticed the blood in the bathroom. It was on the mat I was using to dry my feet and there were drops of blood in the sink. At first I thought the blood might have come from my ears which I had pierced extensively not too long ago, but then immediately i knew it wasnt mine because the stains on the mat were too big for just droplets from my ear, and when i touched the blood in the sink it was caked on already. There was also blood smeared on the faucet. again, however, i thought it was strange, because my room-mates and i are very clean and we wouldn't leave blood.

She told herself that perhaps Meredith was having "menstrual issues" and hadn't cleaned up ("ew"). Since there were no towels in the bathroom, another oddity, Amanda said that she then went into her bedroom to get more, using the blue bathmat like a coaster so she wouldn't have to step on the cold floors. The room had a dresser, small closet, nightstand, and desk, on which she kept her Toshiba laptop. Everything was neatly arranged and Spartan, as if she didn't spend much time there.

Amanda said that she turned on her computer and played some music. After she changed into a blue top, a long white skirt, and black hiking boots, she went into the larger bathroom shared by Filomena and Laura to borrow their hair dryer.

She dried her hair and then made a very unsettling discovery. Not only was the toilet full of feces, but somebody had left a lot of toilet paper in the bowl.

"I noticed the shit that was left in the toilet, something that definitely no one in our house would do. i started feeling a little uncomfortable and so I grabbed the mop out of the closet and left the house, closing and locking the door," Amanda said in the e-mail.

Ironically, Meredith had complained of Amanda's own inadequate toilet flushing habits. Amanda later explained that she didn't know about the "loo brush" that English people use to clean the toilet after flushing. Used to powerful American plumbing, she hadn't realized that the less-forceful European toilets often needed more attention, perhaps even the use of the brush, to do away with all remnants in the bowl.

Amanda hurried back to Raffaele's flat, taking the mop with her. She quickly mopped his small floor. Over breakfast, she described to him "the strange blood in the bathroom, the door wide open, the shit left in the toilet."

As Raffaele later said to police: "She told me that when she got home, she found the door wide open and bloodstains in the small bathroom. She asked me whether I thought it was strange. I said I did, and advised her to phone her friends."

When Marco Brusco, one of Raffaele's lawyers, was asked later if the Sollecito family blamed Amanda for anything, he mentioned this particular moment.

"Well, perhaps, this one thing she might have done differently," said the bearded lawyer, a southern Italian known for his outgoing manners and constant smile. He paused, somber, trying to be tactful, choosing his words with care.

"If only . . . well, if only Amanda could have called the police herself and not gone to Raffaele," he continued in a wistful voice. "That's all, just that one little thing. You see, she barely knew him."

Asked what would gone differently, he explained about the plans for Raffaele's graduation party.

"They thought they'd found a restaurant. Don't you see? He would have been in Milan in a few weeks. He never would have been part of this."

ON November 1, while at Raffaele's, Amanda made a flurry of calls, as her phone records confirm.

At 12:07 P.M., she called Meredith's British phone, but got no reply. Perhaps this was the ringing that Fiametta Biscarini heard, leading her like a homing device to the second cell phone in the garden.

At 12:08 P.M. Amanda called Filomena. The only Italian roommate still in town, Filomena had spent a happy evening with friends at the amusement park, riding the roller coaster and playing games, and then had returned to Marco's flat about 10 P.M. Later, other friends had called, wanting them to go out, but they'd said they were too tired to leave the flat again.

Filomena was frazzled. She'd gotten up later than she'd planned and had borrowed Marco's car to pick up her best friend, Paola Grande. They were heading off to the *Fiera dei Morti* (Fair of the Dead) at Piann di Massiano on Perugia's outskirts, a huge, chaotic affair offering everything from barbecued pigs turning on spits to carnival rides, flower stalls, and a flea market. Filomena picked up Paola later than she'd planned, discovered that she'd run out of cigarettes, and stopped to get them. Then, when they finally reached the fairgrounds, her cell phone rang.

"While we were trying to park the car, I received a call from Amanda, who told me she had slept at Raffaele's house, and that when she had returned to our house, she had found the door open and blood in her bathroom," Filomena said later. "She said she'd taken a shower, that she was scared . . . and that she was going to call Raffaele Sollecito. It seemed really strange to me. I asked her to check that the house was in order and to call the police."

Paola, who overheard this conversation, said Filomena had not told Amanda to call police, a sensible hesitation since Amanda was a foreigner, nine years younger, with limited Italian. At no time did the American girl try to call police. Nor would she have had any need to call Raffaele, since she made all the calls from his flat. The differences in the two accounts may simply be the result of nerves, distress, and a serious language barrier. Amanda's phone records show no calls either to the police or Raffaele that day.

According to Amanda, Filomena told her that she'd gone to a party the night before and had not yet been back to the cottage. Filomena didn't know where Meredith was, but knew for certain that Laura was in Rome.

That meant Meredith had most likely spent the night alone in the flat—and that she was still unaccounted for.

Filomena and Paola entered the fairgrounds and started walking around the stalls. Paola said her friend was agitated and kept her cell phone clenched in her hand. Finally, Filomena called Amanda, who said in the e-mail:

Filomena seemed really worried, so i told her id call meredith and then call her back. i called both of mer-edith's phones the english one first and last and the italian one between. The first time i called the english phone rang and then sounded as if there was distur-bance, but no one answered. i then called the Italian phone and it just kept ringing, no answer. i called her english phone again and this time an english voice told me her phone was out of service.

Phone records showed this sequence:

12:07 P.M. Amanda calls Meredith's phone. No answer.
12:08 P.M. Amanda calls Filomena.

12:11 P.M. Amanda calls Meredith's Italian phone. No
    answer.
12:11 P.M. Amanda calls Meredith's British phone
    again. No answer.
12:12 P.M. Filomena calls Amanda.
12:20 P.M. Filomena calls Amanda.
12:34 P.M. Filomena calls Amanda.

At some point after the last call, Amanda and Raffaele
hurried back to the cottage. Amanda carried her handbag plus
the mop, dropping the latter on the concrete landing in front
of her flat.

Then she unlocked the door and led Raffaele around the
house. He said that they went first into the larger bathroom,
where she showed him the feces, then they went into Filomena's room, which was a wreck. Somebody had rummaged
through the cupboards and thrown clothes on the floor. Most
alarming, a large rock had been thrown through the window
and had fallen under the desk, half-hidden in a Sisley shopping bag.

In Amanda's e-mail, she said:

The living room/kitchen was fine. looked perfectly
normal. i was checking for signs of our things missing, should there have been a burglar in our house
the night before. filomenas room was closed, but
when i opened the door her room was a mess and
her window was open and completely broken, but her
computer was still sitting on her desk like it always was
and this confused me. convinced that we had been
robbed i went to lauras room and looked quickly in,
but it was spotless, like it hadnt even been touched.
this too, i thought was odd. i then went into the part
of the house that meredith and i share and checked
my room for things missing, which there weren't. then i
knocked on merediths room.
    At first i thought she was asleep so i knocked gen-
tly, but when she didnt respond i knocked louder and
louder until i was really banging on her door and
shouting her name. no response. panicking, i ran out

onto our terrace to see if maybe i could see over the
ledge into her room from the window, but i couldn't
see in. bad angle.

Raffaele wrote in his diary:

*There was glass on the floor and the room was a mess.
Amanda's door was open but the room was tidy. Then I
went to Meredith's door and saw it was locked. First, I
checked to see if what Amanda had told me about the blood
in the bathroom was true. I noticed there were drops of
blood in the sink and there was something strange on the
bathmat, a mixture of blood and water, while the rest of
the bathroom was clean. Nothing else was out of place.*

   *Just then, Amanda went into the big bathroom and
came out looking scared. She clung to me and said that
when she was showering earlier, there had been stools in
the lavatory bowl but now it was clean. I wondered what
was going on and went out to see if I could climb up to
Meredith's window. I tried to force the door but I couldn't
open it.*

At 12:34 P.M., Filomena made a final call to Amanda.
   "We spoke to each other for the third time," Filomena
recalled, though it was the fourth call, "and she told me that
the window in my room was broken and that my room was
in a mess." Filomena also misremembered the call as having
taken place at 12:45.
   At 12:47 P.M., Amanda placed the first of five calls to her
mother, Edda, back home in Seattle, where it was 4:47 A.M.
She said, "Mom, I'm okay, I'm home, but I think somebody
might have been in my house." She told Edda about the open
door, the blood in the bathroom, and the unflushed toilet. She
said she couldn't find her roommate, Meredith.
   Edda told her to hang up and call the police.
   Since Amanda was a foreigner with poor language skills,
Raffaele said he would handle the call. First, though, he called
his sister, Vanessa, for advice. She worked in Rome for the
Carabinieri, the paramilitary unit that handles violent crime.

"At the end I think the thing to do was break down Meredith's door," Raffaele wrote in his diary. "We try, but we cannot, then we call my sister and she tells me to call 112 [similar to 911]. I call them and leave the name of Amanda and the details and try to explain briefly the situation. They say they would call back. We pause to wait outside."

At 12:51 P.M., Carabinieri captain Daniele Ceppitelli received a call from a polite Italian boy whose accent indicated that he was from the south, alerting officers to a possible burglary. Ceppitelli was busy juggling calls that day, and he told the young man to call back later.

At 12:54 P.M., Raffaele redialed 112. This call would become a hit on YouTube. The Italian student's voice sounds calm, self-confident. Amanda can be heard clearly in the background, supplying address details.

RS: Hello, good morning, listen, ah . . . someone broke
    into the house through a window and made a big
    mess. There is a closed door.
POLICE: They managed to enter that way, they broke
    a window? And how do you know that's how they
    entered?
RS: You can see the signs. There are also stains of
    blood in the bathroom. They didn't take anything.
    The problem is the door is locked. . . . There is a lot
    of blood.
POLICE: There is a locked door? Which door is locked?
RS: The one belonging to the roommate who isn't here
    and we don't know where she is. Yes, yes, we tried
    to call her, but she does not respond to anyone.
POLICE: Okay, good, now we will send a patrol to
    verify the situation.

FROM this point on, all was conflict and contradiction, a battle of words. Raffaele and Amanda were on one side; prosecution witnesses and police, on the other. All sides agreed that the couple was outside at this point, on the lawn. The disagreement: Had Michele Battistelli and Fabio Marzi, two officers from the Postal Police, hot on the trail of Filomena's cell phone, arrived after Raffaele called the Carabinieri? Or had Raffaele called the Carabinieri after the Postal Police had already arrived, to establish some kind of alibi?

The Postal Police insisted that they arrived first, in a dark, unmarked sedan that they parked outside. They said they saw the two college students standing around, on a sunny patch near the fence.

"They were whispering to each other and told me they were waiting for the Carabinieri," one officer said. "They didn't say when they had called them just that they were waiting for them."

Neither officer saw Raffaele make a call. Later they would insist that they'd actually arrived at 12:35 P.M., shaving ten minutes off the previous claim, which only added to the confusion. This point would be debated and debated until at the end, the two accounts would differ only by five minutes.

"They told me that they had come back to the house and found the front door open and the window of one of the flatmates, Filomena Romanelli, smashed," recalled Battistelli.

Raffaele invited the officers to come inside, where he and Amanda showed them the broken window and the ransacked room with clothes on the floor.

Since Amanda lived in the house, she was given the task of escorting these officers around the cottage. She communicated with them in broken Italian.

"After the police arrived, I brought them into the house, because I thought that they were the people that Raffaele had called," she wrote in her e-mail. The officers were dressed in *Borghese* (plain clothes) not in uniform, which could explain why Raffaele apparently didn't inform Amanda that they weren't the Carabinieri. "And so I showed them that the door was locked, that the window was broken."

Battistelli was a telecommunications investigator unused to burglary or murder scenes, but he made a few quick deductions. "I immediately thought that this had been an attempt to make it look like a break-in," he insisted. He recalled seeing glass on top of the clothes, although the crime scene photos would not show that. From the glass, he said, he deduced that the intruder had ransacked the room first and then broken the window from the inside. He also noticed that small, easy-to-sell valuables were still in place, such as the computer in Filomena's room and a camera in the kitchen.

Meanwhile Filomena still hadn't arrived, even though she was only a fifteen-minute drive away from the cottage. But she had called her boyfriend, Marco, and asked him to rush to the cottage. Since Filomena had his car, he had to call his friend Luca Altieri, Paola's boyfriend, and ask for a ride.

Frank Sfarzo would later comment on the weirdness of this call. Here was Luca Altieri, a complete stranger to Meredith, Amanda, and Raffaele. Suddenly his good friend, Marco Zaroli, called asking for a lift, saying that Filomena's house had been broken into.

"Luca doesn't know, but the script of his scene is already written," Frank wrote on Perugia Shock. "He's not going just to drive a friend to check a theft. He is going on a trip to hell."

The two Italian men, both medium size with brown hair and glasses, arrived at the cottage shortly before 1 P.M. Not long afterward, Filomena arrived with Paola, a stranger to Raffaele and Amanda. Paola said the couple was in Amanda's room when she arrived and they came out to introduce themselves. In the American girl's e-mail, she captured all this activity in a rush:

> Two uniformed police investigators came to our house.
> I showed them what I could and told them what I
> knew. I gave them phone numbers and explained a
> bit in broken English, and then Filomena arrived with
> her boyfriend Marco and two other friends of hers.
> All together we checked the house out, talked to the
> police.

Filomena, wearing a loose top and jeans tucked into high leather boots, hurried into her own room. It was a mess. The broken window was scary, not to mention the clothes thrown on the floor. But her money was still there, plus her designer

sunglasses, the gold jewelry she kept in a drawer in the nightstand, and her laptop computer. She rummaged around, looking for her things, destroying part of the crime scene.

"Stupid burglars," she said to her boyfriend, with a nervous laugh.

"It seemed an unusual theft and we joked that it was not a
professional thief," she later explained. "But we could not find
Mez and there was blood in the bathroom. I was worried."

The Carabinieri still hadn't arrived, but the two Postal
Police officers faced the six young people. By now, the officers had learned about both cell phones. They knew that the
first phone found, the one traced to Filomena, had been loaned
to Meredith Kercher so that she could make local calls. The
police also knew that Meredith, the owner of the second cell
phone, was missing, but they did not suspect that she'd been
murdered. Nobody did at this point. The officers were reluctant to break down Meredith's door without good reason.

Filomena took charge. She said it was very strange that her
flatmate Meredith would be without her cell phones, that she
carried them everywhere. In fact, Filomena couldn't picture
Meredith without the British cell phone tucked into her back
pocket in case her mother, who was ill, needed to reach her.

Still, the two officers hesitated. They were Postal Police,
not Carabinieri. They were not supposed to go around kicking down doors. Before they destroyed property, they needed
to know: did Meredith usually lock her door or not? The two
roommates, Amanda and Filomena, couldn't agree. Actually,
they couldn't even understand each other. Filomena spoke to
the police in rapid Italian. Amanda struggled to explain, in
her bad Italian, that *sometimes* Meredith locked the door.

"Amanda said Meredith always kept her door locked but
Filomena said the exact opposite," Luca would tell police,
without addressing the language difficulties. Later, Laura
Mezzetti, the other Italian roommate, would confirm that,
yes, Meredith would lock her door when she went to see her
parents in London or was away on some other trip.

After the locked door discussion, Filomena stayed with
the police while Amanda went into the kitchen to call her
mother.

Meanwhile, Raffaele stayed with the other Italians, who

were standing in front of the door. Luca asked him why it was already cracked.

"Raffaele said that he'd tried to break it down," remembered Paola. "We asked the police to open the door but they said they couldn't, so we decided to do it."

Finally, with Filomena's blessing, at about 1:15 P.M., Luca gave the door three or four hard kicks. It flew open, knocked right off its hinges.

The room was dark. Everyone except Raffaele and Amanda got a quick look, seeing a terrifying image: blood everywhere. Meredith's beige duvet on the floor, with a bluish foot protruding from the edge of it.

"*Un piede! Un piede!*" yelled Luca and Filomena. A foot! A foot!

Marco shouted, "*Sangue, sangue!*" Blood, blood!

"All I remember was Filomena saying 'a foot, a foot,'" Raffaele would later say. "I was in shock. I couldn't understand what was going on. All I heard was 'a foot, a foot.' I thought there was a foot in her room."

Paola screamed. She took off down the hallway and ran out of the house.

Amanda heard the shouts, from the kitchen. Even her mother could hear the commotion over the phone from Seattle.

"She said, 'A foot, a foot!'" Edda recalled. "So I thought there was a foot in the room. Maybe an animal foot. I didn't know what to think."

Amanda hung up abruptly. A few minutes later, she called back, panic in her voice.

"'They found a body in Meredith's room,'" Edda remembered her daughter saying. "'I gotta go, the police want to talk to me.'"

Amanda headed for Meredith's room, but Raffaele grabbed her and pulled her out of the house.

Inspector Battistelli had heard the screaming, the cries of "*sangue, sangue.*" He ordered everybody out of the house.

Only Luca lingered for a moment. He saw Battistelli, he would later say, go into the bedroom, kneel by Meredith, and lift the duvet to see if she was alive.

Battistelli would swear that he did not enter the room but

only observed the scene from the doorway, that he could see the blood and the lack of movement under the duvet, so he immediately got on the phone to headquarters.

Meanwhile, outside, Amanda was sitting on the ground. "And I could not . . . I was in shock and did not understand what had happened."

CHAPTER FIVE

BAD NIGHT AT THE *QUESTURA*

Friday, November 2, 2007

"One of the English girls, she tells me she wants to kick Amanda. She actually says that."

—Pisco Alessi, Merlin's co-owner

"Did Amanda understand what her behavior would look like to other people? Well, no. She was traumatized, devastated."

—Edda Mellas

FILOMENA Romanelli could not forget the blood. So much blood. It was everywhere, she told a reporter for the Italian newspaper *Corriere della Sera* in the only interview she ever gave. "But what country is this? Why must a 20-year-old girl be killed this way, why does she find herself dead now, without anything, without a future?"

Filomena had set off that morning to spend a pleasant day with her best friend at the Fair of the Dead, only to be literally thrown into a murder scene. Her boyfriend had tried to shield her; when the door came down, he had yelled, "*Via! Via!*" (Go! Go!) after he saw the blood. Then he'd yanked her out of there. But Filomena couldn't forget the nightmare vision: a beige duvet, a ghostly human foot, a sea of blood.

Who would want to kill the dazzling Meredith Kercher, only two months into her Erasmus year? When, why, and how was the murder pulled off? Filomena could think of no enemies that Meredith had. No suspects. Neither could Amanda. They were all strangers, really. "Just settling in," as the American girl put it.

Now Filomena stood around on the cottage's gravel drive, under some trees, trying to explain all this to a bearded officer, while he jotted down details in a little notebook. Her boyfriend, Marco, hovered nearby. So did Luca, keeping his arm around Paola, who looked dazed. Paola could not remember how much time had passed between her scream and the moment when she had finally seen Luca outdoors. There was just a blackness.

But Paola did remember the blood on the wall. That had told her something.

"I could see that the girl had struggled," she said later. "I knew that."

Meanwhile Amanda and Raffaele huddled near Luca's silver car on the other side of the gravel drive. A detective had already placed a white marker on Filomena's window ledge— right behind where they were standing—and he had used red and white tape to block off the entire cottage as a crime scene. *Villetta degli orrori*, "the house of horrors," reporters would call it now.

THE Postal Police ordered all six young people to stay outdoors, thereby sparing them a terrible sight. Inspector Battistelli dialed 118, the unit that handled medical emergencies. He also called the *Squadra Mobile*, the "Flying Squad," the investigative unit charged with identifying suspects and collecting evidence. An ambulance showed up around 1:50 P.M., only minutes after Monica Napoleoni, head of homicide for the Flying Squad. She was a tanned, rail-thin brunette with big brown eyes. Wearing her trademark dark jacket, tight jeans, and tall leather boots, she looked like a double agent from a spy movie and would play a key role in the Meredith murder investigation over the next two years.

The two paramedics who'd arrived in the ambulance hurried inside, not waiting to put on protective gear, but Napoleoni paused on the threshold of the cottage to don gloves and shoe coverings. She followed the paramedics, taking notes and snapping pictures. A little later, Perugia's forensic police also showed up. They wore white protective clothing, looking like Martians, but not all of them covered their hair.

In Meredith's bedroom, the duvet still shrouded everything except for part of her face and one foot. When the rescue workers lifted the covering, they saw her half-naked body resting on a bloody pillow. Meredith's left leg was turned out at a peculiar angle. The killer had removed all of her clothes except for a white T-shirt. Soaked in red, it had been pulled up to expose her breasts.

"It was like a butcher shop," Napoleoni later said of the murder scene. "*Era scannata.*" She was slaughtered.

Amid pools of blood on the terra-cotta tile floor, police found the rest of the victim's clothes, the same ones that her friends had seen her wearing before she vanished the previous evening. All her garments were accounted for: the blue jacket, boyfriend jeans, pale sweater, black underpants, white socks, and red and white Puma athletic shoes.

Someone had hacked off Meredith's bloodstained white bra with a knife and made a point of pulling the duvet up over her throat. When the officers removed the covering, they didn't have to wonder about the cause of death. The killer had stabbed the victim three times in the throat. Two of the wounds were small, as if an assailant had first used the knife to taunt or force cooperation. But the killing blow caused a huge, gaping wound on the left-hand side.

Once investigators had time to study the blood splatters on the tiles, they theorized that Meredith had been assaulted in two locations. First, someone had attacked her just inside the bedroom door, perhaps catching her by surprise. Then, after a struggle, she had been trapped near the wardrobe, where officers found the largest pool of blood. The killer either knocked her down or forced her to her knees—and then stabbed her. Forensics experts would never agree on whether she was stabbed from the front or the back, but small, round droplets of blood on her bra and her exposed breasts suggested that she had been on her back, nearly supine, when she bled to death. The victim's blood had spurted upward and fallen back onto her body and splattered the tile floor. Bloody fingerprints marred the bottom of the wardrobe, where she had struggled for her life, making a vain attempt to pull herself back up.

A tiny metal bra clasp, still sewn to a bit of the cloth, lay under the pillow on which Meredith's body rested. Forensic investigators initially missed it, although it showed up in the video they shot this day, November 2. But forty-seven days would pass before they collected this key piece of evidence. By then investigators had trampled it and it had somehow moved more than four feet across the room, ending up under a soiled carpet, in a jumble of shopping bags and other items that the police had sorted through.

A Japanese print of faraway snowy peaks still clung to the inside of Meredith's door, but the doorknob was stained with blood. A blue-covered novel, Ian McEwan's *Enduring Love*, rested on the wooden nightstand next to Meredith's bed, as did a glass of water and a stack of outgoing mail waiting for a delivery that would never come. Meredith had addressed the top letter to her father and had filled out two postcards for friends. The nightstand's top drawer stood slightly open, as if an intruder had made a quick search for valuables, but Meredith's white Mac computer was still on her desk. Her big brown faux-leather purse sat neatly on top of the narrow bed, along with several schoolbooks and a spiral notebook, but it had been rummaged through and Meredith's cash, cell phones, keys, and credit cards were missing.

On the wall, where she had posted photos of smiling friends, someone had wiped a bloody hand, leaving long red stripes on the white paint. The killer had rested the knife on the bed, leaving a bloody outline on the sheet. A bloody handprint stained the pillow under the victim. Forensic police also discovered two of the missing towels from the little bathroom under Meredith's body, soaked in blood. A third, wadded up and lying on the bed, was only slightly bloody.

Police also found a number of distinct bloody shoe prints in the room, all made by the same Nike shoe, which investigators identified by the concentric circles on the soles. Three of the shoe prints appeared on the tile floor next to the victim. The Nike wearer had also left a trail of bloody shoe prints running down the hallway toward the front-door exit, becoming fainter with each step. The only bloody bare footprint found in the flat was the half print left on the blue mat in the small bathroom.

Investigators would later claim that luminol revealed additional bloody bare footprints in the corridor, but Dr. Patrizia

Stefanoni, the DNA analyst from Rome's Forensic Police Service, could not confirm the presence of blood in any of these random prints—since luminol reacts with many household substances, and she did not conduct a second test for blood. All of these bare footprints detected with luminol were tested for DNA, however, and none of them showed Meredith's genetic profile.

In a few of the police photos, the angle hid the biggest throat wound. In those pictures, Meredith appeared to be simply resting on her back, her brown eyes open, drowsily looking over the scene. An optimist might even achieve a moment of denial, hoping against hope that she could still be saved, but other photos showed the terrible throat wound, the heartbreaking defense wounds, the punctures on her palms and bruised arms, plus blood splatters on her chest, arms, and hands.

The close-ups of Meredith, with her head turned to the side, captured the full ghastliness. Her mouth was swollen and bruised, as if she'd been punched in the face. The two small cuts on her throat were visible, as was the fatal stab wound, a blow so savage that the police later said that only a man could have delivered it.

Still, it's possible to hope that Meredith didn't feel the knife going in. Stabbing survivors often say that they didn't feel the blade; instead, they turned cold, then nauseated, then faint. When they finally lost enough blood, they passed out.

NOW Meredith's story belonged to the police. The press caught the cars arriving, everything from the dark, unmarked sedans of the Postal Police to the shiny blue Carabinieri vehicles, the tires squeaking on the roadway. Soon police officers were everywhere, standing around in plain clothes or dark blue jackets that said "Polizia Scientifica," talking on their cell phones and taking notes. Only a few were allowed into Meredith's room. The Carabinieri, it turned out, had been delayed because the house was difficult to find and they'd had to call Amanda on her cell phone to get directions. Called by Raffaele slightly before 1 P.M., they didn't arrive until around 1: 30 P.M.

Then the media rushed in. "Perhaps, yes, somebody alerted

them, but it's not necessary," a top official said of the press with a shrug. "They follow the police, they know everything they do. They can get there right away."

The photographers snapped Napoleoni when she emerged from the house to question the six young people on the gravel drive. One shot showed her quizzing Filomena, Luca, and Paola over by the trees. In another photo, Napoleoni took a hard look at Amanda and Raffaele. They were standing on the gravel by Luca's car, to the left of the front door.

Other high-profile officers also came early, including Marco Chiacchiera, second in command of the Flying Squad. He burned through three sets of cell phone batteries that day, talking to headquarters.

Shortly before 3 P.M., Public Minister (PM) Giuliano Mignini arrived at the cottage. Mignini would lead the criminal investigation as well as prosecute the case. Known for his controversial group crime scenarios, the burly Perugino was there by chance—simply the prosecutor on call, a name picked off the local schedule.

Mignini shook coroner Luca Lalli's plastic-gloved hand on the threshold of the house of horrors, then both went inside. The forensic police allowed Lalli to lift the cover over Meredith long enough to check for rigor mortis, but, unfortunately, would not allow him to take her temperature, a great aid in determining time of death.

Then came Edgardo Giobbi and other officers from SCO (*Servizio Centrale Operative*), the crack investigative squad from Rome. They would assist the prosecutor in re-creating Meredith's final hours. Bit by bit they'd also built a portrait of Meredith's social set, from the cottage tenants to the English girls, from the bartenders to the customers in Perugia's clubs.

After Giobbi came the forensic police from Rome, wearing the protective white clothes but not always the head coverings. The two teams of forensic police, Perugini and Roman, played major roles that first day. They cataloged items in the bedroom of the murdered British girl, making choices that in retrospect seemed either poignant or odd—like the small tube of Vaseline, used by many women for chapped lips, but flagged by police as a sex aid and then worked into their crime theories. The list of items found in the room included:

- A book titled *Early Modern Europe, 1450–1789*, in English

- Plastic teeth in which fake blood was embedded, designed (police noted) to have "a cinematic effect"

- A black cloak marked "Wildmann," with a high collar, found under the desk

- A small container of Vaseline (to fit in a purse), blue and silver on the outside, found under the desk

- Two envelopes with Royal Mail letterhead and paper tucked inside

- A small purse of "faux leather"

- A beige shoulder bag, apparently bloodstained, containing an iPod, a plastic makeup bag, a black pencil, a pen, red lipstick, mascara, and a crumpled white handkerchief

One of the last officers to arrive was Domenico Giacinto Profazio, head of the Flying Squad. His subordinates showed him around the property, but the forensic police from Rome were already at work inside the cottage and he didn't enter. The chubby, nonathletic Profazio quickly concluded that the murder had to have been an inside job. He simply didn't believe, as he later said in court, that anybody could have climbed through Filomena's window without injury. That day, officers directed him to a window on the opposite side of the house, over the balcony. They were convinced that, had they been burglars, they would have chosen that entry point. Although the garden offered many big rocks to hurl through glass, Profazio noted that the balcony had a chair, a table, and a flowerpot—objects he would've used to smash the window, had he been a thief. His conclusion: somebody used a key to get in.

AMANDA recalled this influx of officers in the e-mail she wrote on November 4. "The police told everyone to get out and not long afterward the [Carabinieri] arrived and then, soon afterward, more police investigators. The police took all of our information and asked us the same questions over and over. At the time I had only what I was wearing and my bag, which thankfully had my passport in it and my wallet, no jacket though, and I was freezing."

Raffaele, seeing that Amanda was cold, gave her his gray parka to wear. He wore jeans and a dark blue sweater, with a long yellow scarf wrapped around his neck. "I stayed close to her because she was shocked and cold," he said later.

He and Amanda paid little attention to the press, who perched on the narrow sidewalk on Viale Sant'Angelo, the busy street where the cottage was located, and in the garage parking lot. Film crews even set up their video cameras so they could get an aerial view, capturing Amanda and Raffaele walking around.

The photographers watched and waited. For a long time nothing interesting happened. They snapped the Postal Police talking to the two young couples, Filomena and Marco, Paola and Luca, over by the trees. But nobody drew the cameras like the blond foreign girl and her tall, geeky Italian boyfriend. The two of them held hands. They whispered. They were standing over by the wooden fence that overlooked the ravine.

The photographers waited and waited. Then came the split-second opportunity. They took the money shot. The lovers kissed, only for about thirty seconds, but the brief footage later became a YouTube sensation.

In the clip, Raffaele faced Amanda. He put his arms around her and pulled her in tight. She lifted her chin. He gave her three little pecks. Then he stroked her arms, as Amanda turned to look in the direction of the cameras. She looked bleak.

"I've seen eyes like that in war zones," a British journalist was overheard saying loudly several nights later to fellow scribes drinking beer in La Tana Dell'Orso. "Pitiless, uncaring." Amanda, he told everyone, had "the eyes of a killer."

Later, the Italian press would call Amanda "Luciferina," the girl with the face of an angel and the soul of a devil.

PAOLA and Luca hovered near the officers, trying to figure out exactly how Meredith died. They were not allowed to listen in on what the police were saying, but Paola edged closer to the front door. When a paramedic came out of the house, she saw him mouth the words "Her throat was slit."

She and Luca didn't share this information with Amanda and Raffaele right away, but Paola did try to help the American girl.

"It was very, very cold," Amanda remembered. "First, Raffaele gave me his jacket, but then the others saw that I was cold, really in shock, so they said, 'Come, and come, let's get in the car and get warm.' And inside that car, we talked more about it. We kept saying 'But what did you see? And who was there?' "

Meanwhile Filomena was on the phone.

"The moment I understood the gravity of the situation, I first called the lawyer in the office where I work," she said later, explaining why her first move was to get a legal buffer between her and the police, even in the earliest part of the investigation. She felt this was necessary, she said, because her family was more than four hundred miles away south in Calabria, down in the boot of Italy.

Amanda, whose own family was several continents away, would face the police without legal representation, as would Raffaele.

Next, Filomena called Laura, the other flatmate. It was about 1:45 P.M.

"Thieves have entered the house and killed Meredith," she bluntly said.

"You are kidding," Laura said. "What are you saying? Are you pulling my leg?"

Filomena repeated her remark. Laura was shocked; she hung up, and then called back again, but her roommate couldn't provide any details except that her own room had been ransacked, yet her jewelry was still there, as were her computer and other expensive things.

Laura was still in Viterbo, near Rome. She called a lawyer in the Perugia office where she and Filomena worked and told him about the murder. She "vented a little, cried a little," she later said on the witness stand. Asked why she had called a lawyer first thing, Laura made a bad joke: "Sure, I was calling in to report 'Yes, attorney, I killed my roommate.' " She added that she had certain worries to discuss with him that day, such as how to reschedule a meeting. "And certainly, I was without a house."

After Laura talked to the lawyer that chaotic day, she rounded up her father and various other family members They headed off to Perugia and the police station. .

Filomena's third call was to Giacomo Silenzi, the downstairs neighbor who'd been dating Meredith. She didn't know his number and had to ask Amanda to get it off her cell phone.

When Filomena dialed Giacomo, he was on the train, headed home to Perugia from his holiday in San Giorgio.

"Meredith has been murdered," blurted Filomena.

Giacomo turned white, said Stefano Bonassi, his friend and flatmate, who was also on the train. Giacomo didn't say anything right away, but just sat there, stunned. He'd never been a talker. Now he simply couldn't find the right words.

"Meredith was found dead," he finally told Stefano. Then he just sat there on the train while the wheels kept pulling them closer and closer to Perugia.

"My stomach dropped," he later told the *Daily Mail*. "I just could not believe it. I had spoken with her for the last time just a couple of days earlier and she had sent me a text saying she was looking forward to me coming back."

He and Stefano got off the train in Foligno, the stop before Perugia. Stefano, feeling the need for an older person to advise them, called a professor, Alessio Ariste. They waited around until he joined them at the train station. Then the trio caught the train to Perugia, only about a twenty-minute ride away. There, Giacomo and Stefano called their parents and waited until they arrived. Finally, they all went together to the police station.

Meanwhile, Filomena was outside the cottage, fretting about her things. Incredibly, she decided to run back inside, somehow getting past the officers, either with their permission or without their noticing. She grabbed her purse first, then ran into her bedroom to collect her computer, once again disrupting the crime scene.

Later, she would insist that she saw shattered glass atop her clothes, which would bolster the police's faked-burglary theory. Michele Battistelli, of the Postal Police, would also claim the glass was atop the clothes; although, as stated, no crime scene photo would ever show this.

Filomena carried her computer out of the cottage and put it into the back of Marco's car. At the *questura*, incredulous police would take it away from her, asking her what she had been thinking, removing objects from a crime scene. When she got it back, something strange had happened to the hard drive and she would be hard-pressed to recover the contents.

SOMEWHAT later, police sent all six young people to the *questura* for questioning. The paparazzi caught a shot of Amanda and Raffaele, looking grim and frightened, in the backseat of Luca's car.

"Why did you shower in a house with an open door?" Paola asked Amanda during the fifteen-minute drive. She didn't get an answer, finally realizing that she needed to speak to the American girl through Raffaele, her translator. Paola asked him what time they had arrived at the cottage. Raffaele said Amanda got there around 10:30 A.M., then she had returned to his flat to get him, and they had come back together to look around.

Then Paola, meaning to be kind, asked if Amanda had somewhere to sleep that night. Raffaele said she could stay with him, but that he'd be leaving Perugia for good on the 16th. Indeed, he had an appointment with a professor on the 14th to discuss his thesis.

Then Raffaele started asking Luca and Paola questions. Was Meredith dead? How did she die? What had they seen? Then Raffaele passed the information along to Amanda, in his garbled English. He told her Meredith's throat had been cut.

"At that point I became a bit, uh . . . I closed myself off a little bit inside," Amanda said later. "I cried a bit because I kept thinking but how is it possible? No, it was too much . . ."

Based on the witness reports, Frank Sfarzo reconstructed this crucial moment on Perugia Shock.

RAFFAELE: Is she dead?
LUCA: Yes.

(Amanda cries.)
RAFFAELE: Did they kill her?
LUCA: Yes, they cut her throat.
RAFFAELE: With a knife?
LUCA: No, with the bread.

"Apart from the great Luca's joke this conversation proves that Amanda cried and that she knew how Meredith was killed," Frank Sfarzo added.

Filomena also saw Amanda cry, but none of the reporters ever did. Nor would the police. So the press would write that the American girl didn't shed a single tear for Meredith.

Luca felt spooked by the whole encounter, even checking his car afterward to make sure that Amanda and Raffaele hadn't left anything incriminating in it.

Amanda Knox had always been eccentric, even by Seattle standards, a strong girl who believed in speaking her mind, in telling all. Her parents had worried about her studying abroad, saying that she sometimes lacked common sense. That was one of the reasons why they'd hoped she would study in Germany, where she had close relatives. Everyone agreed that Amanda was book smart, not street-smart. She prided herself on being her own person, not like anyone else. But from now on her freedom would depend on her ability to behave like a conventional person.

Amanda's tears, like her smiles and kisses, would be badly timed.

"**AN** English student has died in Piazza Grimana," the local radio stations began announcing within an hour of the discovery of Meredith's body. The early reports said the student was female, but the name wasn't known yet, nor cause of death. In fact, locals assumed it was a drug overdose, given the neighborhood.

Meredith's friends heard the radio reports. They called people who might know more. They kept the radio on and waited. What else could they do?

Robyn Butterworth knew Meredith hadn't shown up for

class that day. She was very worried, as she told her room-mate Amy Frost. They called Sophie Purton, the last to see Meredith the previous night. She said she hadn't heard from her either.

Then around 3 P.M. Sophie's phone rang. The caller identified herself as an Erasmus program official, speaking in strained tones, choosing each word carefully, as if her heart were in her throat:

> You are Sophie Purton?
> Yes.
> May we speak?
> Yes.
> The caller paused.
> Do you know a girl named Meredith?
> Yes.
> The police are looking for her. May I give them your
>   number?
> Yes.

Sophie called Robyn. They knew now that the police were looking for a girl named Meredith, but they clung to the hope that their friend wasn't the girl who'd died. Maybe she wasn't answering her phone for a different reason.

"They said the girl was Welsh," Robyn said. "They had her age wrong. They said the girl had died near Meredith's house. So we weren't sure."

Pisco, the Merlin's co-owner, had heard the radio reports about a dead English girl. He called Sophie to see if she knew more. By this time the other English friends had evidently started to gather in Robyn and Amy's flat, to comfort one another and come up with a plan. Pisco said he could hear a lot of crying in the background.

"So I don't stay on the phone . . . just a bit. The girls say, not a good time. Maybe later, we can talk."

Late that afternoon, the girls decided to head out for the cottage to see if they could learn anything. They hadn't gotten very far when the police called Sophie's cell phone. They told her to take the other girls and head over to the *Stran-*

ieri, where a police car would pick them up. That was about a fifteen-minute walk.

They arrived at 5:30 P.M. and hung around in front of the *Stranieri*, on the same street corner where Amanda Knox and her sister Deanna had spotted Laura putting up the flyer about a room to rent. The cottage was just around the corner. It was too terrible to think about.

The British girls faced the newsstand on Piazza Grimana, ordinarily a beehive of activity, but dreary and cold in the November light, with papers blowing across the pavement and cars swirling around. People spoke loudly, in order to be heard over the traffic noise.

One of the Italian men was even shouting. Robyn knew him only as D. J. Naf, but his real name was Pietro Campolongo. He was the bookish-looking Merlin's bartender who'd worn the *Scream* mask on Halloween. Robyn had once seen him throw ice cubes playfully at Meredith. Amy had even told her, "I think he fancies you."

"He was talking in Italian to Pisco," Robyn said, "but I understood the gist of it."

"It is *Meredith*," Pietro was saying. "It is *her*." He provided some details about how the body was found, but Robyn didn't want to hear another word from him.

"As I was very upset and still no one had said it was Meredith Kercher, I told Pisco to tell Pietro to be quiet. So at 5:30 P.M., I still didn't know for sure."

Finally, around 6 P.M., the police arrived to transport everybody to the *questura*, a tall, modern building bunched with other gray buildings behind concrete walls, with a little guardhouse in front.

Officers escorted the young people into the station, where they were either shown immediately into separate interrogation rooms or dropped into a large waiting room to wait their turn. After being questioned, officers placed them in that same large chamber, where they would stay until dawn, with nothing for subsistence but vending machine drinks and cookies.

The room was pale, sterile, Pisco said, like a hospital waiting room.

Meredith's friends kept arriving. Little by little they figured out the truth.

"Nobody ever actually told us Meredith died," Robyn said. "There was just talk about a girl who had died. We supposed it was Meredith because eventually every single person had arrived. We were all there except for Meredith. She was still unaccounted for. And so . . ."

ACCORDING to Amanda, she and Raffaele entered the big waiting room around 9 P.M., after they'd finished talking to police. Robyn remembered seeing them later, closer to 10 P.M. or 10:30 P.M. But then, the whole situation was unreal. Everyone felt traumatized. It was hard for people to "hear."

Amanda did not say much at first. She'd given a statement to the police at 2:30 P.M. and Raffaele had given his at 3:45 P.M. Both were exhausted. The questioning had been more grueling for the American girl because she'd answered first in broken Italian and then, when a translator was provided, had repeated everything so that the police could get it down.

Eventually Laura came in as well, along with Giacomo and the rest of the boys downstairs. Amanda hugged Giacomo. He and Raffaele met for the first time. Eventually the witnesses separated into groups divided by language—English speakers over here, Italians over there. Then, too, the *questura* was large, with many rooms. Paola Grande, for instance, never saw the lovebirds in the station, after dropping them off.

In any case, Amanda and Raffaele were thrown among the English girls, who were feeling very raw, still in the very first phase of discovery and shock.

It was a strange time to meet new people. When Sophie Purton was introduced to Amanda, she tried to embrace her but the British girl later complained that the American "did not reciprocate my hug. She seemed quite cold. She kept her arms at her side."

The truth was that without Meredith to unite them, the loose bonds that connected the young people in the room had already begun to fray. Raffaele didn't even have that much to cling to. He was meeting several of Meredith's friends for the first time. He went around introducing himself. He said he was Amanda's boyfriend and that they'd been at the cottage when Meredith's body was found.

His English wasn't very good, Robyn remembered. He was trying to tell them about the door being broken down, and they had to help him find the word for "kicked." Still, he was calm, quiet.

Amanda, on the other hand, made a startling impression. Her moods ranged from angry when discussing the crime, to playful when interacting with Raffaele. Meredith's friends found Amanda's behavior so outrageous that they nearly dropped their reserve.

"One of the English girls, she tells me she wants to kick Amanda," Pisco remembered. He laughed at the absurdity of it. "She actually says that."

Meanwhile panicked friends and relatives of Amanda's kept calling from Seattle, where it was early afternoon. She was very upset, she kept telling them, saying, "I found the body, I did." The British girls listened in on the calls, finding the agitated American annoying.

"At the police station Raffaele was very quiet, nothing strange, but Amanda was always talking on the phone," Sophie said. "She was very affectionate to Raffaele but she would keep complaining: 'I'm tired. I'm hungry. I'm thirsty.'"

Amy complained that Amanda and Raffaele pushed their chairs together. Amanda propped her feet up on his lap. They made faces at each other, kissing, giggling. At one point, she even stuck her tongue out at Raffaele.

"I wondered for the first time if she were mad," Robyn said. "She literally seemed crazy."

Finally, she moved away from the American girl altogether, unable to bear her energy level. "She seemed proud of finding the body. She kept talking about it. She kept saying there was shit in the toilet. Shit. Shit. Shit."

Since none of the girls had been briefed on how Meredith died, they asked Amanda to provide details.

"What do you want to know, because I know everything," Sophie remembered her saying. Amanda gave her a garbled version, based on what she'd pieced together from Paola and Luca and also from the police when they were interrogating her. She told Sophie, incorrectly, that Meredith had been found in the wardrobe with only her foot sticking out. The only correct detail she had, in fact, was that her flatmate's throat had been cut.

Natalie Hayward, a tall, thin, shy-looking girl from Peterborough, wondered if Meredith had suffered.

"What do you think?" Amanda said. "She fucking bled to death."

"She also yelled, 'Those fucking bastards,'" Sophie recalled, "but I don't know who she meant. I think the murderers. She said she took a shower, and then she realized there was some blood."

At another point Sophia overheard Amanda talking to her Italian roommates. "Threat. Threat. Threat," Amanda kept repeating loudly. "Threat. Threat. Threat."

From November 2 to the 5th, Amanda would take more than sixty phone calls, because the people she felt closest to were far away, on different continents. Raffaele, her boyfriend of six days, was ever ready to be her translator, but he barely spoke English. Her mother, Edda, was her strongest supporter, but she was still a disembodied voice on the phone. To top it off, Amanda no longer had a place to live.

Frank Sfarzo of Perugia Shock, who knew his way around the *questura*, described the strange impression that the American girl made on an interpreter later that night:

> There was an Australian in the police station. Assistant Fabio D'Astolto who left that wonderful land to come be a policeman in Perugia. . . . On the afternoon of November 2 he was called to the *questura*. He got there and started to work as an interpreter for Amanda and the English girls until six the next morning. As an interpreter and a waiter because every now and then he would go to the machine to take some snacks or some beverage for everybody. As an interpreter, a waiter, and a psychologist because that night he assisted Amanda during another terrible moment.
>
> At about 3 in the morning the interrogations of Amanda and everyone else had run without any problem. He tells Amanda they have to go down to the scientific police to take her fingerprints. As soon as they arrive

Amanda starts to nervously walk forth and back, then she
starts to bring her hands to her temples continuously and
hit her head. D'Astolto is worried. He talks to Amanda,
he asks her what's going on, he offers her some water,
some coffee. A nice guy this D'Astolto, it really looks
like he was sincerely worried for that self-hurting girl. He
couldn't know that she was just one step from the abyss.

AMANDA remembered the night quite differently in her
lengthy e-mail. She spoke of fielding many questions after
entering the *questura*.

> I was in a room for six hours straight after that without
> seeing anyone else, answering questions in italian for
> the first hour and then they brought in an interpreter
> and he helped me out with the details that i didnt
> know the words for. they asked me of course about
> the morning, the last time i saw her [Meredith], and
> because i was the closest to her, questions about her
> habits and her relationships.

She didn't mention Sophie trying to give her a hug, but
noted that she was meeting some of Meredith's friends for the
first time.

> i met two of merediths english friends, two girls she
> goes out with, including the last one who saw her alive
> that night she was murdered.

For Amanda, who suffered from stomach spasms, the
questura fare was disastrous.

> i sat around in this waiting room without having the
> chance to leave or eat anything besides vending
> machine food (which gave me a hell of a stomache
> ache) until 530 in the morning.

Meanwhile, the police were endlessly watching her. In
fact, homicide chief Monica Napoleoni would never get over

the fact that Amanda hadn't cried while at the *questura*. None of the men cried either, not even Giacomo, Meredith's boyfriend. Some of the English girls also stayed dry-eyed.

"[Amanda and Raffaele] would make faces, kiss each other, while there was the body of a friend in those conditions," Napoleoni recalled. She said the lovers seemed "indifferent to everything," even though they had been the ones to sound the alarm.

Filomena later told investigators she saw Amanda pass a note to Raffaele at one point. Amanda was also seen scribbling in the infamous green notebook:

And so I'm at the police station now, after a long day spent telling how I was the first person to arrive at the house and to find my flatmate dead. The strange thing is that all I want to do now is write a song about this. It would be the first song that I've written and it would be about someone who died in a horrible way for no reason. How morbid is that? I'm starving. And I'd really like to say that I could kill for a pizza but it just doesn't seem right. Laura and Filomena are pretty shocked. Raffaele too. I'm angry. At the start I was scared, then sad, then confused then really fucked off and now . . . I don't know. I can't concentrate. I didn't see her body and I didn't see her blood and so it almost seems like it didn't happen. But it happened, in the room right next to mine. The blood was in the bathroom I used to have a shower today. The front door was open because of the wind and now I haven't got a house and am without a person that was part of my life and I don't know what to do or think.

DJ Johnsrud said Amanda always dealt with her emotions by jotting them down. Composing a song at such a moment might seem strange to many, but Amanda would see it as a sign of respect. "Music is everything to her. She would think that writing a song would be a great way to honor somebody."

The fact that Amanda wrote "I could kill for a pizza," a common expression meaning merely "I'm hungry for pizza," would cause her great harm in Italy, where the phrase was taken literally. "If she would kill for a pizza, what else would she kill for?" startled pundits would actually debate on national TV.

Police sent Raffaele and Amanda home at 5:30 A.M., telling them to report back at 11 A.M. When the *piccioncini* (lovebirds) finally reached Raffaele's flat on Corso Garibaldi, Amanda said she "ate something substantial, and passed out."

ALESSANDRO Capponi, a reporter from *Corriere della Sera*, reached Filomena at nine that first night, coaxing her only interview out of her. Identified as "Filomena R." in the article, she told him that she'd already spoken to police for five hours (and, in fact, she would ultimately be there for another eight hours, until her release around 5 A.M.).

"Filomena R. answered the phone, speaking with a weak voice, and, above all, weeping, wrote Capponi. "She doesn't want to talk. She confides in an acquaintance in Perugia, who calls her to ask about Meredith. 'She was a girl who came to Italy to study, and that's what she was doing, studying, learning. No enemies, no suspects. She was a [twenty-one] year old student who can become nothing now.' "

Filomena continued "crying and asked questions that have no answers: 'How is it possible to live happily like this? When you are not secure even at home, how is that possible?' Asking questions and not expecting answers: 'In what country do such things happen?' "

In the same *Corriere* story, Capponi spoke to several of Meredith's Italian friends, saying they were "sitting around, watching, praying, blaspheming," evidently at the *questura*.

"I knew Meredith, yes," said Pietro Campolongo, the Merlin's bartender who had offended Robyn by loudly talking about the girl's death. "I was at a party with her not long before. . . . She was frequently with her friends, strolling around, at home, in the usual places, Merlin's, La Tana, places where there are hundreds of people every evening."

The friends described Meredith as very pretty, sunny, and strong. "Sociable, determined in studies, never showy. Very nice, of Indian background, an amber complexion. She liked to dance, to go out, to live like a twenty-[one]-year-old: some evenings slightly drunk, perhaps, but in her past, there is nothing to hide," Pietro noted, adding that "Meredith, for example, did not even smoke cigarettes."

"She loved Italy," stressed the *Corriere* reporter. "Everyone who knew her says the same thing. Who knows what great things she might have achieved?"

ACROSS the English Channel, Meredith's loved ones were trying to reach her, leaving frantic messages that police would discover on her British cell phone:

Please call us. Don't make us worry. Please call.

At 5 P.M. London time, a long night of horror had begun for John Kercher, a tall, silver-haired man who wore dark blazers with light-colored turtlenecks and puffed on filtered cigarettes in times of stress. His ex-wife, Arline Kercher, had called him from her hospital bed to tell him that TV newscasters were reporting that a British student had been murdered in Perugia, a girl, but that they didn't have a name or photo yet.

Amazingly, Italian police never did tell the Kerchers that their daughter was dead. Her parents had to call around to find out for sure. John tried to reach Meredith's cell phone at least twelve times that night, but he kept getting her recorded message. At 5:30 P.M., he finally heard her phone ring, but nobody answered. Then he decided to use his reporting skills, calling newspaper desks all around London, working his media contacts. After about two hours he at last reached someone who knew the student's name. But the reporter hesitated, not wanting to be the one to break the awful news.

Yes, the name going around is Meredith.

John Kercher dropped the phone. He couldn't believe it. He clung to one last hope. What if there was another Meredith studying in Perugia?

He made his way to the family home in Coulsdon, where Meredith's siblings, Stephanie, John Jr., and Lyle, were already contemplating the baffling, horrific loss. Only Arline, still in the hospital, wasn't there. But by this time she'd spoken to the Foreign Office and knew that Italian authorities had identified Meredith's name and cell phone number.

At 9 P.M., the family was gathered around the TV. Meredith's photo popped up on the screen. Nobody spoke. They all hugged one another.

"Meredith is so beautiful, so witty," he told the *Sun* that night. "We love her so much. I'm just stunned. We're devastated. I'm in total shock. I can't get upset, I can't cry, I can't get angry."

The most gut-wrenching task lay ahead of them. Somebody had to identify the body. So Arline, Stephanie, and John made plans to fly to Perugia on November 6, 2007.

"I can't bear to think about it," he said.

BECAUSE of John Kercher's devotion to his daughter, police were able to use his last call to make a rough estimate of when the murder had occurred. They knew Meredith and Sophie had parted ways right before 9 P.M. Meredith had walked home alone and gone into the cottage. That much was clear. Then, shortly afterward, Meredith's call to her mother had been cut off. At 10 P.M., someone used her British cell phone to try reaching her bank. Nobody answered a 10:13 recorded call from that bank, sent to the same phone. Police traced both calls back to the area near the cottage, but something strange happened when they studied John Kercher's call, which had occurred just after midnight. The phone seemed to ping in a new location.

Frank Sfarzo knew every dip and rise in the hilltop town. When he heard about that last sad call, he suddenly "saw" the path that the killer or killers must have taken with the cell phones. The stairs up Via della Pergola provided the fastest escape route back into the old town, but that route ran right past the too-public basketball court. So the killer would probably head uphill through back roads until he reached a small door in the wall. It opened directly into the Corso Garibaldi neighborhood, only steps from Rudy's flat and not far from Raffaele's. But Frank Sfarzo discovered that the door had been locked on November 1, as it was most nights. So in order to avoid detection, the attacker would need to aim for an open gate higher on the hill. As he wrote on Perugia Shock:

We can imagine the murderer wandering through the town, with the adrenaline in a circle, with the blood on his clothes, wet with cold sweat. Wandering in the town, wandering out of the town, out of the world, through via della Pergola, via del Bulagaio, via Andrea da Perugia, via Sperandio, roads not streets, where nobody walks, where only a fugitive runs in the night with death in his heart. Afraid to be recognized by someone passing by with a car, the murderer is thinking what to do with those cell phones. His mind is in confusion, his hands are shaking and the panic makes him unable even to realize how to turn off the cell phones. Then maybe before entering back into the town, into Corso Garibaldi, he gets rid of them by throwing them into what looks like wild nature, but which is instead the well groomed garden of Elisabetta Lana.

CHAPTER SIX

STUDENTS FLEE, THE PAPARAZZI RUSH IN

Saturday, November 3, 2007

"On Saturday night plainclothes policemen were seen in the student bars around the city, interviewing anyone who may have seen Miss Kercher on Halloween night."

—BBC News

"Investigators say the killer probably broke in through a window, locked Meredith's door after killing her and then escaped in a hurry, leaving the front door open and throwing the phones into woodland as he fled."

—*Sunday Mirror*

THE Italians dubbed the murder *Il Misterio di Meredith*, "the Meredith Mystery." The entire country reeled from the shock. How could such a beautiful young woman, with no enemies, die so brutally in the *Bel Paese*? *La Stampa* captured the full horror: "She would have been twenty-two years old on December 28. Meredith Kercher, who was from London, crossed the English Channel only to die in Perugia, in an old house in the old town."

Inventive reporters turned the murder into an action movie about two plainclothes Postal cops who uncovered the vicious murder of a British student while chasing down lost cell phones. No mention of Luca Altieri kicking down the door. The flatmates came into the plot as mere stragglers, returning from a holiday weekend to hear the terrible news.

Murder was rare in the hilltop town, which residents invariably described as *tranquilla*. When the local police did investigate the murder of a woman, they usually discovered that a husband or boyfriend had done the deed. In 2007, they'd already jailed Roberto Spaccino in the sensational "Barbara case," accusing him of killing his pregnant wife, Barbara, following a long period of domestic abuse, the details of which kept spilling over into the press. They hadn't solved the disappearance of Sonia Marra, an Italian student from the University of Perugia who'd vanished the November before Meredith's stabbing. Sonia had last been seen leaving her apartment with a man dressed in black, probably a lover. The Marra family did "not even have a body to cry over," lamented her sister, Anna, who was certain that Sonia was murdered.

As tragic as Sonia's disappearance was, however, it didn't sound like what residents feared most, a random act. What if, they asked themselves, a killer broke into the cottage to rape or steal? What if Meredith's death was the work of a sex maniac? Then nobody was safe.

The headlines on the bright metal newsstands along on the Corso only fed the fear:

Sgozzata Studentessa In Camera Di Letto, "Female
   Student's Throat Cut In Bedroom"
Studentessa Ventenne Era Seminude In Camera,
   "Twenty-year-old Female Student Was Half-Naked
   in Her Room"

Somebody posted a macabre ad in Italian on the wall of the *Stranieri*, offering Meredith's room for rent for 220 euro a month, calling it large and airy, with a spectacular view, and saying that an "English girl, hopefully Erasmus" should call as soon as possible. The telephone number given was Meredith's date of death.

THUMBING through Thomas Mann's *Death in Venice* was the closest to tragedy most exchange students in Italy ever came. Their time in Perugia typically had all the charm and realism of a summer fling. In fact, investigators had to work at lightning speed to question students who knew Meredith. The sound of suitcases being wheeled across the cobblestones reverberated throughout Perugia.

Robyn Butterworth left on November 3, 2007, the day after Meredith's body was found. So did Amy Frost. Not only did they feel the need to be around their families, but they were terrified that somebody was targeting English girls. Over the next few days most of the Meredith's friends left the Umbria capital, needing to put the English Channel between themselves and the murder. Robyn and Amy eventually completed their year abroad, but in Bergamo, another medieval college town about two hundred miles away from the crime scene.

"They never came back to Perugia," Merlin's co-owner Pisco Alessi said, though the girls did eventually come back for court. "It was too stressful for them, the reporters, everything. No tranquility, they said." Indeed, some of them didn't even pack up all their possessions. They just fled.

Sophie Purton stayed put, but her parents flew in to stay with her. The BBC's Christian Fraser reported that police had refused her permission to leave the country, because she'd been the last person to see the victim alive. Like Raffaele and Amanda, she was "a person informed of the facts" and police needed her cooperation.

Amanda certainly felt frightened, as she told friends, but she wasn't ready to leave Perugia. "This could happen anywhere" she'd said at the *questura*. Now she eagerly awaited the arrival of her mother, Edda, on November 6. They planned to stay together in a hotel until they found new lodgings for Amanda. Edda also wanted to help her daughter restock her wardrobe, since Amanda literally had only the clothes on her back.

Meanwhile, Filomena was staying at her boyfriend Marco's place; Laura, with a friend named Maurizio Pace, just a temporary arrangement. Amanda hoped to live with them again, but they hadn't had time to discuss it.

LOCAL merchants worried about the economic fallout if students continued to leave. Mayor Renato Rocchi insisted that the police would resolve the case quickly, telling *La Repubblica* that he felt no need to spur on the police, since they were fully committed. Perugini could "expect the perpetrator to be identified early and punished in an exemplary manner."

Police chief Arturo De Felice, the commander of the entire Perugia police force (outranking even Profazio), said he knew that locals wanted the crime solved in a flash. The silver-haired commander, dark circles under his eyes, announced that "all investigative tools, strengths, and skills have been put into place to arrive at an early solution."

The lights in the *questura* blazed nonstop. Investigators coordinated by Giuliano Mignini, in his dual role as prosecutor and investigator, were trying to reconstruct the last hours of Meredith's life. They grabbed names off her Facebook pages, looked through her phone records, and questioned her friends.

They knew Meredith had last been seen alive at 9 P.M. on November 1, heading home, on foot. Had she met someone? How had she spent her few remaining hours?

They called in Pisco and other bartenders to pick out the faces behind the Halloween masks. They also studied the CCTV footage from the parking garage, hoping to spot Meredith coming home on the night of her death or her killer approaching the house.

On November 3, Marco Chiacchiera—second in command of the Flying Squadron and head of the organized crime division—announced a massive manhunt. "We have a hundred officers on the ground," he boasted. He and Monica Napoleoni, head of the homicide unit, coordinated the massive effort, along with Domenico Giacinto Profazio, head of the Flying Squad, and Edgardo Giobbi, from SCO, the Rome-based serious crime unit.

Investigators searched the cottage grounds for a murder weapon, saying it could be a knife, a screwdriver, or even a shard of glass. The forensic police, similar to CSIs, worked around the clock, photographing and bagging the evidence to be shipped off to Rome for analysis. Their finds included footprints, handprints, blood samples, and even the feces from the larger bathroom.

Detectives found themselves in both lucky and unlucky circumstances. The best way to determine time of death was to pinpoint when the victim was last seen alive. They knew Sophie had parted from Meredith around 9 P.M. on November 1, but beyond that, their best weapon would have been taking Meredith's temperature—and that's where their bad luck began. The coroner hadn't arrived until early afternoon on November 2, and the forensic police hadn't allowed him to take a temperature reading until their own tasks were completed (at around 12:50 A.M. on November 3), more than twelve hours after Meredith's body was found and presumably more than twenty-four hours after her death.

By that time "the rice was cooked," to use the expression that Dr. Henry Lee once coined to describe the botched evidence collecting in the scandalous O. J. Simpson case.

MEANWHILE, reporters from all over the world swarmed the cottage. They mounted cameras on the narrow sidewalk on Viale Sant'Angelo, where locals tied bouquets of long-stemmed roses to the rails. Sightseers perched on the sidewalk and leaned over the railings, trying to get a view of the house's back side, where Amanda and Meredith had lived side by side.

"That's where the two rich girls lived," some Italian onlookers would say of the remodeled back end of the house, equating foreignness with plentiful cash.

Later, the wealthy absentee owner of the cottage would complain that she owned "the most famous house in Italy" and yet could not collect any rent. For more than a year and a half, the once bustling cottage would remain cordoned off as a crime scene.

The press also ransacked Meredith's Facebook page, before anyone thought to lock it. Reporters grabbed the photos of her dressed as a vampire and flashed them on TV screens and in newspapers around the globe. The shot of Meredith in the Count Dracula cape, clowning around with the guy in the *Scream* mask, popped up all over the Internet.

By far the best plunderer was England's notorious *Daily Mail*. Nick Pisa's story "Police hunt killer after British student is found butchered and part-naked in Italy" came with four photos swiped from Facebook, including one of a smiling Meredith posed against the bricks at La Tana Dell'Orso, with a caption reading "Bubbly: but devoted to her studies."

A trench-coated, whirling dervish of a reporter, Pisa turned in copy for many different publications. He'd found the victim's Facebook photos even before police had released her last name. He gleefully explained his technique to Dublin Institute of Technology graduate student Michelangelo Felicetti for a paper called "Crime and the Media: The Sensational Case of the Murder of Meredith Kercher." Pisa explained to Felicetti that he had learned that the murdered girl's name was Meredith and then searched the Web for a class list, finally finding one for the University of Perugia. There was only one Meredith from England. Now that he had a name, he checked out Facebook and was thrilled to find so much information available, including photos of her, snapshots and names of her friends, and more. Soon he and many other reporters would shine this same flashlight on Amanda and Raffaele.

Italy's *La Repubblica* also featured the bittersweet photo of Meredith at La Tana. The twenty-one-year-old Erasmus scholar, beaming with joy, is seen in a stylish gray dress. Her "faux leather" brown purse, left on the bed at the crime scene, can be seen perched on a wooden chair.

On November 3, Chiacchiera of the Flying Squad said that police were hoping the Halloween photos would lead them to Meredith's killer, perhaps a man she'd met that night. They suspected that she'd had consensual sex, because they'd found her half-naked, atop a pillow on the floor, and except for the tiny defense wounds on her hands, they'd detected no signs of a protracted struggle. Officers hoped coroner Luca Lalli, who'd scheduled an autopsy for the next day, would be able to clear up the sexual assault issue.

Meredith's British friends found all of this speculation insulting. They were fairly certain that she hadn't phoned or texted anybody that last afternoon at Amy and Robyn's. She'd also borrowed a history book to study that night. And before Meredith and Sophie parted ways, they had agreed that they were tired and looking forward to a good night's sleep. Moreover, Meredith hadn't been dressed for a romantic encounter, but in athletic wear and minimal makeup. Nor had she set up a romantic scene at the cottage, lighting candles and laying out wineglasses.

The British girls said no man other than Giacomo had ever entered Meredith's bedroom. Filomena Romanelli, one of the Italian flatmates, went further, portraying the British girl as a sexless student, all study and no romance. She called Meredith's relationship with Giacomo "a sentimental attachment."

Meredith's confidant, Merlin's co-owner Pisco Alessi, also offered a Giacomo-free view of Meredith's world. "She was nice, cordial, but very reserved and she did not have a boyfriend," he told *La Repubblica*. "She was happy to be here and she liked Perugia a lot. Her only worry was her Italian, which she still didn't know very well."

He said Meredith always went out with other girls, and always in groups. She was not the type who'd meet a man in a bar and invite him into her bed.

"She was very proper. She was careful about what she did."

Although Chiacchiera said investigators suspected that a man had committed the murder, he stressed the fact that they were considering all possibilities. "We are now questioning all of Kercher's friends, male and female."

Police questioned Giacomo thoroughly, of course. He considered his two-hundred-miles-away alibi "cast-iron," but he had lawyered up, just like Filomena and Laura.

Soon police would draw a circle around Meredith's social set and tighten it like a noose.

BY this time, the Meredith Kercher mystery had drawn Frank Sfarzo back to Perugia from Florence. He'd noticed the cute little house on Via della Pergola many times; he thought the location was dangerous, because an out-of-control car could have spun right into its windows. He was also fascinated by the people caught up in the plot. He called his blog Perugia Shock because the murder had stunned the town. He thought locals would feed him tips and photographs, but they did not. They hated the media circus and wished the reporters would all go home.

They already had their share of worries. In fact, the Umbrian capital was struggling with an explosive mixture of recent immigrants, university students, and locals. Police were also battling a rise in stabbing, prostitution, and drug dealing.

Meredith's murder only added to the general feeling of uneasiness about the safety of Perugia's streets. "We tell girls who are studying in Perugia not to walk home by themselves, but this has really shocked us," Esteban Garcia Pascual, the Peruvian co-owner of La Tana Dell'Orso, told reporters.

One of the few aboveground bars in town, La Tana claimed to have "Perugia's best wine selection." The arched ceilings and brick accents gave it the cheerful feel of a Napa Valley wine-tasting room. It also had small tables on the street, spread with bright yellow tablecloths, where one could enjoy a rich Bolognese lasagna while watching happy-looking students stroll up and down cobblestoned Via Ulisse. For Amanda and Meredith, that winding street had provided the quickest route up from the cottage into the historic center, a steep climb through the Etruscan Arch.

Esteban described Meredith as a regular customer with dark good looks. "A really nice, smiling girl coming here for live music and drinking with her English girlfriends," he told the *Independent*.

For Esteban and his English wife, Lucy Rigby, the days before and after Meredith's murder were bizarre. Lucy, a striking young woman with soft blue eyes and upswept blond hair, had suffered a violent attack at La Tana on October 30, just days before the stabbing.

At closing time, a drunk Albanian had picked a fight with another man near the front door. The drunk had grabbed a large ceramic vase and flung it at the other man, who ducked. The vase hit Lucy instead and gashed her forehead, and she'd ended up in the hospital.

Earlier that same night, Meredith had been in La Tana with Raffaele and Amanda and a couple of the British girls. Lucy, originally from Shrewsbury, England, remembered the customers because they made such a strange grouping: the "small, quiet American girl, drably dressed," accompanied by her much taller, plain-looking Italian boyfriend, and the British girls in their pretty clothes, talking among themselves.

Lucy was surprised by the British girls' aloofness. "They could hear my accent. They knew I was British. But they had no interest in me. After a while I didn't try to engage them."

During the two hours that this group shared a table, they said little and drank less, only a liter of white house wine. When the check came around, they pooled their money, paying entirely in coins. Then they went their separate ways.

Because Lucy worked behind the scenes in a kitchen area most of the time, she wasn't sure who the girls were. After they left, she complained to Esteban about the two-liter, two-hour, unfriendly table. Her husband told her not to worry. The English girls were good customers. Meredith often waved at him as she headed home to the cottage. She and her friends loved to dance, Esteban said, and they often came into La Tana to get the tickets to local discos that he, like other bartenders in Perugia, dispersed. These prized tickets provided free entree to the big discos on the outskirts of town, reached by a special bus on Saturday nights.

"Those girls can stay as long here as they like," Esteban told his wife. "I know them. They are regulars."

British reporters had trooped into La Tana right after the murder to do two stories in one. They wrote about violence in a beautiful town, about the drunk who'd attacked a British bar owner in her own establishment—and about the British girl who'd lost her life shortly afterward. Like other bartenders, Esteban gave a flurry of interviews after Meredith's homicide, with mixed results. Like many other locals, he disliked the way reporters described Perugia.

The British press had dubbed the rocky hilltop town "the new Ibiza," after the leafy tropical Spanish island known in the UK for drug-fueled fun in the sun, while even the Italian *La Repubblica* insisted that "a world of studies, parties, drugs, drink, sex, pubs, and discos" awaited visitors in Perugia.

"Now I know where I want to go for spring break," an online commenter wrote on the National Public Radio site in the U.S.

Locals also coped with urban legends. A rumor went around that Perugia bartenders had concocted a cocktail called a "Bloody Mez," modeled after a Bloody Mary—supposedly the victim's favorite drink. Her friends, on the other hand, said that Meredith preferred the more stylish Mojito, a delectable mix of lime juice and tequila, spiked with rum and other ingredients.

The Bloody Mez rumor disgusted Esteban. "The police came to see me," he said later. "They know us. We have good relations. They say, we know you wouldn't do this terrible thing, but people are upset and we have to ask. Do you have this drink?" He rolled his eyes. "Of course I tell them we would never do anything like that."

IN South London, TV reporters posed in front of the pale, semidetached Kercher house for their broadcasts. With dark wood accents and diamond-paned windows, the house stood on a spacious street in Coulsdon, an upscale neighborhood in Surrey. John Kercher lived in a red-brick apartment in Croydon, a short drive away.

"Behind closed curtains the family mourns," said a BBC reporter in front of the house. As she delivered her short report, well-dressed men and women were visible speeding by her, keeping their heads down. She identified them as friends and relatives who'd come to help the family cope with the loss. John Kercher could be seen, opening and closing the door.

Reading the next-day newspapers couldn't have helped the family cope with its grief.

"Police hunt killer after British student is found butchered and part-naked in Italy," said the *Daily Mail*. The best known of the racy tabloids, it had the schizophrenic habit of salting useful information into the hyperbole—so it couldn't simply be ignored. A lean, factual article on the Kercher case might appear one day; an overblown, nearly fictional account the next. The *Mail* also excelled in hard-to-obtain crime scene photos and paid for "exclusives," a reflection of its deep pockets. All of the London newspapers quickly became obsessed with the Kercher stabbing, from tabloids like the *Sunday Mirror* and the *Sun* to broadsheets like the *Times*, the *Independent*, the *Guardian*, and the *Daily Telegraph*.

Energized Fleet Street reporters found Perugia the perfect launchpad for astonishing coverage. Not only did Italy's police stations and lawyers' offices leak like broken-down yachts, but the country was offshore of British laws that crimped pre-trial publicity.

The Kercher case also satisfied the newspapers' appetite for the next big thing. Since May 2007, tabloid journalists had chased the sensational Madeleine McCann missing toddler case. An exquisite little blond girl with huge, unforgettable blue eyes, Madeleine had vanished from a luxury resort in Portugal where her glamorous-looking parents were vacationing. Unscrupulous British reporters felt free to float rumors, believing that their country's libel laws didn't apply offshore in Portugal. The steamy *Daily Express* and *Daily Star* even alleged that McCann's parents were involved in their daughter's disappearance. Later, lawyers would force the tabloids to print front-page apologies and pay out damages to the parents, whose lives they had made a living hell.

The Internet increased the tabloid damage dramatically, since stories that once would have been read only in the United Kingdom now sped around the world. Conspiracy theorists on message boards lapped up every detail.

Now the rumor was that the most vicious tabloid reporters had descended on Coulsdon and were trying to dig up information on the victim's sex life. In "Meredith Murdered by 'Scary Movie' Nut," the *Daily Star* claimed that a film called *Scary Movie* had inspired the British girl's murder.

"The spoof film, which featured six students being murdered by a killer in a Scream mask, was one of the 21-year-old's favourites," the story began. "Some of her pals dressed up as the film characters for a Halloween fancy dress bash less than 48 hours before she was killed."

Typically, the *Daily Star* relied on anonymous sources described as "insiders," who conveniently backed up the story. "Last night detectives were probing the possibility the exchange student's killer was a movie copycat. . . . Sources close to the investigation said: 'It's a terrifying theory. It would mean others' lives may be at risk. The killer in the film did not stop at one.'"

* * *

TRIBUTES to Meredith also came rolling in, even in the tabloids. When the *London Evening Standard*'s tacky "half-naked" story appeared online, it attracted a poignant comment from Meredith's aunt, Sarah Jennings. She noted that Arline suffered from renal failure and needed to go on the kidney machine regularly. Hence the cell phone Meredith always carried in her back pocket. It turned out the British student had nearly canceled her year abroad over worry about her mother, but Arline had insisted that her daughter follow her dream.

"Mez was my niece, a young thoughtful person kind to everyone especially her family and friends," wrote the aunt, adding that "whoever did this has wrecked several lives as we all loved her, she did not deserve this as she is a quiet shy person who despite the pictures was reserved and loved life. She will be missed by me and my family and all her relatives."

The *Guardian* offered a glimpse of Meredith's by-then-locked Facebook page. "The picture Meredith had chosen to use on the website showed her smiling into the camera, dressed in a shiny red top and leaning into her close friend, Noita Sadler, whose own Facebook page simply said she was 'lost without her.' "

Residents of London, where stabbing deaths were common, nevertheless expressed astonishment that such a vicious crime could occur in an Italian hilltop town. Former Erasmus scholars also weighed in, saying they couldn't believe Perugia had become dangerous.

Leeds University sent representatives to Perugia to help students cope. "We will remember Meredith as a beautiful, clever and happy young woman, who was serious about her studies and popular with her peers," a spokesperson said.

MEANWHILE DJ Johnsrud, over in China, was concerned because Amanda had missed their Skype appointment at 4 P.M. on November 2. He knew Amanda wouldn't forget an appointment. He decided to check her Facebook page and saw a startling message she'd left for all her friends:

"My roommate has been murdered."

DJ didn't know how to cope. "When you hear horrible news like that, you'd think you'd be stunned into silence, but instead you can't quit talking about it. You can't think of anything else," he said, sympathizing with Amanda's talkativeness that first night in the *questura*. "I went to a birthday party that night and I could not shut up. Finally, I removed myself, so I wouldn't depress the hell out of everyone else."

MEANWHILE Rudy Guede was keeping a low profile. A friend spoke to him on November 2, so he was definitely in Perugia the day that Meredith's body was discovered. He couldn't have missed the firestorm over her death. Not only did he live just a ten-minute stroll from the cottage, but he would have seen the TV cameras, the reporters swarming the town center, and the students clustered on the street corners, reeling from the news.

But that night Rudy once again headed to the Domus. When the disk jockey asked for a moment of silence to honor Meredith, Rudy kept on dancing. Meredith's friend Pietro Campolongo said the extroverted young man was dancing alone.

"People kept their distance from him because he smelled like he hadn't washed."

Now, on November 3, Rudy Guede came up at the *questura* for the first time. Stefano Bonassi, one of the boys who lived in the downstairs apartment, mentioned him in a witness report. Stefano was a serious-looking young man who spoke slowly but had a fine memory.

He told investigators about the two times Rudy had been over to the cottage.

"One guy who came to our house was tall, skinny, and he always wore basketball shoes and baggy trousers. He was nicknamed Body Roga," Stefano said. The nickname was apparently a reference to Dejan Bodiroga, the Serbian basketball star. Rudy also went by "the Baron." Police asked Stefano what size shoes Rudy wore, but he didn't know. They were looking for a shoe to fit the bloody Nike print by the bed.

As if he sensed a storm brewing, Rudy told friends that

same day that he was headed to Milan. They weren't surprised, because he liked to go to the fashion capital for dancing and to visit his aunt in nearby Lecco. Rudy was unhappy in Perugia, according to his friends, feeling depressed, drinking more often. He was also having girl troubles and maybe needed to get away to sort things out. Rudy liked Nordic girls, one friend said, but they did not reciprocate his passion. To make matters worse, Rudy's landlord was looking for him. She'd asked him to present a letter of employment, because she was worried he wouldn't be able to pay his rent. Since he'd been jobless since late August, Rudy had no way of providing such a document.

On November 3, he split town, skipping out on the rent. He threw a few things into a backpack and caught a north-bound train. That night he showed up at the Soul to Soul disco in Milan, which offered everything from hip-hop to reggae music. There Rudy met a young woman named Veronica Volta, and he told her that he was going to Germany to look for work.

Perhaps he had good reason for not lingering in Milan. Six days before Meredith's murder, police had arrested him there, after he was discovered sleeping in a children's nursery school armed with an eleven-inch knife lifted from the facility's kitchen. He said he'd broken in only because he needed a place to sleep and he wanted the knife for self-protection.

When police searched him, they discovered that he was also carrying a stolen cell phone and laptop computer, both of which had been swiped from a lawyer's office in Perugia. The burglar had broken in through a second-story window. Rudy claimed that he'd purchased the items from somebody at the Milan train station, however, and after police took mug shots, they let him go. He stayed in Milan only one day and then headed for Germany.

"He just needed to be somewhere that wasn't Perugia," said his lawyer, Nicodemo Gentile.

Rudy wore Nikes. So did Raffaele.

DETECTIVES, led by prosecutor Giuliano Mignini, were already speculating that the murder was an inside job, beginning with the fact that they believed the broken window had been staged. The problem was that, short of a confession, this would always remain a theory. The Postal Police had been the first responders, not the Carabinieri, and they weren't trained to handle violent crime. By the time the Carabinieri arrived, a herd of young people had tromped through the house, sans head coverings and protective "booties" over their shoes. The Postal Police had even asked Filomena and Amanda to go into their rooms and rummage around to see if anything was missing. Filomena had disrupted the broken glass in her room twice.

In Umbria, where gyms were as rare as Vietnamese restaurants, investigators doubted that anyone could climb twenty feet up a brick wall and enter the house through Filomena's window. Or that a burglar could throw the 8.8-pound rock through the window in the first place. In fact, investigators described the window as if it were the Khumbu Icefall on Mount Everest. They glossed over the open shutters, visible in the earliest newspaper photos, not to mention the grilled window directly below Filomena's, which beckoned to mischief makers as a handy little ladder.

Later, private investigators would wonder if the parapet right by the front door might not have offered a perfect launching pad if one wanted to throw a rock big enough to break a window. The ravine below the house, where prowlers had been spotted on two occasions, offered plenty of similar stones.

Nevertheless, police never wavered from their contention that the window had been broken from the inside to fake a burglary. Once they decided the break-in had been staged, they saw only two possibilities: either Meredith had let a trusted person into the house, or somebody she trusted had used a key to get in.

AT 11 A.M. on November 3, Raffaele and Amanda showed up at the *questura* as the police had requested. But detectives told Raffaele that they didn't need him. Instead, they drove Amanda back to the cottage. In most of the press photos taken that day, Amanda looked pale and upset, wearing a black fleece jacket over the same blue top and white skirt that she'd worn the previous day. Her hair, parted down the middle, appeared more brown than blond. She was biting her nails in one shot; in another, she stood near the steps of the cottage, looking small but serene in her white skirt, talking to prosecutor Mignini.

In the most widely circulated photo, Amanda pressed her hands together, a gesture that her friends said she often made when upset. All around her were male police officers, in plain clothes, seven in all. One officer had his hand raised to his forehead, pushing his hair back as if in anguish.

That day, cops quizzed Amanda not only about the boys downstairs, "the neighbors," but also about Meredith's sex life, an experience she found weird and unsettling, as she wrote in the long e-mail sent to friends and family:

> At the house they asked me very personal questions about meredith's life and also about the personalities of our neighbors. how well did i know them? pretty well, we are friends. was meredith sexually active? yeah, she borrowed a few of my condoms. . . . does she use vaseline? for her lips? what kind of person is stefano? nice guy, has a really pretty girlfriend. hmmm . . . very interesting. . . . we'd like to show you something, and tell us if this is out of normal.

The police insisted that Amanda go downstairs with them. The day before, Perugia homicide cop Lorena Zugarini, a blonde with a prison matron build, had kicked down the door to the boys' ground-level apartment. There, police had found blood spots in several different places, even on the light switches, which turned out to be from the cat with the bleeding ear. They also had photographed Giacomo's marijuana plants, as green and sturdy as cornstalks, which he kept in a room with a special lock.

In the e-mail, Amanda said the rooms were tidy, because the boys had thoroughly cleaned them before leaving on vacation, though Stefano's room had been stripped of linens, which Amanda found odd. His comforter had been shoved on top of his bed. She saw blood drops on it.

So she told the police that, yes, the blood was abnormal. Also, she said, usually Stefano made his bed.

Under prodding, she said Meredith and Giacomo had been seeing each other a few weeks. Meredith never mentioned any fights and, anyway, Giacomo was a calm person. The couple seldom appeared in public. Meredith liked to go out with her British friends, while Giacomo was more of a homebody. Sometimes Meredith went to his room; other times, he came to hers. Yes, Meredith said she had fun on Halloween, but she hadn't mentioned meeting anybody new. She never went out at night alone, only with roommates, Giacomo, or her English friends. None of the girls had given their boyfriends keys to the house.

THAT night Raffaele took Amanda strolling around the center, not realizing they were being watched. Yet police were posting surveillance cameras everywhere in Perugia, trying to cut down on drug dealing and street violence. All over Italy, in fact, the cameras were on. Two years later, *La Nazione* would call Perugia "a city increasingly similar to the bugged rooms in the reality show 'Big Brother,'" with "cameras rolling, electric eyes ready to spy on every piazza and alleyway in the heart of town."

At 7 P.M. on the evening of November 3, Amanda and Raffaele went to buy some underwear for her at a boutique in the center called Bubble. She was still unable to retrieve her things from the cottage, and her mother hadn't yet arrived with more clothing. She was likely tired of wearing the same underpants.

Raffaele accompanied Amanda into Bubble, where he was badly outnumbered by teenaged Italian girls in trendy clothes, chattering away, while loud music thumped through the store. CCTV cameras, clearly visible in the entryway, protected the clothes from shoplifters.

The cameras caught the lovebirds in the second room— smiling, touching, staring into each other's eyes. At one point

Raffaele gave Amanda a quick kiss. She sorted through the schoolgirl T-shirts, tank tops, and lingerie. She was still wearing her black fleece jacket and white skirt and carrying her usual patterned shoulder bag.

Afterward the lovers grabbed a pizza and then headed over to the Perugia flat of Maurizio Pace, the young man with whom Laura was staying. Filomena was also there, with her boyfriend, Marco.

"We talked a little and listened a little, trying to say how we were, because clearly we had all been shocked a little," Laura said. She had trouble following Amanda, though, because she broke into rapid English when she got upset and Laura couldn't keep up. She found the twenty-year-old that night both "annoyed and annoying."

Amanda kept complaining that she felt tired, and that she'd not had a break since Meredith's body was found. She was sick of the police—the repetitive questions, the need to discuss the scene in the cottage, the nasty assertions about Meredith's sex life. What was it with the Vaseline, anyway?

Laura didn't know. This was the first time she was hearing anything about Vaseline.

Amanda continued to rant about the police, saying that they were becoming more belligerent, shouting even. She was tired of the pressure. Laura became increasingly exasperated and wished Amanda would just stop talking. In her e-mail, Amanda gave her own version of the events:

> It was a hurricane of emotions and stress but we needed it anyway. What we have been discussing is basically what to do next. We are trying to keep our heads on straight. First things first though, my roommates both work for lawyers, and they are going to try to send a request through on monday to retrieve important documents of ours that are still in the house. Secondly, we are going to talk to the agency that we used to find our house and obviously request to move out. It kind of sucks that we have to pay the next months rent, but the owner has protection within the contract.

* * *

UNBEKNOWNST to Amanda, police had called Sophie Purton into the *questura* for the second time that night. She was about to offer them a voice from the grave.

Sophie faced the A-squad of investigators, including Domenico Giacinto Profazio, head of the Flying Squadron; Edgardo Giobbi, from the Rome-based serious crime squad; Monica Napoleoni, chief of the homicide squad; and Rita Ficarra from the narcotics squad. They kept Sophie there until 11:10 P.M.

They began by grilling the twenty-one-year-old Leeds student about Meredith's social set. Profazio said he was determined at that time "to gather as much information as possible about the victim and persons who lived with her and in the floor below. We tried to reconstruct her movements and that of her friends until the time of death."

Most of all, he wanted the name of every single man who'd ever crossed Meredith's threshold.

The British girls went out together four or five times a week, to movies, to dinner, to pubs, Sophie began. They always watched out for one another and made sure everyone got home safely. She was sure that Meredith had only Giacomo in her life. She would have told her friends if she'd met someone new. They didn't have many secrets. They were just young girls, far from home, happy in Perugia, before all this started.

Sophie began to hedge, though, when asked about hashish, that popular intoxicant. She said that *if* Meredith smoked it, then she must have been with her roommates or *other* friends, and she hadn't confided in Sophie. As for Amanda, perhaps she smoked the stuff. Sophie wouldn't know, though apparently Amy Frost had said she might. And, yes, Sophie had smoked marijuana herself—but not in the city of chocolates and jazz.

"Very well," the officers said. "Now tell us about Hicham Khiri." He was the twenty-eight-year-old Tunisian man the English girls knew from the clubs. They called him "Shaky" because of the way that he shook when he danced. Once at the Domus, Shaky had dropped his trousers in front of Meredith to show off his underpants. His idea of a joke. Sophie doubted that Meredith had ever opened the door to Shaky, but she couldn't rule that out.

Not by coincidence, police had already questioned Hicham. He'd described seeing the British girls at the gigantic Gradisca, a seven-bar disco club outside Perugia, at 4 A.M. on October 14. That night Sophie had been very drunk and had vomited in the bathrooms. Meredith and Robyn were hard-pressed to get her home. They'd come on the Saturday night bus and faced a twenty-five-minute ride back.

"It was Saturday and I was with a friend called Abdel," Hicham had told investigators. "I could see that all the staff from the Merlin was inside and lots of foreign women students. There's a bus for them every Saturday. As we were leaving the car park at the end of the evening, we met Meredith and Sophie—Sophie was drunk—with another woman I didn't know. Meredith asked me if we could take them home, given the state Sophie was in."

Since the girls had known Hicham for some time, they weren't worried about riding in his spacious car. His friend Abdel did the driving. On the way home Meredith asked Shaky, in Italian, why he was at the club. He said he had three jobs. He worked as a chef at the Gradisca and in two clothing stores in Perugia.

"Hicham tried to hug and kiss me on several occasions," Sophie said, rather sweetly, when the officers pressed her about this unusual young man, "but I always refused until, finally, last Wednesday, he did kiss me."

"Very well," said the investigators. "Now let's talk about that Halloween."

Sophie said that she, Robyn, Amy, and Meredith had partied together all night. Meredith had fun, but Sophie never saw her with any particular man.

Then detectives asked her about two young Italian guys who'd been at Merlin's but not in costume. In a photo on Sophie's Facebook page, these two olive-skinned boys were seen laughing and hugging Meredith. She was smiling, fake blood all around her mouth.

Sophie said she remembered that photo well. She'd taken it herself. Why? Because her friend Meredith had looked so happy at that moment. The Italian boys had been dancing next to her, in a sea of ghosts, pirates, and witches. When the music stopped, they gave Meredith a squeeze, and she had laughed.

After Sophie took the picture, the boys departed. They didn't get any more hugs.

The investigators then switched over to Pisco. The Merlin's *barista* had a reputation for being a ladies' man. Yes, Sophie knew him. They texted each other at least once a day. Meredith knew him, too. Yes, of course, she had his cell number. Pisco was a good friend.

The officers fell silent. Sophie took a deep breath. Then she turned a klieg light on Amanda Knox, a girl she had met only once.

"I want to tell you some of the things Meredith said to me about Amanda," Sophie told the officers. "I think they're important. Meredith told me Amanda would sometimes bring men back to their house. I don't know how many there were. Meredith mentioned one man in particular who works in an Internet café. That's where she said she met him. Meredith thought the man was strange. At the time, she didn't give me any more details. I don't know how old he is but I can say that at least one other man was taken back to their house, although I don't know what nationality these people are."

Sophie did add a qualifier, but it never made it into the press. "I think, for Amanda, some of these men were only friends." Then the British girl took a wild, erroneous guess: "As for the man who works in the Internet café, they might have slept together."

"Sophie Purton was the first to reveal that the murder house has always had lots of visitors," *Corriere della Sera* would later declare. "Police officers then decided to interview Amanda Knox, the American student," the reporter added.

Indeed, they would summon her to the station the very next morning.

AMANDA had never been a night owl, but that evening she couldn't sleep, even in Raffaele's safe little flat on Garibaldi.

So she decided to take action. She sat on her boyfriend's bed, fired up his computer, and tapped out a long e-mail describing the events of the past few days. She wrapped it up at 3:30 A.M., Italian time, and sent it to all twenty-five people in her online address book. Perugia police would have it in their hands within two weeks, because a former employer would hand it over to the Seattle police, who'd forward it to Italy.

"I had to let off steam somehow, because the whole situation was so heavy that I couldn't sleep," Amanda said later. She had always scribbled down her thoughts as a way of understanding them; her mother had stored hundreds of her diaries back home in Seattle. "So I needed to write. I needed to let off steam by writing, especially to the people who were worrying about me. . . . Then I felt better."

Amanda's keyboarding skills had always been hellacious, her fingers unable to keep pace with her thoughts, but even for her, the e-mail contained a startling number of typos, misspellings, and errors. Like Filomena, Amanda even got Meredith's age wrong.

This is an email for everyone, because id like to get it all out and not have to repeat myself a hundred times like ive been having to doat the police station. some of you already know some things, some of you know nothing. what im about to say i cant say to journalists or newspapers, and i require that of anone receiving this information as well. this is m account of how i found my roommate murdered the morning of friday, november 2nd.

The last time i saw meredith, 22, english, beautiful, funny, was when i came home from spending the night at a friends house. It was the day after Halloween, Thursday.

Amanda traced the path of discovery, beginning with the last time she spoke to Meredith and ending with the fractious talk she'd just had with Laura and Filomena, the Italian roommates.

Ive been talking an awful lot lately and im pretty tired of it. . . . I still need to figure out who i need to talk to and what i need to do to continue studying in perugia, because its what i want to do. Anyway, thats the update, feeling okay, hope you all are well.—Amanda

CHAPTER SEVEN

TOO MANY MEN, THE ITALIANS SAY

Sunday, November 4, 2007

"Less than two hours after Amanda listed male visitors, Stefano Bonassi entered the police station. He was able to describe one visitor as a lover of Amanda's."

—*Corriere della Sera*

SOPHIE Purton's revelations had focused on one "strange" man—not a soccer squadron—but police summoned Amanda Knox to the station on Sunday to explain herself. In a 2:45 P.M. statement, Amanda readily listed the small number of male visitors she'd brought to the house. Only one of them was a lover, although police would assume she'd slept with all. In Italy "bringing men home" had an almost exclusively sexual connotation. Anytime Perugia police heard about a man "coming over," they factored "for sex" into their crime scenario.

Indeed, the victim hadn't been spared this speculation either. "The most plausible hypothesis we have is that Meredith met someone at the Halloween party," Marco Chiacchiera, second in command of the Flying Squad, had told the *Telegraph* only the day before. "She expressed a desire to meet him again. She had been to a friend's house on the night she was murdered but decided to make her own way home to meet him."

Now all eyes were on Amanda Knox. Even though Sophie

couldn't possibly know who Amanda had slept with, investigators concluded, erroneously, that the American kept a busy bedroom in addition to her weeklong romance with Raffaele.

"She did not deny that there were visitors," *Corriere* said, when Sophie's statement was leaked. But the "strange man" Sophie had referred to turned out to be Juve, Amanda's coworker at Le Chic. Meredith may very well have found Juve strange, but he was no stranger. In fact, he was insulted when police asked if he'd ever had sex with Amanda—a friend, he said, nothing more.

"We sometimes danced salsa together, but I have a girlfriend and nothing ever happened," he told an English tabloid. The photo he posted of himself on Facebook showed a man with large features and a halo of curly, receding dark hair. Dressed in a black leather jacket, he had his arm draped around a plainly clad girlfriend. He described himself as an admirer of Al Pacino, the musical group the Guardians, and the Palestinian cause.

Ironically, Amanda and Meredith had discussed Juve in their last conversation, because he didn't approve of Raffaele. Meredith had told her roommate to ignore Juve and follow her heart.

"Juve's been to our house at least five times," Amanda said in her witness report. "The last time was on October 31. He knew Meredith because he met her at the bar with me. Juve never tried to hit on me. He's got this habit of hugging and touching even when he's not drunk."

Later, Amanda explained in court that Juve came over to listen to her play guitar since the only instruments she had access to belonged to Laura and couldn't be taken out of the house.

"The other men I brought back are one called Spyros, only once in October when he met Meredith; Daniel from Rome—I don't know his phone number—who came twice. The second time he said hello to Meredith and spoke to her."

Spyros Gatsios was Amanda's Greek pal from the Internet Point, a big, black-haired local with warm manners and many friends. He hadn't seen Amanda since Halloween. After hearing about her roommate's murder, he had texted her twice.

Later, he would turn those messages over to police and the y surface in *Il Messaggero*, offering a chart of Amanda's moods after the murder.

> AMANDA (November 3. 9.57 a.m.). My housemate
> was killed the night before last. I was the first to go
> home and call the police.
> SPYROS (November 3. 11.28 a.m.). I know. I saw
> the latest news. I wanted to call you. . . . it's really
> shocking. . . . if you need a hug tell me so, sweetie.
> AMANDA (November 3. 11.30 a.m.). Maybe later,
> thanks. Today I still have to speak with the police
> for a while.
> SPYROS (November 4. 4.19 p.m.). What are you doing,
> sweetie? I hope you're well, if you need
> anything call me. I am in the bar where you don't
> like having coffee.
> AMANDA (November 4. 6:19 p.m.). With the police in
> my house. I am very tired.

"THE list of people who visited the women is a long one," said *Corriere*, notwithstanding the actual shortness of the list. The newspaper noted that Stefano Bonassi, one of the boys downstairs, had told police that Amanda had sex with Daniel de Luna, a childhood friend of theirs from The Marche.

That was enough for police to summon Amanda back from the waiting room. Yes, she said, she did bring Daniel home that one time, but that was before she'd met Raffaele. It turned out that Daniel was studying in Rome at the *Università degli Studi di Roma*. In the fall of 2007, he had stayed twice with the boys downstairs. The first time, in September, he'd met all of the girls except for Meredith, who'd been away in London.

On October 20, Daniel had returned to stay with the boys. They decided to go clubbing with Meredith, Amanda, Amy Frost, and a few other students. Stefano also invited his girlfriend. They all headed for the Red Zone, a rowdy disco where college students partied amid throbbing red neon palm trees under a revolving glitter ball. Daniel danced with Amanda;

Giacomo, with Meredith. They had such fun that they didn't get home until 5:30 A.M.

"Red Zone, that's the place where girls become approachable, it seems, maybe with some chemical help," wrote Frank Sfarzo of Perugia Shock. "Giacomo kisses Meredith and Daniel kisses Amanda. When they come home Meredith goes to sleep with Giacomo and Daniel with Amanda."

When questioned, Amanda was perfectly willing to discuss Daniel, even though investigators treated this *avventura della notte* (one-night stand) as if sex were a gateway crime to murder. Search as they might, police would never find another male who'd had sex in Amanda's bedroom, not even Raffaele, since she was always at his place. Nevertheless they did not hesitate to paint her as, well, a whore.

"Amanda is not ashamed of having sex," said Madison Paxton, her UW friend. "She's responsible about it and doesn't make a big deal about it—she's not obsessed with it, she's not into nontraditional things. She's like most other twenty-year-old Seattle female college students when it comes to sex."

Madison said Amanda liked Raffaele because he *wasn't* like the other Italian boys she'd met. "He was nice to her. He treated her with respect. He was kind."

ALAS, being open about sex was not an Italian trait, even in the twenty-first century. Newcomers expecting to enter a Fellini movie soon discovered Italians were a passionate people, but with intricate sexual mores. Italy was not only a Catholic country, but also the home of the Vatican, the epicenter of the faith. Religion had a prominence in public life shocking to most Americans. Huge crucifixes hung in courtrooms. Children prayed in the schools.

On the other hand, abortion was legal; divorce, common. In Umbria, ads for married couples looking to "swing" with other couples appeared in local newspapers. Prostitution flourished in Perugia. Beautiful, hollow-cheeked girls from Eastern Europe charged about 30 euro (about $43) per transaction, worked a grueling 10 P.M. to 2 A.M. schedule, and turned their earnings over to pimps. Transsexuals also made up part of the trade, according to *Corriere dell'Umbria*.

Despite the stereotypes about large families, modern Italians married late and had one of Europe's lowest birthrates, usually one child per family. Many women engaged in premarital sex, though they frowned upon casual hookups, publicly at least. Single women inevitably presented themselves as serially monogamous, hesitating to discuss sexual experiences casually over dinner, with strangers, or in public settings.

"You can do what you like, but nobody can know about it," said Judy Witts, an American writer who came to Italy when she was thirty, married an Italian man, and put down roots in Tuscany. "Italian women also resent the foreign women who come to Italy and have sex with Italian men. Local women have to guard their reputations. They can't just sleep around. For the foreigners, what happens in Italy, stays in Italy. They don't have to worry about their reputations because they are not 'at home' and nobody will ever know."

In Perugia, a young man might stop a foreign woman on the Corso, address her in delightfully accented English, pretend to be a little shy, suggest a drink or an espresso and, if all goes well, perhaps a special pasta dish in a *ristorante* where he knows the chef. All of this leading to her bedroom.

Certainly, a seduction attempt on the Spanish Steps in Rome can be an interesting cultural experience for many female tourists. "But it's not true that all foreign women lust after Italian men," said Amanda Castleman, an Italian-American who first became an expat via UW's Rome Program. She married a fellow alumni, then returned to Europe for eight years, including two in the Eternal City. "That's a stereotype, which some locals buy into. As a travel writer, I've talked to hundreds of expats and travelers in Italy. They complain the men can be very crude, especially on the street. The creeps—called *pappagalli* (parrots)—often target women traveling alone. In their culture, this signals availability more than independence. So they hiss and bully and fondle—behavior that's 100 percent unacceptable normally. No wonder many travelers head home with complaints about another stereotype: 'Italian stallions.'"

American women blogging about their Italian study-abroad adventures described dancing in discos only in groups of other women, all of them watching out for one another, fending off the Italian guys who pinched and grabbed. Many said they were scared to walk alone after dark, even in upscale neighborhoods in Florence and Rome.

Zach Nowak, in *The Little Blue Book*, a "how-to" guide to Perugia life, wrote that Italian men are crude with foreign women because they believe the newcomers are looking for adventure, hoping to do things in Italy that they wouldn't do at home for fear of retribution. Having decided that foreign women are easy, the local men abandon all subtlety.

No one doubted female Italian students led more cloistered lives than their foreign counterparts. Witts said that the Italian girls that one saw strolling the Corso, always in groups, probably had curfews at home (even as early as 11 P.M.). Dressed appropriately in brightly colored scarves, soft woolen sweaters, and tight jeans, they strove to act like the sort of girls whom an Italian boyfriend would bring home to his mother. If they'd had sex, it was most likely with the boys from back home, their first loves, the boys they envisioned marrying. The sex was probably carried out in the backseats of cars, for want of a better place. Many still lived with their parents.

Even Italian boys must be discreet in tiny Perugia, where the night truly has a thousand eyes. The Romeos of the Corso, chasing after foreign girls, probably had girlfriends back home whom they saw on holidays and to whom they would return once their college years were done. They weren't eager to advertise sexual liaisons, lest word trickle back to their hometowns. Once a male student got a reputation as a player, then he might have trouble attracting fresh partners in Perugia. Even the foreign girls would be wary. They would catch on and tell all their friends.

"You can tell people everything, but you must leave half of it out," said one female University of Perugia student who lives near Piazza Grimana. "These Perugia people, they are not especially warm. No, they can be very cold. You can live by them for years and they will not offer you even a glass of water. But if you are a young unmarried woman, then you have to watch out. They will report everything you say and do."

The woman used to invite a young man over to her flat, a friend, just for lunch. A neighbor who'd barely nodded to her on the street waited until her brother came to visit and then informed him that his unmarried sister was entertaining men in her home.

"My brother did not care, but it was very embarrassing," she said. "It was none of his business. Why should I have to explain anything to him?"

Other Italian women are quick to say their country is more modern than critics suggest. "Italian women do have men over, to study with or do work with or other things," said a female reporter based in Rome. "It's perfectly okay. It's just that Meredith didn't like it."

Judy Witts noted that the cottage offered entertainment possibilities that many Italian accommodations do not, since it had a nice big kitchen/living area where guests could be comfortable. "For most foreigners, male and female, the street is the only place to socialize, because sitting in coffee shops or bars is expensive," she said. "So the *passeggiata*, the stroll along the Corso, is the way to meet somebody new in any town. Amanda was no different than any other girl in Perugia, but her 'private' notes and thoughts were exposed. Out of context, I think, which would make anyone look bad."

Ironically, perhaps, the United States is by far the world's most popular destination for foreign students, welcoming more than 600,000 per year. Americans, too, socialize by their own playbook. They do not like to be watched or judged. They enjoy having friends of both genders. They are out to meet as many people as possible. Savvy university recruiters boast about the richness of their schools' social life. A survival guide for foreigners at Emory University, a private school in Atlanta, Georgia, addresses the inevitable cultural shock, even needing to explain the behavior of American women to foreign students:

"Their relaxed and more independent attitude may be misunderstood by people whose native culture is more restrictive of women's activities. It is not unusual, for example, for unmarried women to live by themselves, to share living space with other single women, or to go to public places unescorted."

THAT Sunday, November 4, Giacomo Silenzi was also summoned to the *questura*, where he talked about his relationship with Meredith:

Even though I really liked her, I didn't feel at all jealous about her. Me and my friends often use hashish and marijuana but not other drugs. Meredith used hashish, too, and we often took it together, either on our own or with other people in the house. Usually, we got the drugs in the center of Perugia, on the steps outside the church in Piazza Novembre, but I don't know the names of the pushers. We'd go into town to get some anytime we wanted it. I don't recall the women ever buying any. Usually, us men bought the drugs. Joints, and alcohol as well. The women would often come home drunk.

Why would Giacomo describe his time with Meredith so joylessly? Perhaps he feared being taken for a jealous lover, the kind of person who might stab a girl in a murderous rage. His statement might also reflect Perugia's perplexing sexual code, as difficult for a foreigner to decipher as the Latin Mass.

Merlin's co-owner Pisco Alessi offered some insight into Giacomo's boorish behavior. Meredith was definitely a "nice girl," he said, and given his many years of serving drinks to college students, this was not guesswork. Girls often came into the bar with a certain look in their eyes, he explained, making it easy to tell what they were seeking. But Meredith wasn't like that. She didn't hand out her phone number or go home with strangers.

Still, Giacomo would surely see her as a foreigner, somebody in town only a short time. Their relationship was not necessarily monogamous. They hadn't even reached the point of discussing past loves. They shared a *storia*, a story, a common arrangement in Perugia, where young people are constantly arriving and departing at the train station. Who wished to risk heartbreak over something that could end in tears and scenes at the ticket counter? Sure, Giacomo might sleep with a foreign girl. He might ask her to water his marijuana plants. But he wouldn't hold hands with her on the Corso or call her his girlfriend, no matter how tenderly he might treat her in private.

"One day Meredith is walking on the Corso with me, she is complaining about Giacomo," Pisco recalled. "She says he ignores her when he sees her away from the house. And, then, who do we see? Giacomo. Yes, he's coming toward us. Can you believe it?" Pisco laughed. "He does the very thing she says. He looks. He doesn't smile. He doesn't speak. Nothing."

WHEN Meredith's image lit up TV screens in London, it triggered the memory of the British journalist Francesca Steele. In the *Times* online, she recalled hanging out with Pisco and other local luminaries like Patrick Lumumba (then a DJ) on the church steps during her own student days. She explained that the bar owners had befriended her, unlike the Italian girls whose company she'd sought. In fact even her Italian roommate, Silvia, couldn't afford to be seen with her in public.

It was nothing personal, her roommate explained, but people would gossip. They would say Silvia had a drinking problem and "that I am like you, an English girl."

Francesca, meanwhile, "was rather in awe of a group of bar owners and their 'crews.' By night they were tending a bar, or rather, one would be giving away drinks at one of the bars they ran while the others would be entertaining girls. Always foreign girls, mind, since, as my flatmate Silvia explained, an Italian girl wouldn't have touched them."

Like many newcomers, Francesca found the bartenders delightful. Indeed, when Pisco took a liking to a girl, he could solve many problems for her. Need a place to live? He knew someone who was renting. Furniture moved? He'd send a crew right over. Feeling blue?

Come hang out with us, he would say. Let's get an espresso. Let's have a beer.

When Francesca returned to Perugia a year after she left, she wandered along Corso Vannucci and saw Patrick and Pisco sitting on the steps of the Duomo, "surrounded by a gaggle of giggling girls. It was laughably familiar, and the group seemed all the more harmless for its predictability. As a friend remarked as she looked at pictures of Meredith out on the town with people we used to know: 'She looks just like we did. Sociable. Happy.' "

Amanda's day at the *questura* was far from over. Around 3 P.M. interpreter Aida Colantone came in to translate the American girl's latest statement into Italian. She found

Amanda sprawled on a chair, leaning her head back. Colantone thought she looked wrecked, pasty, done in, and she spotted a small red mark on Amanda's neck, noticeable because of Amanda's pallor.

The interpreter didn't think the mark was strange (although the police would jump to that conclusion), but she did worry about the girl's overall health.

"*Come stai?*" she asked Amanda. How are you?

"Not well," Amanda said with typical frankness. "I can't eat. I can't sleep. And my period just started."

Colantone took the student downstairs, treated her to a cappuccino from a machine, and grabbed a coffee for herself. She offered Amanda a brioche, but the girl said no thank you and shook her head.

When they returned to the upper levels of the station, the seemingly friendly Colantone put the American girl into a bugged room. Raffaele was, as usual, waiting around for his girlfriend and he was allowed into the room, too. Colantone listened in on their conversation, but heard nothing useful or suspicious.

Finally Raffaele left the room and asked the police if he could get a pizza for Amanda. They said fine. He called their favorite place, only to discover that it didn't deliver. The lovers were "desolate," the interpreter said in her report, because they were so hungry. There was only one solution: Raffaele would have to pick up a pizza somewhere and bring it back to the *questura*. He left on this errand.

Not long afterward, around 4 P.M., homicide chief Monica Napoleoni informed Amanda that she needed to return to the cottage again. Laura and Filomena were also going with her. In fact they soon joined Amanda in the bugged room. The microphone picked up their comments. One of them came in saying that she hadn't felt well for days. The other asked Amanda how she was.

"Not well," the American said, complaining that the police were "treating me like a criminal." She then mumbled something about not lying.

"Where is Raffaele?" one of the roommates asked.

"Out getting pizza," Amanda replied.

The trio then talked about someone named Giorgio, who had not entered their flat, Filomena stressed. Then Laura brought up her friend Maurizio, the boy that she was staying with. She asked Amanda how the police had known about him. Amanda said she didn't know. Laura stressed that he had never entered their flat either.

They were interrupted by police officers, who came to drive them back to the house of horrors. Colantone, the interpreter, came with Amanda, as did Monica Napoleoni. When they got there, the place was crawling with journalists drawn, moth-like, to the Kercher case. The reporters hung around on the narrow sidewalk and across the street, hoping for a juicy quote or a sexy photograph. The girls hurried in, managing to avoid the throng. All of them found it painful to return to the house.

Napoleoni escorted Amanda into the kitchen, insisting she look through the knives in the cutlery drawer.

"Do you see any knives missing?" the officer asked.

"No, no," the girl managed to say, meaning that the house had many knives and she simply couldn't tell. She struggled to breathe. Then she had an attack of nerves, like the one she'd experienced earlier in the day in the *questura*, when interpreter Colantone had become concerned enough to take her downstairs for a cappuccino. Now Amanda collapsed on the couch and started to sob.

"During the inspection of the house, Amanda began to tremble," Colantone said later. "She was made to sit down. She was greatly upset. I remembered that she cried, also."

Homicide chief Napoleoni reportedly became concerned enough to ask the coroner, also in the cottage that day, to come see if the girl needed medication. Later, Amanda would say she broke down at that point because the full force of Meredith's death suddenly hit her. She was also sickened by the questions the police kept asking, especially "What kind of sex did Meredith like?"

This breakdown was a "crisis of crying," she said later, adding that she "felt very, very scared, even to get near the house. All the emotion that I had been keeping inside me escaped, because I'd had a shock, an inability to understand what had really happened. I didn't want to accept it and so . . ."

* * *

SOMETIME before 7 P.M. Amanda arrived back at the station. Raffaele was there to greet her, to no one's surprise. Investigators thought it was strange how the lovers always traveled in a pair. Police would "invite" Amanda, and Raffaele would show up. To detectives, the couple looked like co-conspirators. Touching, kissing, whispering, flirting. They thought the girl had the stronger personality; complaining loudly of hunger, thirst, fatigue, boredom.

Police spoke of Amanda's "virginal beauty." She looked glossy, like an American girl in a magazine. Investigators felt that a girl like that could persuade a malleable boy to satisfy her every whim. The rumor was that some lower-ranked officers had to be careful when encountering the American girl, lest they lose objectivity. Those huge blue eyes. The sweetness, fake or not.

The couple didn't know it, but Edgardo Giobbi was monitoring their behavior through his minions, especially their words and facial expressions. Head of the Rome-based serious crime squad, he noticed every little thing. As he later explained in a British documentary, he ran his investigations on pure psychology, believing that detectives could establish guilt or innocence by "closely observing the suspect's psychological and behavioral reactions during interrogations. We don't need to rely on other kinds of investigation as this method has enabled us to get to the guilty parties in a very quick time."

How investigators could apply the psychological approach in a town like Perugia, with its huge language gaps and rainbow of conflicting cultures, was the question. Certainly, Italian detectives had never met anyone like Amanda Knox before, with her West Coast–fringe, flower-child, honor-student, soccer-playing, first-generation-German personality. The more they tried to fit her into an Italian mode of behavior, the more perplexing they found her.

But why was Giobbi suddenly so intensely interested in the turtledoves?

"As soon as he arrived from Rome, Giobbi noticed, as did everyone else, that the door wasn't forced open, and he thought that the broken window was a staging," wrote Frank Sfarzo on Perugia Shock. He said Giobbi's attention focused on the guys from the Marche because of the blood in the downstairs apartment. However, the Roman cop lost interest once the drops turned out to come from Giacomo's cat with the cut ear. Investigators did travel to San Giorgio, of course, to check out their alibis, but they cleared all of them.

"Amanda and Raffaele's behavior was suspicious. Always whispering to each other and all the things we know. Apart from the kissing and the whispering Raffaele, at the police station was, according to Giobbi, always classy." The only time Raffaele showed attitude, according to Giobbi, was November 4, when he insisted that he finally be allowed to deliver pizza to Amanda, who'd evidently had nothing to eat all day.

"For Amanda, a different story," wrote Frank Sfarzo. "Not exactly classy, not exactly controlled, not exactly sensitive."

Homicide inspector Monica Napoleoni was happy to show the lovers into a bugged room that night. No doubt she found them maddening. The phone taps had failed to reveal anything incriminating. When Amanda wasn't talking about being scared and tired, she was trying to score some pizza. She and Raffaele seemed to live on nothing else.

At 7 P.M. interpreters strapped on their earphones yet again and translated for the investigators. It was near impossible to penetrate their weird mix of Italian and English. At first, they appeared to be discussing Juve, Amanda's buddy from Le Chic, who had helped Amanda find the job. At another point, Amanda brought up Hicham, aka Shaky, the Tunisian who knew the English girls.

AMANDA KNOX: (in Italian) I know, but he's a bit crazy when he's . . . (she hesitates, stumbles in Italian and continues in English) When he thinks about breaking off a relationship with a woman (incomprehensible) . . . strange to me. He says he trusts his girlfriend but he doesn't like it when he sees her talk to a man he doesn't know. Even if they've just split up . . . (incomprehensible). He looks at her and gets crazy. And . . . but then he. . . . He's terrible. He says he doesn't mind seeing his girlfriend, even

if he's talking to a man he doesn't know, but then
he gets arrogant with me.

RAFFAELE SOLLECITO: (in English) This is ridiculous.

AK: (in English) I don't like him anymore frankly.
I mean: it was nice of him to find me a job and I
liked it when he played the guitar with . . .

RS: Hang on, are we talking about . . . (he hesitates)
your friend from Le Chic or . . .

AK: (she interrupts him) Friend from Le Chic?

RS: I'm not talking about the one that . . .

AK: Who?

RS: I'm mean the one that . . .

AK: Spyros?

RS: No. Shaky, Shaky, eh, eh (laughing).

AK: I don't like him. He's not . . . I detest that man
(laughing). He tried with me.

Investigators also discovered that Raffaele told Amanda
jokes to cheer her up, hence the giggling. First he told her a
funny story in "stunted English," about a prank he'd pulled
when he was fifteen. Then he translated several vulgar
expressions from Italian into English: *Vaffanculo* (Fuck you),
Li mortacci tua (To your lousy ancestors).

The lovers chuckled over that.

Then Amanda turned somber, telling Raffaele that she'd
been to the cottage, where the cops asked if any knives were
missing. Before she could say more to Raffaele, her father,
Curt Knox, called her cell phone and she filled him in on the
house visit. She was at the *questura*, Amanda told him. "It
was frustrating," she said, spending so much time there, "just
waiting around."

Then Edda called. Amanda told her, too, about the house
visit. Then she handed the phone off to Raffaele, who told
Edda that he had a photo of himself and Amanda, which he
would send to her. Amanda got back on the phone. She asked
her mother to call her when she arrived in Italy so she'd know
about what time to wait for her at the Perugia train station.

At one point Amanda spoke a little German to an unidentified caller, most likely her second cousin Dorothy Craft Najir,
a motherly woman who was very concerned about Amanda.

She said it wasn't normal for police to bring a witness back to the station each day. Amanda now shared her grievances with Dorothy, which were picked up on the wiretap.

"Even at Raffaele's, Amanda says she finds no rest," read the report. "Calls come in from police, from journalists. She says police asked her to remember who came to the house. They asked her about Meredith's sex life and she says, 'What? I don't know. That I don't know.' "

Raffaele got on the phone with the cousin. She evidently asked him to take care of Amanda.

"I can do nothing when we are at the *questura*," he said. "They are squeezing my brain, literally kicking me in the head."

Amanda told her cousin that she had class on Monday. She thought the police might keep her in town for at least another month, until December, which was okay. But she wanted to regain some semblance of normal life. She hoped the police understood that she couldn't be at their disposal all the time.

The bugged session ended there.

CORONER Luca Lalli had wrapped up Meredith's seven-hour autopsy around 5 P.M. Outside the building, he found reporters waiting for him in the darkened parking lot.

"Any signs of sexual activity?"

"No comment." The tall, stooped-over Lalli smiled and fiddled with his car keys as the reporters kept pressing him. They knew he wasn't actually supposed to talk to the press. Finally, he hinted that, yes, he'd found something that he needed to discuss with the prosecutor.

Richard Owen, a tall, gray-bearded British reporter, who covered the murder for the *Times* of London summed up the confusing day: "Luca Lalli, the chief forensic science officer in the case, dampened down speculation in the Italian media that Ms Kercher had been raped. He said only that there were 'possible' signs of sexual activity . . . [and that] preliminary findings had produced 'interesting elements' but declined to elaborate further."

Later, Lalli's findings would prove very interesting indeed. Like other Rome-based reporters, Owen was covering many other stories. He placed Meredith's murder within the larger context of Italian life, especially the country's attempt to deal with foreign immigration from North Africa and Eastern Europe. As he wrote in the *Times*:

"Fears rose yesterday that Ms Kercher's murder would fuel rising xenophobia in Italy. There is widespread belief among local Italians that the assailant could have been an immigrant. Their suspicions followed the murder last week of a 47-year-old Italian woman in Rome. A homeless Romanian immigrant from a makeshift camp is being held on suspicion of her murder."

MEANWHILE prosecutor Mignini was taking a great interest in Amanda Knox. Since he was in charge of the overall investigation, he heard about her every move. When he'd first seen her on November 2, she'd reminded him of the girl next door, but that was before the kissing video, her loud discussions with the English girls at the *questura*, and Meredith's complaint about Amanda bringing men over.

Is the American girl telling us everything she knows? he was wondering. Could she have been involved? Is she covering for somebody else?

He had started to suspect a woman might be involved, Mignini said later, because the body was covered, an act of compassion that he saw as uniquely female. But according to John Douglas, who worked for twenty-five years as a criminal profiler in the FBI's elite Investigative Support Unit, covering the victim is typical of a *young* murderer, not specifically a female one. In Douglas's seminal book *Mind Hunter* he tells detectives who find a covered body to look for a young male suspect (since men commit most murders) who hadn't crossed this line before, an immature person who could still feel remorse and wished to cover up his terrible work. A burglar may break into a house only to rob, Douglas said, but if he finds a woman alone, he may launch a sexual attack. If the woman screams, the burglar may run away or kill the victim in a panic; his behavior isn't predictable.

On November 4, a *Republica* reporter leaked a very big story: "Autopsy: Meredith raped, perhaps by two," boldly claiming that "Meredith struggled with the killer—or killers—who would compel her to have sex."

The reporter noted that he wrote this story after he saw coroner Lalli meet with the prosecutor and investigators at the cottage on November 4, where they discussed the autopsy's "interesting developments." When pressed, however, Lalli would always say that he could not confirm either a rape or multiple assailants. *La Repubblica* reporter could not know it, but he was witnessing the birth of Mignini's *gioco erotico* (sex game) theory of the crime. All that awaited was the casting of the characters, including the criminal mastermind.

The reporter watched both Lalli and Mignini poke around that day. "A visit that made me think of a turning point, because with them was a young woman, it seems, one of the friends of the victim."

Who could that girl be but Amanda, making her first appearance in the press?

CHAPTER EIGHT

INTERROGATIONS, HIS AND HERS

Monday, November 5, 2007

"The killer may have the appearance of a friend. That is the hypothesis that is gaining ground . . . or at the very least that the girl opened the door without suspicion."

—*Corriere dell'Umbria*

"**I'M** falling to pieces," Amanda e-mailed to a Seattle buddy three days after Meredith's body was found. She could get no rest, she explained. Police summoned her to the station every day and bombarded her with the same questions. Who came to the house? Who acted suspiciously? Who did she think killed Meredith?

Amanda said she no longer felt safe, even in daylight on the streets of the old town. "When I talked with my family after everything happened, either in the *questura* or outside, my stepfather told me to be very, very careful," she said later, "because maybe someone knew Meredith was alone at home that night and that person might've been watching the house and would know how to find me, and he could be crazy. And I was scared because they hadn't caught whoever did this. And I was just frightened in general to be alone."

At first Amanda did have an escape route. Her German cousin, Dorothy Craft Najir, had urged her to take a break from school and come stay with her.

"Amanda sounded scared and confused, and I had the feeling she needed her family," Dorothy recalled. "She was terrified that someone was going around killing girls." When Amanda assured her cousin that she wanted to stay in Perugia, Dorothy suggested she seek advice from the American Embassy. "She replied that everything was okay, and she did not need help because she was cooperating and wanted to help the police with their investigation,"

However, Amanda was now forbidden to leave the country, because she was an important witness, a "person informed of the facts." When she told Dorothy that, her cousin flew into a panic and urged Amanda to rush over to the American Embassy, "where you will be safe."

By November 5, Dorothy had called Amanda a half-dozen times on a wiretapped line. Eavesdropping police discovered that the American girl had German relatives who could provide a safe haven. They'd also learned that the American Embassy might get involved and that Amanda's mother, Edda, would arrive the next day.

So if investigators suspected Amanda had anything to do with the murder, they knew that they had to act quickly.

AMANDA'S friend DJ Johnsrud had heard nothing from Amanda since November 2, when she'd missed their Skype appointment and left the Facebook message saying that her roommate had been murdered.

More than any of Amanda's family or friends back home, DJ could understand her isolation. He was in China, deep into a new culture, surrounded by strangers, and unable to rely on his native language. So that Monday, November 5, he decided to call the Seattle girl and find out what was going on. He tried to reach her cell phone via his computer, but the complicated program kept acting up. Finally, the call went through.

Since Amanda was getting ready for class, Raffaele answered her cell phone. That was a disaster. Raffaele barely spoke English and DJ could scarcely make himself heard over crackling on the line. So the ever-polite Raffaele waited for a minute, and then hung up.

Many people might have felt jealousy at that moment, but DJ insisted that he had not. Yes, he would've preferred to be the guy he'd seen in the kissing video, comforting Amanda, but they had split up. That was official. They had a deal.

"Amanda is her own person," he explained later. "She is free to do as she wants. Besides, I like Raffaele. From what Amanda told me, he was very kind and respectful towards her."

So when Raffaele hung up on him, DJ ignored the awkward situation and called back. This time he got a clear line. Raffaele again picked up the call, but he handed the phone over to Amanda.

She told DJ that she was exhausted and tired of talking to the police. She was also afraid to stay in the flat alone or even to walk the half block from Corso Garibaldi to her class at the *Stranieri*.

So he agreed to stay on the phone while Amanda made that five-minute trek. He continued talking to her until she reached ancient Palazzo Gallenga, rising over Piazza Grimana like a battleship.

Then they said good-bye and she hung up.

Nearly a year would go by before DJ heard her voice again.

ALTHOUGH police would interpret Amanda's going to class as indifference to Meredith's death, Amanda said that she went hoping to achieve some normalcy, a wish shared by her two Italian roommates, who both went to work that same morning. Amanda showed up for Italian class around 9 A.M. She apologized to her professor, Antonella Negri, for having nothing better to wear than a blue tracksuit, and took her usual seat in the front row of the ornate classroom.

Negri, an elegant woman with coiffed blond hair, remembered the American as a "model pupil, diligent, and active in class." She was always punctual, the first to arrive, impressive because "everyone knew she worked in Patrick's bar. She gave guitar lessons to a girl from Kazakhstan, and she was always punctual about that, too."

On November 5, however, Negri noticed Amanda wasn't her usual bubbly self; she rested her head on her arms and looked very upset. Still, she managed to complete the class assignment, to write in Italian a "casual or formal letter to whomever you chose."

"*Ciao, Mama*," Amanda began her assignment, neatly printed on lined notebook paper, explaining that she was writing to Edda despite knowing that she'd be arriving the next day, because she "didn't have the best of weekends."

The British tabloids would castigate Amanda for not focusing on Meredith's murder in this letter, but in it she clearly stated that she was a witness and was not allowed to talk about the crime. She said she could talk about her "situation"—locked out of her house with only her purse and one set of clothes, "living with a friend" near her old home, and trying to figure out how to get her own life back.

As translated, from the Italian:

> *I don't have my clothes or any of my things. I have only what I had in my hands when the police ordered me to leave my house immediately, after we found Meredith. I have nothing. I am without a plan and, often, I feel emotionless. I only know that I am always nervous. I need to talk to my boss because I can't work at night anymore. I need to reconstruct my life, but I feel like I've forgotten how I lived before. I hope you will be able to help me. Maybe we can go shopping for some new clothes and you can meet my roommates. Perugia is truly a beautiful city and I want to show you everything. . . . Despite my situation, I would like to remain in Perugia. I know that you want me to come back with you to the United States, but I am not finished here. I am not afraid of Italy. I am not afraid of anything in particular. I am afraid because I am confused. What happened is a mystery to me.*

Amanda's professor read the letter aloud to the other pupils. It stunned and shocked them, she said, to have a fellow student so close to a murder investigation. She remembered Amanda talking to her after class, keeping her head down, looking distraught.

Edda never received the letter. Negri turned it over to police. Eventually Edda would see bits of it in mangled form posted in British tabloids. There, Amanda would be "the girl who went shopping only seventy-two hours after her room-mate's death." A creative *Daily Mail* reporter translated the letter from the Italian, rearranged the sentences, and gave the University of Washington student a British accent:

"I'm on edge. I can't stop thinking about Meredith's death. What I really want, Mum, is for you to take me shopping."

Later, a British girl who was in class that day would criticize Amanda in a UK documentary, saying the American girl hadn't looked sad enough; Amanda hadn't cried during class or acted as the student felt she would done in the same circumstances.

"Students do not normally sit at the front of the class, but Amanda always did," her teacher told the *Telegraph*. "She seemed a sweet and innocent girl. She spoke of Seattle, her city, which is actually twinned with Perugia. She promised to do a project on her city, to talk about its history and attractions. However, she was unfortunately unable to finish it."

AROUND 1 P.M. on November 5, Amanda had a fateful meeting with Patrick Lumumba, her boss at Le Chic. She was standing in front of the *Stranieri*, getting ready to return to Raffaele's place on Corso Garibaldi. Patrick waved to her, flashing his big smile. He picked his way through the swirl of traffic to talk to her.

Patrick had learned of Meredith's death on November 2, the day her murder was discovered. Around 6 P.M., several customers came into Le Chic, where he was bartending. They said a foreign student had died, "a girl of Indian origin."

Right away Patrick thought of Meredith, whom Amanda had brought into the bar a few times. He remembered the British girl as vivacious. They'd had only one actual conversation, about Polish vodka. Meredith said she knew how to make a Mojito with it. Patrick offered to let her "guest host" at Le Chic one night with her friends. So when he heard about a British girl dying, he called Amanda around 7:30 P.M. She was at the *questura*.

"Is it true that your friend, the English girl, is dead?" Patrick asked Amanda in Italian.

"Yes, it's true," Amanda said, adding that she couldn't stay on the phone because she was with police. Before she hung up, though, she asked Patrick how he'd heard the unbelievable news and he explained about the customers.

Now Amanda told her boss that she needed to quit her job, because she was afraid to work at night, especially in the same neighborhood where her friend had died.

He responded graciously, saying, fine, don't worry. Then he mentioned that big-time reporters from the BBC and other networks were having trouble finding English-speaking students to interview. As he recalled that conversation:

PATRICK: Would you be interested in talking to
    reporters?
AMANDA: No, absolutely not. My roommates and I
    have agreed not to talk to anyone.
PATRICK: *Scusa.* Of course, of course, excuse me for
    asking. And how are you doing?
AMANDA: I have spent a long, long, long time with
    the police. It is very difficult, exhausting.
PATRICK: Look, it is normal for the police to do this. It
    isn't magical, it is normal that they ask these ques-
    tions, and I think that you have to understand that.

According to Amanda, Patrick then asked what the cops were saying about the murder. Finally, she told him that she couldn't talk anymore. She was tired and needed to go meet Raffaele.

"You are a good person," Patrick remembered her saying. "And you have helped me a lot." She hugged him and said good-bye.

Later, Patrick's lawyer, Carlo Pacelli, would describe this moment as "the Judas kiss."

That afternoon Patrick handed out flyers on the Corso, helping to get the word out about a candlelight vigil that evening for Meredith, organized by Perugia's bartenders.

"Meredith? No, Meredith, I did not know her," he told *Il Messaggero* that same day. "She certainly didn't deserve to die like this." He refused to give out Amanda's cell number, saying, "My conscience would not allow that." He said she "was shocked" and unable to work in his club anymore.

* * *

MEANWHILE, Amanda had returned to Raffaele's flat. She was there at 2 P.M., when the maid came to do her weekly cleaning. Yes, she later said, she saw Amanda there. She also noticed the drippy pipe under the sink. It was a chronic problem, leaking a bit every time the water was turned on. For that reason, Raffaele had installed a bucket under the sink. When the maid saw it, it was almost full of clear water.

As usual she cleaned the floor with Lysoform, a powerful detergent popular in Europe, with a very strong smell.

THAT night at 8 P.M., more than one hundred mourners carried red votive candles down the Corso to honor Meredith. Pisco Alessi, Pietro Campolongo, and other bartenders marched with the foreign and Italian students. They brought a giant photo of Meredith to place on the church steps.

"With greatest love from all your friends in Perugia, *addio*, Meredith," it read.

The procession stopped at Fontana Maggiore. The leaders draped the giant portrait over the church steps, where Meredith had often stopped to chat with friends. When everyone was in place, the students placed the glowing votive candles around the portrait. They clapped politely. TV cameras captured young women in winter coats and colorful scarves, holding on to each other, wiping their eyes. The stoic male students, dressed in black, stared at the ground.

The mourners stood there for a long time, watching the candles glow, while the video cameras rolled, repackaging the sadness for the nightly news.

None of the cottage flatmates were pictured in the photographs. They were trying to stay away from the media, it was said, and wished to avoid any public spectacle.

NOT long afterward, Edgardo Giobbi, from the violent crime squad in Rome, sprang into action. A thin man with nondescript features, he was an important officer. He came to the station in preppy cotton shirts with khaki pants, looking like a Silicon Valley executive.

Later, he boasted that *he* gave the order to have both Amanda and Raffaele brought to the station for questioning that night, based on his psychoanalysis of their behavior. The Perugia Flying Squad officers would claim that *they* summoned Raffaele and that Amanda tagged along, like an uninvited guest.

"Every time I invited one of them the other would soon follow," said Profazio, the head of the Flying Squadron. He'd watched them carefully because he believed they'd turned their cell phones off on November 1 to conceal their whereabouts, although they could simply have left them at Raffaele's and achieved the same goal. Moreover, the officers only knew about the switch-off because Amanda and Raffaele had provided that information, and they'd never described a "simultaneous turnoff." Amanda said she turned off hers after Patrick called. The ever-vague Raffaele did so "sometime later."

In any case, Giobbi said that he was "mathematically sure" that he gave the order to bring both students in. "At that moment our attention was on Amanda and Raffaele. I decided that we needed to hear them together in order to study their reactions."

Raffaele got the call around 10 P.M., according to Amanda. "We were at the apartment of a friend of his, who lived near Raffaele's, and we were having dinner with them, trying, I guess, to feel a little normal, when the police called Raffaele," she said later.

Raffaele asked for permission to finish eating before they came in, a request that didn't endear the couple to the officers, although they granted it.

Unbeknownst to Amanda, Giobbi had been suspicious of her since November 3, when police had brought her back to the cottage to lead them around. Giobbi said she'd acted strangely when he handed her protective shoe covers. Supposedly she made "*la mossa*," a seductive hip swivel performed by sex bombs in Italian musical comedies.

"Hoopla," he claimed the American girl had said. Or "oopla" or "voilà." Nobody could agree.

Amanda later said she couldn't remember this incident. And one had to wonder where an American girl could possibly have seen *la mossa* during her brief time in Italy. Nevertheless, Giobbi said "it was very unusual behavior and my suspicions against her were raised."

Now, around 10:15 P.M., Amanda and Raffaele showed up at the *questura*. The police split them up right away. They escorted Raffaele into an interrogation room, while Amanda was allowed to settle in a sort of side room near the elevator.

She started doing her Italian grammar exercises in a green notebook, later to be leaked as the "green diary" in *Amanda e gli Altri*, because it contained ten pages of Amanda's private thoughts.

"My mom is arriving tomorrow," Amanda jotted down. Then she drew a miniature sun. "I'm very happy about that. I actually ate dinner with Raffaele's friends. But now I'm very tired. I don't want to stay."

Raffaele's night was not getting off to such a smooth start. Police were exposing him to a high-pressure interrogation. The questions came very rapidly. The officers were loud and threatening. Homicide chief Monica Napoleoni led the interrogation, assisted by three Flying Squad officers. Meanwhile, in a nearby control room, Giobbi, Profazio, and other high-ranking officers were pulling the strings. Periodically, Napoleoni would leave the interrogation chamber to give them an update. Prosecutor Giuliano Mignini was also kept in the loop, since he was at the very top of the investigation, although he remained at home for an undisclosed number of hours.

The officers hammered Raffaele about Amanda, saying that she left his flat on November 1, and that he was covering for her. They said he had lied about the Postal Police, that they'd gotten there before he called the cops.

I want a lawyer, Raffaele said at one point.

That won't be necessary.

Then please, stop the interrogation, so that I can speak to my father.

No, no.

Instead the police kept hammering him. How could he give Amanda an alibi? Hadn't he been smoking hashish? Wasn't he asleep part of the time? How well did he know this girl after six days? Why was he covering for her?

At some undisclosed time past 10:30 P.M. (perhaps after a number of hours), Raffaele "crumbled." In a written statement he suddenly "remembered" that Amanda had left his flat on November 1. He said he'd told police *un sacco di cazzate*, a "sack of shit" because she'd asked him to lie for her and "I didn't think about the contradictions."

Raffaele seemed "confused and nervous," said police officer Daniele Moscatelli, who was in the interrogation room much of the night. He became suspicious when the Italian boy crossed his legs and Moscatelli could see the concentric circles on the bottoms of his shoes. He took them away from Raffaele, to see if they matched the bloody footprint by the bed. Later, Raffaele complained that he'd had to stand around barefoot all through the night.

Cops also searched the Italian student's pockets and discovered that he was carrying a switchblade. This was a daily habit. Raffaele was, as he put it, "a fan of weapons and knives." Pocketknives were, in Italy at that time, something of a fashion accessory, especially in the south. But even though his father had specifically warned him not to bring a knife to the station, Raffaele had scoffed, saying that the police were too stupid to search him. The truth, it later turned out, was that he'd been too stoned to remember that he had the knife in his pocket when he got the call to come into the *questura*.

Now he gave the police the keys to his flat, saying they could check his computer, and they'd be able to see that he'd been on it when Meredith died. An officer did head over there and did get on his computer. Later, Raffaele's lawyers would contend that the officer could have accidently deleted traces of the Italian student's computer use that would aid his alibi.

Frank Sfarzo of Perugia Shock speculated on what would "crumble" the sheltered doctor's son and make him change his story:

> We don't know how and why they got him to do that. We can just imagine a typical dialog in an imagined police station about your whereabouts for an imagined crime

evening. You can have been saying for four days that you were with your girlfriend at home. But maybe on the 5th day they ask you what have you been doing at home? And you may say that at one point you were sleeping. And they maybe tell you that so, from that point you didn't see your girlfriend. And you maybe answer that of course from that point you didn't see your girlfriend, you were sleeping. . . . But you told them the right thing, that from one point, in the evening of the crime, you didn't see your girlfriend. Just an imagined example, among the many possibilities, of how to stop covering for somebody.

Amanda, meanwhile, was not worrying about Raffaele robbing her of an alibi. At 10:39 P.M., she called Filomena on her bugged cell phone and police listened in.

"*Bella, bella*," Filomena called Amanda in her sweet, bell-like voice in that final phone call, before everything changed between them.

"Amanda told me that she was at the police station after having accompanied Sollecito there and she then asked if Laura and I intended to live with her again and said that her mother was arriving and she wanted to meet me," Filomena said later.

Shortly afterward, Officer Rita Ficarra entered the *questura* and saw an incredible sight: Amanda Knox, a University of Washington junior, doing a cartwheel in an Italian police station. Yes, a cartwheel right there, in the hallway by the elevators. Did she do the splits as well? Nobody would ever agree on that.

Ficarra was shocked. A short, tense woman with hard eyes and brown hair, she had spent many hours with Amanda over the past four days, questioning her, observing her behavior. She and many other officers had been working around the clock, trying to find Meredith's killer. Now she rebuked the American for horsing around in the station, where exhausted police were trying to solve her friend's murder.

Later, Amanda would try to provide an explanation, one that might have flown in countercultural Seattle, where yoga was very popular. She said that she'd gotten a stiff back from sitting and had gotten up to stretch. She had executed several yoga moves when a handsome young police officer from Rome approached her.

According to Amanda, the conversation went like this:

OFFICER: How did you get to be so flexible?
AMANDA: I took gymnastics in school.
OFFICER: Can you show me some moves?
AMANDA: I sure can.

For Ficarra, this was just another example of the American girl not understanding where she was or how she was supposed to behave. Doing what she liked, whenever she liked, without consideration for others.

Somehow Monica Napoleoni, who'd disliked the American girl on sight, had also managed to witness the cartwheel. She said she'd left Raffaele's interrogation room at that very moment to get a bottle of water. Lorena Zugarini, the muscular blond officer, had also seen the one cartwheel. She said she'd been strolling around the area near the elevator. Many other officers heard about it, too, including Giobbi and Profazio, the big guns who were directing everything from their control room.

SHORTLY after the cartwheel, at perhaps 11 P.M., Ficarra and Zugarini joined Amanda at the table where she was doing her homework. Ficarra said it was time for a frank discussion. She wanted a list, and she wanted it now, of every male who'd ever come into contact with Meredith. Who was she friendly with? Why was that so hard to remember?

Amanda clicked open her cell phone. Ficarra jotted down names and telephone numbers from the contacts list. She pressed for details. "When did you meet him?" "How?" "Why?" "What relationship did he have with Meredith?"

By 11 P.M., Ficarra had "a list of subjects indicated by Amanda," which included Juve, Patrick, Spyros, and Shaky among a few other names. Then, at the very bottom, sort of as an add-on, Amanda also mentioned another boy, although she didn't give a name or contact information. As Ficarra jotted down:

Amanda reported finally another South African young
man of color, short, who plays basketball in the court at
Piazza Grimana, and who had on one occasion frequented
the house of the young men living in the house (Giacomo,
Stefano, Riccardo, and Marco) and on that occasion she
was present as well as Meredith.

Rudy Guede was in Germany at that very moment. On
November 4, police in Munich had stopped him for some
minor violation. He had given them a false name—Kevin
Wade—and they'd let him continue on.

Ficarra did not follow up on these leads. Nor did she let
Amanda go back to her homework. The tough-looking officer
worked for the Perugia narcotics squad.

"You have not been honest about your drug use," she
accused the American girl. "You lied about the marijuana."
This was not guesswork, since Ficarra had access to the witness
reports. Certainly, Amanda smoked the occasional *spinello*.
But police usually didn't have a problem with personal use.
They had enough trouble trying to catch the dealers.

Ficarra now wrote:

Amanda, in the same circumstances of time and place,
affirmed also that, contrary to what she said earlier, she
had used a drug substance of the type hashish, together
with her boyfriend Raffaele. Of the latter she claimed to
know, because he had confided in her that in the past he
had made use of cocaine and acid, but presently would
limit himself to "smoking." She also pointed to two problems of "depression-sadness" from which Raffaele suffered. For the procurement of the "smokes," Amanda
reported that she also turned to Laura, her roommate,
who would act as a go-between with third parties.

The two officers told Amanda that they were taking her to
an interrogation chamber on the third floor.

At that point, Amanda said, the police stepped up the questioning. They kept asking her to repeat and repeat her versions
of the same things she'd been saying for days. What she and
Raffaele did on November 1, the night of the murder. How

they found the body the next day. And, of course, who did she think the murderer was. She said she still didn't know.

At 12:30 A.M., police interpreter Anna Donnino entered the station. She'd been in bed when she was called in, and since she lived near Lago Trasimeno, it had taken her an hour to get there.

When she came into the room, she saw Amanda with the police officers Ficarra, Zugarini, and Ivano Raffo, a police officer from SCO in Rome. They were all in place, then, to witness the key event: Ficarra insisted that Amanda produce her cell phone, read off all of her text messages, and spill the goods on each one.

Evidently Amanda had been calm as long as she was talking about what she had done at Raffaele's on the evening of November 1, but Donnino saw her break down over the text messages. The first one was heartbreaking under the circumstances, the sweetly worded text from Meredith on Halloween, signed with an "x," a kiss. It marked, as Frank Sfarzo wrote, "That possibility to go out together, an occasion that will never occur."

The next message was time-stamped 8:35 P.M. The police could see the number it was sent to, but no name popped up. They demanded to know who Amanda had sent it to. She said she could not remember. It was, of course, the text to Patrick.

Certo ci vediamo più tardi buona serata! "Okay see you later good evening!"

Who did you send it to? Ficarra asked.

Amanda shook her head. She deleted all her received messages, she explained later, keeping only those that she sent.

Since Meredith had last been seen alive at 9 P.M., the officers took a keen interest in this message. In fact, more and more of them started crowding into the room. Donnino, the interpreter, was not a neutral observer because she worked for the police. She never left Amanda's side. She raised her voice. So did the others. And the questions came faster now.

"Dirty liar!" Amanda said they called her whenever she couldn't remember a fact. A female officer with chestnut-colored hair came up behind her, she claimed, and hit her twice on the head.

Then Monica Napoleoni, the assistant police chief with the

spy-novel looks, came into that room, armed with a sledge-hammer of bad news. Amanda could forget about having an alibi, she told Ficarra. Raffaele wasn't covering for her any-more. He had "broken."

Raffaele's new alibi began the same way as Amanda's, but then it took a drastic U-turn. Now he claimed he wasn't with her all night, that they had parted at 9 P.M. in the center. She had not returned until 1 A.M. Somehow he had forgotten that she'd been seen by Jovanna Popovic at his flat at 5:45 P.M. and 8:45 P.M. He had also invented an 11 P.M. phone call from his father that didn't exist.

His new statement read:

> I've known Amanda for two weeks. She's been sleeping at my apartment since the evening we met. On November 1, I woke up at about 11 a.m. I had breakfast with Amanda and then she left. I went back to bed. I got to her place at 1 or 2 p.m. Meredith was there but she left in a hurry about 4 p.m. without saying where she was going. Amanda and I went into town at 6 p.m. or so but I can't remember what we did. We were in the town center until 8.30 or 9 p.m. At 9 p.m., I went home on my own while Amanda said she was going to Le Chic because she wanted to see some friends. That's when we said goodbye.
>
> I went home, smoked a joint and had dinner but I can't remember what I ate. At about 11 p.m. my dad called on my home line. I remember that Amanda hadn't returned yet. I surfed the Net for another two hours after my father called and only stopped when Amanda got back, at about 1 a.m., I suppose. I can't remember what she was wearing or if she was wearing the same clothes she had on when she said goodbye before dinner. I can't remember if we had sex that night.

For both Amanda and Raffaele, this was a disaster. He had left her unprotected from 9 P.M. to 1 P.M., the crucial hours. And who could give him an alibi now? Not Amanda. He'd already called her a liar and said she wasn't with him half the time. He'd also claimed that he'd been on the phone with his dad at 11 P.M. on his landline, which would also be proven false.

"Napoleoni let Amanda know that Raffaele wasn't covering her anymore," wrote Sfarzo of Perugia Shock. "He had betrayed her, she must think. She was legally naked at that point. She had no alibi. A betrayal (a *presumed* betrayal) that must have turned Amanda crazy."

Giobbi, the Roman detective, had remained in the control room with Profazio, the head of Perugia's Flying Squadron. Giobbi was helping orchestrate the his-and-hers interrogation rooms, though he never stepped inside those rooms. He didn't need to, because the officers kept going back and forth. Everything that needed doing was being done.

Now he could hear screaming. Screaming coming from the room where officers were interrogating Amanda—two, three, four officers, maybe more.

This was the start of a new mystery. What happened in those twin interrogations rooms that night? Why had Amanda's boyfriend turned on her? Why did she scream?

Give us a name, the police shouted at Amanda. You know the name. Give it to us.

Amanda sobbed. "He's bad, he's bad," she allegedly said.

Then she gave them a name.

CHAPTER NINE

AMANDA NAILS PATRICK

THREE PEOPLE IN DEEP WATER
Tuesday, November 6, 2007

"It's an ugly story in which people whom this girl had in her home, friends, tried to force her into relations that she didn't want."

—Interior Minister Giuliano Amato

AT 1:45 A.M. on November 6, Amanda Knox accused her boss, Patrick Lumumba, of murder. Her statement named him as the killer in one "confusedly" given sentence. The American girl spoke in English, which interpreter Anna Donnino translated into Italian for Rita Ficarra, who wrote up the report in Italian police parlance. No audio or videotape of the November 5/6 interrogations would ever emerge from the *questura*, either for Raffaele or Amanda. Thus the entire evening would remain a case of they said/police said.

Retranslated back into English from the Italian, Amanda's statement read:

> On Thursday, November 1, on a day when I normally work, while I was at my boyfriend Raffaele's place, at about 20.30, I received a message on my cell phone from Patrik, who told me the club would remain closed that night because there weren't any customers and therefore I would not have to go to work.

I replied to the message telling him that we'd see each other right away. Then I left the house, saying to my boyfriend that I had to go to work. Given that during the afternoon with Raffaele I had smoked a joint, I felt confused because I do not make frequent use of drugs that strong.

I met Patrick immediately at the basketball court in Piazza Grimana and we went to the house together. I do not remember if Meredith was there or came shortly afterward. I have a hard time remembering those moments but Patrick had sex with Meredith, with whom he was infatuated, but I cannot remember clearly whether he threatened Meredith first. I remember confusedly that he killed her.

The Patrick story pivoted on the text message that Amanda sent to him on November 1, but Ficarra didn't pull Amanda's actual words off her cell phone. Instead she paraphrased "Okay see you later good evening!" as "I told him that we'd see each other right away" ("*Ho risposto al messaggio dicendogli che ci saremmo visti subito*"), completely changing the meaning.

As perplexing as this statement of Amanda's was, it marked a huge step forward for the officers. Not only had the American girl now admitted that she left Raffaele's flat on the night of the murder, but she'd also placed herself at the crime scene. Her story now lined up better with Raffaele's new story, because in both versions, Amanda left the flat. However, the police still didn't have a coherent tale. Raffaele now said that Amanda had left his side at 9 P.M. to join her friends at Le Chic; she now said she left at 8:30 P.M. to meet Patrick at the basketball court. Neither version accounted for Amanda being at Raffaele's at 5:45 P.M. and 8:45 P.M. to greet Jovanna Popovic.

By naming Patrick, Amanda had created a legal quagmire for herself. Under Italian law, failing to prevent a crime was considered the same as participating in it. As police chief Arturo De Felice would soon explain to reporters:

"Even if I was drinking a beer and watching soccer while this was going on in the next room, I would be responsible for it."

Given the American girl's rudimentary Italian and ignorance

of Italian law, she was unlikely to understand that she had now crossed the line from "person informed of the facts" to suspect. Had she simply stopped talking, her 1:45 A.M. statement couldn't have been used against her in court (only against Patrick), since she'd made it as a witness. Police needed her to repeat her "declarations" as a suspect, to set them in stone.

To safeguard witnesses, Italian law required police to provide lawyers at this point. Later, police would claim that Amanda told them that she didn't need a lawyer. She, however, remembered the conversation like so:

Do I need a lawyer?
No, that would only make things worse for you.

The American student also claimed that police warned her that she was facing thirty years in jail, a life sentence in Italy, if she didn't cooperate.

Enter Giuliano Mignini, the high-profile prosecutor assigned to the case. Only he could sign a detention order for Amanda—or Raffaele or Patrick, for that matter. Having been informed by phone that Amanda had "broken," the bearlike, pipe-smoking Mignini drove immediately to the *questura* and entered her interrogation room, where he found the American girl sobbing uncontrollably.

Mignini, the father of three teenaged girls, had a fatherly, folksy manner at his disposal, but during interrogations he could be very forceful, accusatory, threatening. In fact, his fiery interrogation techniques were captured in the nonfiction bestseller *The Monster of Florence*, written by American novelist Douglas Preston and Italian journalist Mario Spezi, both of whom had run afoul of the prosecutor while researching their book. They did not share Mignini's belief that Satanism was behind the "Monster of Florence" serial murder case (the slaying of seven couples over the course of several decades, all of whom had been caught in the act of making love in the Florentine hills). Mignini, after linking those crimes to another murder case he was prosecuting in Perugia, not only accused Spezi of interfering with his investigation, but also had him thrown in jail for twenty-three days. He hauled Preston in for questioning too (after which the celebrated thriller writer prudently decided to pack up his family and leave Italy).

Mignini had not emerged from such battles unscathed. In fact, while prosecuting the Kercher case, both he and former Perugia police chief Michele Giuttari would be on trial themselves for abuse of office and wiretapping charges related to their involvement in the Monster of Florence investigation.

UNTIL 10:30 P.M., Amanda Knox had just been an American college student, scrawling Italian grammar lessons into a green notebook. Now she had signed a statement accusing her boss of murder. She had placed herself at the murder scene. And now she faced Mignini.

Four more unaccounted for hours went by. "It was not the lounge of Lady Windermere there, with the tea on the hour and the cookie aside," wrote Frank Sfarzo of Perugia Shock.

According to Amanda, it was more of the same. She said the interrogators kept yelling, "You met Patrick. You know you met Patrick! What did you go there for?" She said that interpreter Donnino stood behind her, shouting things in her ears. Officers kept coming in and out. Sometimes as many as ten officers grouped around her, all shouting. Prosecutor Mignini made "suggestions" about what she might have heard or seen at the cottage.

All of which would be heavily denied in court. In fact, Mignini would always question Amanda about naming Patrick, as if he hadn't witnessed any of the events, as if he hadn't even been there.

JUST before dawn Amanda signed a 5:45 A.M. statement, both streamlining and embellishing the Patrick story. An officer wrote it down for her in Italian:

> I want to voluntarily report what happened because I'm deeply disturbed and very frightened of Patrick, the African owner of the pub called "Le Chic" on Alessi street where I work occasionally. I met him on November 1 at night after I sent a reply to his message with the words

"see you later." We soon met at about 9 P.M. at the basketball court in Piazza Grimana. We went to my house on Via della Pergola No 7. I cannot remember exactly if my friend Meredith was already in the house or if she came after, but I can say that she disappeared into her bedroom with Patrick while I think I stayed in the kitchen. I can't remember how long they were in her bedroom but at one point I heard Meredith screaming and I was scared and covered my ears. I do not remember anything after that. I have a lot of confusion in my head. I do not remember if Meredith screamed or if I heard any thuds because I was in shock, but I could imagine what was going on.

After so many hours, the word "voluntarily" had an odd ring. This version mentioned confusion, but not drugs. The actual text message appeared, but was shortened to "*ci vediamo*" (see you later). Amanda's meeting with her boss now took place at 9 P.M., not 8:30 P.M. Again, the basketball court, shrouded and scary at night, was chosen as a meeting place. After "suggestions" from the prosecutor, Amanda now also mentioned a scream and thuds, but said, confusingly, that she couldn't remember them. Amanda briefly described the conversation she had with Patrick outside the *Stranieri* on November 4, claiming that he wanted to know what the police were asking her. Then she pulled Raffaele's alibi:

I'm not sure whether Raffaele was also present that night. I remember I woke up at home with my boyfriend in his bed in the morning and that I went back to my home where I found the door of the flat open.

At the bottom of the document, the officers present from the Flying Squad and SCO made an unusual observation: "At the end of her statement, Knox repeatedly covered her face with her hands and shook her head."

AS soon as Amanda signed the 5:45 A.M. statement, she calmed down, according to police. She wiped her tears. Ficarra led her down to the cafeteria and encouraged her to help herself to pastries and espresso, whatever she liked. Later, other officers supposedly teased Ficarra about the royal treatment she provided to the American girl, such as offering her brioche and not making her wear the handcuffs required of suspects. They insisted that every amenity was provided.

Alternatively, Amanda would say she was not "treated like a person" until after she'd signed on the dotted line. No food, no water, no bathroom breaks or naps.

In any case, once she returned from the cafeteria, police put her under arrest.

Prosecutor Mignini's detention order built colorfully upon the statement, placing Amanda at the murder scene and accusing her of helping to carry out a rape that, according to the coroner, might not even have occurred.

"The sexual relations between Meredith and Patrick must be considered violent in nature," Mignini wrote, "considering the particularly intimidating atmosphere in which it occurred and Knox must be considered a contributor to Patrick in the infliction."

Amanda, it turned out later, did not really understand that she was under arrest. She'd thought she would be allowed to go home after she signed the statement. But either she convinced herself, or the police convinced her, that they were keeping her at the station for her own security.

Prosecutor Mignini also signed arrest orders for Raffaele and Patrick, using Amanda's words.

According to *Corriere della Sera*, "Her account is confused, it's understood that the girl has not told the whole truth. But the prosecutor believes that her statements are still good enough to sign the detention order also against the two men."

The entire Flying Squad, at least thirty-six officers, showed up to watch the American college student be cuffed, processed, and carted off to jail. "This was because the entire mobile patrols squad had taken part in the investigation of this very serious, bloody crime," said Manuela Comodi, a local prosecutor who would join Mignini much later in the process. "It does not mean that there was physical aggression or mobbing."

As the police scrambled to process her paperwork,

Amanda suddenly told Ficarra that she wanted to give her a "gift." She asked for pen and paper so that she could write down her thoughts. Ficarra was happy to oblige. Amanda then scrawled a four-page *memoriale* in English, a voluntary declaration made in her large, loopy writing.

Ficarra's pre-prison report described this disorganized, peculiar, bewildering document:

> After her detainment and subsequent to being transferred to Capanne Prison, Amanda Knox asked for writing paper with the aim to produce a written account that she had the intention of handing over to the undersigned before her transfer to prison, asking that it be read by all the police. The undersigned then received the alleged manuscript in the English language of Knox and informed her that the writing, after translation into the Italian language, would be sent to the Judicial Authority proceedings.

In this handwritten mishmash of emotion, Amanda expressed great shock and perplexity about what she'd just done. She described the Patrick story as a "vision," nothing more.

Ficarra couldn't read what Amanda had written, though, because she didn't speak English; so she handed it off to an interpreter and slapped handcuffs on Amanda.

Unbeknownst to Amanda, the police had already locked up Patrick Lumumba. Lorena Zugarini had left the *questura* shortly after Amanda signed her first statement at 1:45 A.M. accompanied by the high-ranking Daniele Moscatelli and other cops.

These officers staged a pre-dawn raid on Patrick's house. They pounded on his door, disturbing the entire family, including Patrick's beautiful common-law Polish wife, Aleksandra Kania. Their toddler son heard the pounding and ran to the door, followed closely by his father, who'd been preparing a baby bottle.

Later, Moscatelli hedged and said he couldn't remember whether or not the bartender had been wearing pajamas when he was disturbed.

"Certainly he was not dressed for the evening, I can say that."

Patrick opened the door to an intimidating sight. Police cars were everywhere, as were armed officers. They rushed into the flat, yelling insults, he later said. They handcuffed him in front of his terrified wife and crying son. His arrest was so public that when he was hustled outside, a neighbor claimed to have heard him shout, "I haven't done anything wrong!"

Raffaele Sollecito, meanwhile, had continued to proclaim his innocence, telling police that he had stayed home on November 1, the night of the murder; it was chilly outside and he had had no intention of leaving his warm and comfortable flat. Far into the night the police had hammered him. They continued to insist that the flick knife he had been foolish enough to bring to the station was the murder weapon. They also doubted his "I was on the computer when Meredith died" alibi, but it was too soon for them to have done a thorough computer check. Most seriously, they claimed that the Nike shoes Raffaele had worn to the station matched the bloody footprint by Meredith's bed.

"I was barefoot until I arrived home, where they gave me a pair of my shoes that was there," he later said. "I walked around barefoot at the police station and onto the street."

Afterward the officers escorted the Italian prisoner back to the *questura*, where a spectacular show was about to begin.

PART TWO

UNDER LOCK
AND KEY

CHAPTER TEN

FROM PERP WALK TO PRISON

Tuesday, November 6, 2007

"A police convoy, ten cars long, blasts through the streets, sirens blaring. Police wave to the grateful crowds and raise their fists in triumph."

— Daily Mail

"An American woman who traveled to Italy to comfort her daughter following the slaying of her British roommate was told during the journey that her daughter was being detained as a suspect."

—Associated Press

THAT sunlit fall morning, police staged a once-in-a-century perp walk, a United Nations of pain and embarrassment. They insisted that the murderers of Meredith Kercher, who had died alone on her bedroom floor, bleeding, choking under a beige duvet, were not the night dwellers, the drug pushers, or the thieves from the alleyways, but the people next door—the smart ones, the good kids who went to college.

The unforgettable images of Raffaele Sollecito, Amanda Knox, and Patrick Lumumba would be splashed on TV screens all over the world. The video became a YouTube favorite, an Italian take on *The Beautiful and Damned.*

Through a set of double doors at the *questura*, police thrust the suspects onto the world stage, one by one. Flanked by plainclothes cops, a prisoner would hover in the doorway long enough for a photo opportunity. Then the officers would haul the prisoner down the steps, across the sidewalk, and into a separate squad car, bound for Capanne Prison, eighty miles away, on the pine-studded plains near Rome.

First up, Raffaele Sollecito. The Italian university student was dressed in the same belted gray jacket that he had loaned to Amanda on November 2, the one she wore in the kissing video. Raffaele had pulled the hood over his head, concealing his upper body. A popular perp walk technique in Italy, where making a *bella figura*, a good impression, is important at all times. Raffaele might look clumsy, foolish even, an Italian reporter explained, but at least his face would not show up on TV. He could be any young Italian man in designer jeans and running shoes.

Next, the biggest prize. A handcuffed young girl dressed in the casual clothing of an American college student: a black fleece jacket, Chicago White Sox sweatpants, hiking boots, a big patterned shoulder bag, and a gray wool hat.

The cops had pulled the hat down over Amanda's blond hair and blue eyes, a maneuver that her handcuffs kept her from performing. The cops who escorted her had also conducted the all-night interrogation. Rita Ficarra, the brown-haired officer with the hard face, held her tightly by one arm. Lorena Zugarini clutched the other.

This mismatched trio paused in the doorway. A good-looking young police officer with a stylish goatee came up behind them, balancing an unlit cigarette on his lower lip, looking excited, jazzed up.

Snap, snap went the cameras. The videotape rolled.

Ficarra scowled. She yanked the wool cap even farther down over Amanda's face. Then Ficarra and Zugarini hustled the prisoner to a squad car and waited while she slid into the backseat. Before they slammed the door, they allowed a photographer one last shot. Amanda faced the camera, the cap still hiding her eyes. Her skin was very pale, her mouth slightly open. She looked perplexed, weary, as she waited for instructions.

Later, Zugarini would insist that Amanda gave her a good-bye kiss on the check, that they were just two women at that point, not cop and prisoner. She felt certain that they had parted on good terms.

Then it was Patrick's turn to face the flashbulbs, clad in a thick brown sweater and jeans, his hair in short dreadlocks. He had no way to hide his face, because he was handcuffed and nobody had loaned him a cap. One of Perugia's most recognizable citizens, he stood in the doorway, his face clearly visible. Only hours before he had been a business owner, a spouse and proud father, asleep in his bed. Now he was a suspected murderer, paraded in front of the cameras, and nobody would ever forget that.

As the officers escorted him into a squad vehicle, he stared defiantly into the cameras.

ONCE the doors slammed on the last prisoner, a celebration began. Police wanted to send a message, to tell the townspeople that they had the killers in custody, detectives had solved the Meredith mystery, and Perugini could finally sleep well again. So they lined up the vehicles, switched on the headlights, and honked the horns in jubilation. Instead of driving directly to the prison, they headed uphill into the old town, horns blaring.

"I have seen police behave like this only once before, and that was when they arrested one of the country's most notorious Mafia dons," a startled local told the *Daily Mail*. "They were celebrating, saying, 'Look at us, look at what we have achieved.'"

POLICE Chief Arturo De Felice wrapped up the event with what British correspondents called a "presser" in the *questura*'s white briefing room, where a gigantic blue banner proclaimed "Polizia di Stato," a salute to the Perugia police. Investigators had drawn a standing-room-only audience by sending out a sizzling press release, promising to reveal the identities of Meredith Kercher's killers.

In a navy blue suit, crisp shirt, and striped tie, De Felice displayed the confident manner and tousled white hair of a mayoral candidate about to swing into a stump speech. He presided over a long rectangular table of blond wood, flanked by high-profile police officers in plain clothes, from Domenico Profazio to Monica Napoleoni and Edgardo Giobbi from Rome. Another row of case-related officers, including Lorena

Zugarini, stood behind him in blue vests that said "*POLIZIA*" on them in big letters. The only major player missing was prosecutor Giuliano Mignini, the maestro of the investigation. He was hovering somewhere outside the briefing room and would be photographed exiting the building with the other big shots.

De Felice waited until the rumpled-looking reporters, cell phones pressed against their ears, settled into the bright blue chairs. Then he delivered a cocktail *esplosivo* straight from prosecutor Mignini's desk, telling them that the English girl had died fighting off a sexual attack, launched by a trio of friends.

The stunned reporters stared at one another, shaking their heads, muttering "*Dio*" and "*incredibile*." Here they'd spent fruitless days trying to wring anecdotes out of increasingly hostile students. Now they had a story that practically wrote itself.

"Kercher killed after refusing orgy," the *Times* would announce that night.

As the reporters aimed their microphones in De Felice's direction, he wove them a cinematic saga about a long, dark night at the *questura* that had ended in a total victory before dawn. Everything had come together when the American girl made a "partial confession."

"She crumbled. She confessed. There were holes in her alibi."

De Felice didn't explain how the prosecutor could weave an orgy-gone-wrong story out of Amanda's baffling "confession" about a single attacker, a scream in the night, and a murder she didn't see because she was in the kitchen. A story, moreover, that she was already trying to recant. In the four-page *memoriale* scribbled just before her arrest, she remembered, correctly, that she'd actually texted "good evening," after "see you later" to Patrick on the night Meredith died. She claimed that she saw a "vision" of him entering Meredith's bedroom, nothing more—a vision she said she had never seen until the police pressured her at the *questura*, even hitting her a few times, evidently during the run-up to that fateful 1:45 A.M. statement in which she named Patrick.

In regards to this "confession" that I made last night, I want to make clear that I'm very doubtful of the verity of my statements because they were made under the pressures of stress, shock, and extreme exhaustion. Not only was I told I would be arrested and put in jail for 30 years, but I was also hit in the head when I didn't remember a fact correctly. I understand that the police are under a lot of stress, so I understand the treatment I received.

However, it was under this pressure and after many hours of confusion that my mind came up with these answers. In my mind I saw Patrik in flashes of blurred images. I saw him near the basketball court. I saw him at my front door. I saw myself cowering in the kitchen with my hands over my ears because in my head I could hear Meredith screaming. But I've said this many times so as to make myself clear: these things seem unreal to me, like a dream, and I am unsure if they are real things that happened or are just dreams my head has made to try to answer the questions in my head and the questions I am being asked.

AT the press conference, De Felice talked a good game, but he didn't have the aces he wanted to flash. He could only tell reporters what *might* be true. The forensic results from the Rome lab wouldn't be in for another three or four days. Detectives couldn't nail down DNA, blood-spatter evidence, or other crucial elements. They didn't know who'd left the bloody handprint on the victim's pillowcase or the feces in the toilet. And although they swore that Raffaele had left the bloody Nike print by the bed, they couldn't be sure. His flick knife hadn't been tested yet for blood or DNA, so they referred to it as "compatible in the abstract."

"So what's the motive?" a reporter yelled out.

De Felice flashed a tight little smile and stared through his thick black glasses directly into the TV camera.

"The motive is sexual, very much so, that is one of the grounds for the arrest."

This was another shocker, since just the day before, coroner Lalli had toned down speculation that Meredith was sexually assaulted, saying only that he'd found "interesting elements." Lalli had also told the *Telegraph*, "I can confirm that Miss Kercher may have been sexually active before the death, but it was definitely not a rape." That same day, DeFelice himself had urged patience, saying it would be sixty days before he would have the "technical information" to back up the autopsy results, meaning feedback from court-appointed experts.

Although De Felice didn't explain this puzzling turn of events, his remarks had one very welcome effect, finally putting to rest the "Meredith Had Sex with Her Killer" stories.

"She was a victim, nothing more," the police chief assured the press, stating what was most obvious. Calling the British student "morally innocent," he said that the coroner hadn't found alcohol or other drugs in her bloodstream.

Then he stressed the foreignness of the crime, ticking off the nationalities involved, beginning with the British student, the murdered *studentessa inglese.* Even Raffaele, from the southern part of the country, came across as an outsider, as did Patrick, despite being a popular bar owner, homeowner, and longtime resident. They were not Perugian. Not even Umbrian. In fact the Italian press would always refer to Patrick as "the Congolese." Raffaele would be "the Barese" or "Pugliese," designating him as from Bari, in the Puglia region. As for middle-class Amanda, reporters everywhere would place "spoiled," "privileged," or "entitled" before "American," in implication if not always on the page. The fact that her arrest came in the final years of the Bush administration, wildly unpopular in Europe, did nothing to help her. When she spoke of pressure from police, Italian reporters would often bring up waterboarding and other abusive interrogation techniques practiced at Guantánamo Bay.

De Felice called cell phone records vital to the investigation, insisting that Italian investigators could pinpoint the location of calls with laserlike accuracy, even within narrow Piazza Grimana, where distances were measured in yards. He claimed that all three suspects had lied about their whereabouts on the night of the crime.

"If I told you I was in Rome, but the record showed I was in Paris, then you might begin to ask questions," he said, listing cities nearly seven hundred miles apart, in different countries.

Amanda was the linchpin of police strategy, he said. She had "crumbled" when police confronted her with the Patrick text, which the police chief shortened for reporters to "see you later." He also claimed that she had set up the meeting with her boss for 8:35 P.M., which would mean that she had left Raffaele's flat, met Patrick in the basketball court, escorted him to the cottage, waited around until Meredith got there at 9 P.M., overheard her screaming as she was being murdered—and yet somehow also managed to be in Raffaele's flat at 8:45 P.M. to greet his friend Jovanna, acting cheerful and calm.

"Initially the American gave a version of events we knew was not correct," De Felice said, seeming to underline the police role in implicating Patrick. "She buckled and made an admission of facts that we knew were correct, and from that we were able to bring them all in."

He conceded that he didn't know specifically who did what, but under Italian law, that didn't matter.

"They all participated but had different roles," he said.

De Felice told reporters that Raffaele Sollecito had also "crumbled." Not only had he admitted to lying, but he had also blamed the falsehoods on his American girlfriend.

Indeed, changing alibis and pointing fingers at others seldom did a suspect any good in the police station or in court.

As for the suspects' civil rights, De Felice boasted that they wouldn't be allowed to see lawyers until their first hearing. *Il Messaggero* would later spell out Mignini's role in this action, noting that "the magistrate who coordinates the police investigation has prohibited the meeting between the suspects and their lawyers until the moment when the three appear before a judge."

Since the suspects had given conflicting stories, police

would also throw them into solitary confinement to prevent opportunities for collusion. They would be treated like rounded-up Mafiosi until their first hearing, the seriousness of which could not be exaggerated. Under Italian law, a judge had to confirm the arrests within the next few days. If the judge said yes, then the prosecutor could hold the prisoners, suspected of murder and sexual assault, for up to a year without charges while the investigation went forward.

They could meet their lawyers at their first hearings, said De Felice, which would be soon enough.

"We will not question them today. They would have to reflect upon what they have told us."

Then the police chief wrapped things up with a bang. "We felt the weight of this city, which was asking us to solve the case and do it quickly. The case was not cracked overnight, no, but in five days. That is fast enough."

Caso chuiso, he declared. Case closed.

THAT same day, Meredith Kercher's bereaved parents, John and Arline, and her older sister, Stephanie, made their first appearance in the old town, meeting with everyone from prosecutor Mignini to Chief De Felice and the mayor. Wherever they went, it was a mob scene. Reporters poked sound booms and video cameras into their faces, nearly knocking them over, shouting their names.

They traveled in a trio: black-haired Stephanie, who shared her sister's large brown eyes and beautifully sculptured face; John Kercher, tall, nervous, puffing on cigarettes; and Arline Kercher, ashen and frail, dignified, her dark hair parted down the middle, her eyes bleak behind large, thick glasses.

While mother and daughter went into the morgue to identify Meredith's body, John decided that he could not bear the anguish. The last time he'd seen his daughter, they'd gone out for coffee in London and she'd showed him a new pair of boots she had just bought. He wanted to remember her like that.

Dressed all in black, the Kerchers faced rows of camera-flashing reporters that day in a press conference organized at the Sangallo Palace Hotel by the British ambassador to Italy. The small hearing room had rows of plastic chairs arranged, as if in a church, with an aisle down the middle. Chattering reporters had filled all the seats; they also leaned against the walls and sat on the floor. The clicking of the cameras and the flashing of the bulbs continued as Stephanie squared her shoulders and took deep breaths.

"Nothing can prepare you for the news we received on Friday evening and it has taken this long for us to feel able to express our thoughts," she said. "Mez, as she was fondly known to us and to those who knew her, was someone very special, a twenty-one-year-old student who was into her studies, worked hard, and enjoyed spending time socializing with her friends and family.

"As anyone who had been lucky enough to have known her would testify, she was one of the most beautiful, intelligent, witty, and caring people you could wish to meet.

"Nothing was ever too much effort for her, a loving daughter and sister and a loyal friend."

Stephanie said that the family took comfort in the fact that Meredith had achieved her Italian dream and reached a happy point in her life. "In closing we would like to appeal to anyone who may feel they have any information, no matter how trivial it may seem, to contact their local police and to help us bring to justice the person who has destroyed so many lives."

Wax from the candlelight vigil still clung to the church steps when the Kerchers stopped by to see the makeshift shrine. Red rosebuds, petals, and notes of remembrance had been tucked in among the votive candles. Arline, John, and Stephanie lingered by the fountain for a long while, while the press captured their still, stark faces. John lit a candle for his daughter and scrawled on a torn sheet of lined paper:

"Love you forever, Meredith, all my love, Dad."

That evening, mourners lit more candles for Meredith on the church steps. Students drifted into the bars, into Merlin's,

La Tana Dell'Orso, the Shamrock; they gathered on the Corso to smoke and chat, feeling bolder now that police had cleared the streets of killers.

Just outside the high stone walls, cars churned on Sant'Angelo, and the view over the valley was as hypnotic as ever. Mourners had tied bunches of white lilies to the iron railings of the darkened cottage, where eight young people had once lived.

FOR the families of the suspects, November 6 felt like a day without end. All a blur, as Edda Mellas would say later.

Aleksandra Kania, Patrick's wife, was stunned and frightened. She spent the hours quietly with their son, believing completely in the bar owner's innocence.

In Bari, nearly three hundred miles south, Raffaele's father, Francesco Sollecito, learned of his son's imprisonment when he saw news stories on the Internet. He made immediate plans to travel to Umbria, accompanied by a lawyer.

"At this moment I cannot speak to anyone," he told the press, "but I am convinced with absolute certainty that my son has nothing to do with this affair."

Raffaele's aunt Rosaria Achille, spoke with the same conviction. "He is a wonderful boy," she said. "Sensitive, very discreet, polite. A boy who has always been timid and afraid of disturbing others. Quiet, walking on tiptoes so as not to announce his presence."

Edda Mellas, Amanda's mother, was normally known for her cheerful ways and wry sense of humor. Like Amanda, she was a bookworm, a morning person. She had flown out of Seattle on November 5, the day that Amanda began her final questioning. Her plane was diverted to Switzerland and landed on November 6. That's where she learned that her daughter had been arrested. Her husband, Chris, reached her by phone to tell her the news.

"I was physically ill and went into the bathroom and threw up," she said.

She was stuck in Switzerland for five hours, walking around the airport in disbelief. Finally she flew on to Rome

Left:
Twenty-one-year-old British exchange student Meredith Kercher was murdered on November 1, 2007, only two months into what was supposed to be a study-abroad adventure. Franco Origlia/Getty Images

Below:
Meredith was found stabbed to death on her bedroom (top window on right) floor in the "house of horrors," a converted farmhouse on Via della Pergola.

Candace Dempsey

Her flatmate Filomena Romanelli's window (upper left near the front door) was broken that night, either to facilitate entry or to fake a burglary.

Candace Dempsey

Left:
Amanda Knox (center) poses with Italian flatmates Filomena Romanelli (left) and Laura Mezzetti (right) on the day they met, before any of them knew future flatmate Meredith Kercher.

Deanna Knox

Right:
Twenty-year-old University of Washington honor student Amanda Knox planned to spend her junior year abroad polishing her Italian; instead she was accused of killing her British roommate.

David Johnsrud

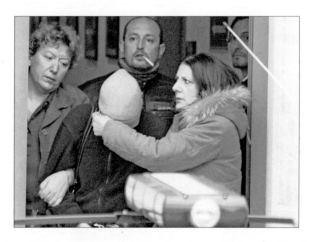

Amanda Knox, a wool hat hiding her face, is escorted from the Perugia police station after her arrest for Meredith Kercher's murder on November 6, 2007. Officers Lorena Zugarini (left) and Rita Ficarra (right) steered Knox's all-night interrogation.

STR/AFP/Getty Images

Meredith Kercher's British friends in Perugia (left to right): Robyn Butterworth (in back), Sophie Purton, Amy Frost (head bowed), Samantha Rodenhurst (smiling), unidentified woman, Helen Powell and Jade Bidwell.

AP Photo/Stefano Medici

Left:
American writer and Perugia local Zachary Nowak, seen here in front of Fontana Maggiore on Piazza Novembre.
Candace Dempsey

Right:
Pasquale (Pisco) Alessi, pictured here on Corso Vannucci, a friend to Meredith Kercher and co-owner of Merlin's Pub, a local Perugia bar where Meredith had partied on Halloween, the night before her fatal slashing.
Candace Dempsey

Top:
Amanda Knox, arriving at the Perugia courthouse for her first pretrial hearing on September 16, 2008. She had been in jail for almost a year by that time, and her trial would last until nearly 2010.

Federico Zirilli/AFP/Getty Images

Bottom:
Raffaele Sollecito, an Italian computer science major and the son of a wealthy doctor, was accused of helping Amanda, his then-girlfriend, murder Meredith Kercher.

Paolo TOSTI/AFP/Getty Images

Patrick Lumumba, a former bar owner and popular Perugia local originally from the Congo, sued Amanda Knox for slander after she falsely accused him of murder in a "confession" she later blamed on police pressure.

Candace Dempsey

Rudy Guede, a Perugia resident originally from the Ivory Coast, escorted by Interpol agents on December 6, 2007, after being extradited from Germany on suspicion of Meredith Kercher's murder and sexual assault. On October 28, 2008, he was convicted of both crimes in a fast-track trial separate from Amanda and Raffaele's, though the trio was accused of conspiring. His initial sentence of thirty years was reduced to sixteen on appeal.

TIZIANA FABI/AFP/Getty Images

Only five days after Meredith Kercher's brutal death, her mother Arline (left), father John (center), sister Stephanie (right), arrived in Perugia for the family's first press conference. "We are utterly devastated by the loss," said Stephanie Kercher.   STR/AFP/Getty Images

Meredith Kercher's family crafted this remembrance for her funeral at Croydon Parish Church, South London, on December 14, 2007, over a month after her murder in Italy.

Peter Macdiarmid/
Getty Images

Left:
Prosecutor Giuliano Mignini outside the Perugia courthouse.

Right:
Prosecutor Manuela Comodi. Visible behind her (left) is Francesco Maresca, the lawyer for the Kercher family.

Left:
Luciano Ghirgha, one of Amanda Knox's lawyers, told reporters that his client had "nothing to hide. She will respond to everything and leave no stone unturned."

Right:
Italian investigative journalist Frank Sfarzo, creator of the Perugia Shock blog, the only reporter to cover every single court date.

All photos on this page by Candace Dempsey

Amanda Knox and Raffaele Sollecito head into court for the final day of rebuttals. A jury convicted them and sentenced them to twenty-six and twenty-five years in prison, respectively, shortly after midnight on December 5, 2009.

AP Photo/Luca Bruno

The Knox/Mellas family outside Capanne Prison the morning after Amanda Knox's conviction for murder and sexual assault. They vowed to appeal. Left to right: Amanda's sisters, Delaney, Ashley, and Deanna; mother, Edda Mellas; father, Curt Knox.

AP Photo/Pier Paolo Cito

and boarded a train for Perugia. Her daughter couldn't pick her up at the station, obviously, and Edda wasn't allowed to see her. But other people helped Amanda's mother, from visiting Seattleites to public officials and locals. The City of Perugia even put her up in an apartment at first. The locals were kind, as they would always be kind, even when her face became world famous as the mother of a murder suspect. Perugia people were discreet; they nodded at her and other family members when they saw them on the street—and then let them go about their business.

Edda was a schoolteacher; she knew how to organize, to get things done. But on this first night there was nothing she could do, not even watch TV. Every time she switched it on, she saw Amanda caught on film, handcuffed, with the wool hat pulled down over her eyes. Edda strained to understand what the newscasters were saying, but it was impossible. She didn't speak a word of Italian.

That night, her daughter's first night in Capanne Prison, Edda stood at her apartment window long after dark, looking down at the street. Even at 3 A.M., she could still see people walking by, but they seemed to occupy an entirely different world. Later on, she would struggle to describe this experience, to put it into terms that an ordinary person could understand. The best she could say was that a glass wall seemed to separate her now from all other people, from any kind of normal situation, and it seemed like this would be a permanent change.

Meanwhile, Amanda's father, Curt Knox, was also making plans to fly to Italy, to help Edda win their daughter's release. They did not question her innocence. Ever.

"We are one hundred percent certain that she had nothing to do with this," Curt would tell reporters time and time again.

The chasm between the Kercher family and the Knox/Mellas families was deep and wide. The two families would be in the same room only once, under supremely ugly circumstances. The Kerchers bore the greatest pain, but the other family endured its own peculiar agony.

"They got the worst call," Curt would often tell reporters,

"the worst call you could ever get. We got a *different* call. We still have hope for our girl."

The *Independent* captured the horror of both predicaments: one family visiting a morgue, the other a prison. "Public sympathy greeted the arrival in Italy of Meredith Kercher's broken parents, who called their daughter 'Mez,' " noted the reporter. "Her father John, a freelance journalist, was clearly touched by the support he received from the press pack covering the crime.

"But another distraught couple was also making their way to Perugia. When Amanda Knox's bewildered parents arrived from far-away Seattle, the wide-eyed, middleclass pair were visibly struggling to make sense of a nightmarish situation."

The reporter was one of the first to accurately portray Amanda's social status. She was not the "child of privilege," as the networks called her, just because her father was a Macy's executive. Her parents had separated when she was three, and Curt had a second family and two more daughters to raise. The Knox/Mellas families lived as well-educated, middle-class Seattleites do—in nice circumstances on safe streets, not on waterfront estates, where billionaires like Paul Allen, the Microsoft cofounder, kept yachts bigger than the average Seattle house.

WHILE the suspects' families dealt with their anguish, Giacobbe Pantaleone, the prison director, boasted of offering his notorious prisoners every comfort, which somehow included stripping them for full medical exams and taking them to be psychoanalyzed.

"All three were tested psychologically," he said, "and the girl is particularly confused but that is only logical and normal under the circumstances."

Besides the shock of imprisonment, the three also had to deal with solitary confinement, which can cause feelings of claustrophobia, depression, and panic if prolonged. Yet these same prisoners would need to clear their heads—and quickly—if they hoped to get out of Capanne. Not only did they have only a few days to prepare for their all-important hearing, but they faced a year in jail without charges if the judge confirmed their arrests.

Barred from legal representation, Amanda hadn't yet learned what any dime-store lawyer could've told her:

Stop talking. You will only hurt yourself. Don't say another word.

CHAPTER ELEVEN

THE MYSPACE KILLERS

Tuesday, November 7, 2007

"Murdered Meredith: Flatmate's 'crazy' boyfriend poses with a meat cleaver and bleach"

—*Mail* Online

"Foxy Knoxy: Inside the twisted world of flatmate suspected of Meredith's murder"

—*Daily Mail*

AMANDA'S friend DJ Johnsrud said she was baffled by what had happened to her. "She placed a lot of faith in the investigators' hands and they abused it. When this thing first happened, everyone Amanda knew was calling her up and telling her to come home. Some people even warned her that she was probably considered a suspect because she was so close to Meredith. But she kept telling people, no, I want to stay and help the police find out what happened. I have to think she regrets that decision now."

DJ had been in his Chinese dorm room when he heard about Amanda's arrest.

"A girl knocked on my door and said, 'I'm sorry about your friend.' I didn't know what the heck she was talking about, so I checked the news."

He switched on his computer and did a search on Amanda's name. Hundreds of headlines popped up.

"American Student Held in Study Abroad Probe"
"I Heard Meredith Scream and Covered My Ears"
"Student Murdered After Refusing Sex"

"I went into hysterics for about twenty minutes," said DJ. "It was absolutely inconceivable that Amanda would do something like this. My mind just couldn't process it at all. I still can't believe what has happened. Then I just crashed for several days. I didn't want to be with anyone. I couldn't take anything in."

IN Seattle, people who knew Amanda were stunned by her arrest, from her teachers and friends to former employers. This was a girl, her relatives said, who couldn't even kill a fish. She always threw them back after she caught them.

British reporters awakened her Seattle friends in the middle of the night, plucking their names off Facebook and then yanking their phone numbers off the UW student directory.

Two of Amanda's close friends, Andrew Seliber and Ben Paxton, said the *Daily Mail* offered $40,000 if they would talk about her personal life, but they'd declined.

Many of Amanda's friends learned about her arrest when they switched on their TVs and saw her in handcuffs, wedged between two tough-looking female cops, or when they saw her exchanging little pecks with an Italian guy in a bright yellow scarf, with light hair and wire-rimmed glasses, reminiscent of Harry Potter.

Amanda's outraged parents took quick action, locking her Facebook and MySpace pages, but tech-savvy bloggers had already grabbed the codes and mirrored her social networking pages on their sites.

Reporters with British accents started hanging out at the University of Washington, looking for dirt on Amanda. They drove by the house of Edda and Chris Mellas in West Seattle and then headed over to the nearby house of Curt and Cassandra Knox, a larger, more expensive dwelling a few miles away. Edda and Chris Mellas became used to coming home to find their curbside mailbox wide open and their mail strewn on the ground; letters from Amanda they'd never seen then popped up in British tabloids. One enterprising photographer even shadowed Curt Knox as if he were a rock star, snapping his photo while he was filling his car up with gas at a neighborhood station.

British reporters also searched Seattle's criminal records, turning up a $247 noise violation fine that Amanda had paid for hosting a loud going-away party shortly before she left for Europe. The *Daily Mail* managed to reconstruct this typical student party as an evening of debauchery that ended in guests running out into the streets, throwing rocks, and staging a street riot. That would have made front-page news in Seattle, if true. Instead, an officer came to the door, Amanda greeted him, and he handed her a ticket. She paid it. End of story.

WHILE the Seattle girl's relatives claimed she wouldn't hurt a minnow, a very different picture of her—and Raffaele— emerged in the press. They became the "MySpace Killers," avatars of their former selves, poster children for what shouldn't get put on the Web.

"It was a feast," said a high-profile tabloid reporter, one of many who had a joyride on the Internet. Reporters would also link Meredith's murder to other young people, in stories like "Dangerous Games of the Facebook Generation."

In fact, reporters were already writing about the lovers— who'd met at a classical music concert and had inserted a Harry Potter book and the dewy *Amélie* film into their alibis—as if they were the trench-coated shooters at Columbine High or groupies of Charles Manson, popular comparisons that conspiracy theorists on the blogosphere also made.

Amanda's nickname, "Foxy Knoxy," would sell a million newspapers. She'd used the childhood nickname as her MySpace alias, a moniker that her soccer teammates had given her because she crouched like a fox on the field. Obviously, it had a sexier meaning when applied to an adult. Headline writers couldn't resist the infinite variety of its uses:

"She's Not Foxy Knoxy, She's Just My Little Girl"
"Foxy Knoxy's Got Some Moxie!"
"Why Foxy Knoxy Gets No Respect"

Most Europeans knew that "foxy" meant sexy, but the Italians didn't really get that the "Knoxy" was just a rhyme on Amanda's last name, with no hidden meaning. They would translate "Foxy Knoxy" as *Volpe Cattiva*, or "Evil Fox," meaning sneaky or unscrupulous. None of this would do the Seattle girl any good when she went before a judge.

Nor would a date rape story that Amanda wrote for a UW writing class and posted on MySpace. Called "Baby Brother," it was about a younger brother who committed a sexual assault and then described it to his older brother. This sophomoric effort came with a clumsily described rape, overheated language, and B-movie dialogue from the younger brother, who thinks he "knows what girls want." But the story didn't glorify the rape. Edda Mellas insisted that Amanda's professor had told the class to exaggerate, to add shocking effects.

Yet never had such a juvenile attempt at shock fiction gotten so much literary analysis around the globe. Pundits portrayed Amanda as a girl turned on by sex and violence; they insisted that she wanted to witness a rape or somehow participate. Only a few pundits noted that Stephen King and other respected people write about murder for a living and have never killed anyone.

"Anyone who's ever read a handful of college-level creative-writing assignments knows that date rape is a cliché of the genre, as is someone-punching-someone-else-in-the-face," wrote Christopher Frizzelle, in an analysis of Amanda's work that appeared in the *Stranger*, a popular Seattle weekly. "These are the sorts of conflicts that creative-writing students cook up because they're taught that the first thing they need to do is cook up conflict." He also pointed out that the story had been online for a year and gotten only one comment.

Amanda had also made the mistake of posting a video of herself on MySpace showing her at a small Seattle party, giggling and acting tipsy.

"I drank one and a half shots," she said into the camera. "One and a half shots, okay?"

This would be a mere aperitif in Perugia, where shots often went for a euro a pop during Happy Hour, and as her friends pointed out on the video, a real drinker wouldn't have stopped at one and a half.

The drinking video lit up YouTube. It seemed no one could resist the chance to see an actual murder suspect, Amanda Knox, clowning around with friends. The footage fed into her new image as a good-time girl with a taste for booze as well as pot smoking. Some reporters went so far as to claim, inaccurately, that she'd been a Seattle bartender. She was too young even to drink legally in the U.S., let alone work in a bar, but she *had* "pulled" espresso during a part-time gig as a barista in a coffee shop, like thousands of other young people in caffeine-crazy Seattle.

According to friends, Amanda was actually a light drinker, an impression shared also by Giacomo Silenzi, Meredith's boyfriend, in his witness report. He said that Amanda smoked a joint and drank sometimes, but not to excess. Her Seattle friends said she preferred to throw tea parties and drank lots of chai, a sweet, spicy Indian tea.

Amanda had also put up photos of her European travels, including an unfortunate one where she posed clutching a machine gun in a German museum, under the even more unfortunate caption "the Nazi within."

"She was just kidding around," insisted her sister Deanna, who had taken that photo.

Truth be told, reporters probably found Amanda's lavender MySpace page distressingly sweet at first. Not only did she refer to her mother as "my greatest hero," but her "Foxy Knoxy" photo showed her in an outdoorsy outfit—denim shirt and wool cap—smiling as she held up a tiny plastic bear. Her interests were mainstream, even vanilla.

> I love things like good wine, rock climbing, backpacking long distances with people I love, yoga on a rainy day, making coffee, drinking tea, and lots of languages. I'm twenty years old and I like new things. Ooh, and soccer, and roller coasters, and harry potter, and . . .

Yet pundits around the world could not resist the question: Who is Amanda Knox? They offered only lady-or-the-tiger extremes. Devil or angel. Whore or Madonna. Killer or saint.

Amanda became "the dark angel" in the Italian press, which recast her schoolgirl sexual escapades as evil, dubbed her "a huntress of men, insatiable in bed," and insisted she *diavolessa fissata con il sesso*," a she-devil obsessed

Yet this same young girl, so apparently generous with her sexual favors, was also said to have no feelings. For Italians, even her blue eyes were a strike against her. "Icicle Eyes," they called her.

Alexandra McDougall, a UW friend, scoffed. "I have never been afraid of Amanda's eyes. I love looking into them. They are not evil. They are beautiful and kind."

Eventually she and other friends created "Free Amanda and Raffaele" Facebook pages to push for the couple's freedom. Anne Bremner, a prominent Seattle lawyer, also helped found a support group called Friends of Amanda to halt perceived character assassination and misrepresentation of forensic facts.

But in the beginning, many supporters were too shocked to speak out. So it was startling to see their rare comments on the Web, including this one from the *UW Daily* site on November 16, 2007:

Dearest Amanda,

We love you so much and hope you're okay. Sorry everyone is making up stories about who you are—it's insane what people can make up by misinterpreting a photograph or a story, huh? Though I must say, it is pretty funny to imagine you as a drunken, slutty, pothead. Yeah, this is ridiculous. I'm not sure how you can take a beautiful, kind, energetic, loving, sensitive, outdoorsy, rock-climbing, yoga-doing, smiley, bouncy, academic, wonderful girl and portray her as a lunatic with no soul.

Well, dear, we've got your back, and we know who you really are.

Love you so much.
—you know who we are

MEANWHILE, British reporters were making a heroic effort to turn Raffaele's blog—the stilted outpourings of a small-town doctor's son—into tabloid fodder. He'd told readers that he was five feet ten inches tall and had green eyes and blond hair (rather than his actual light brown), that he liked vacationing in Jamaica, relaxing on the beach, and kickboxing. His tastes veered toward the corny, and he eschewed the very cultural references that some online critics pointed to as inspirations for the crime. His favorite film was *Hamlet*, not *Natural Born Killers*. He enjoyed listening to the Eurhythmics' "Sweet Dreams," not the Charles Manson-esque "Helter Skelter."

The *Sun* insisted that "disturbing Internet pictures of the Seattle-raised suspect, who fantasized about drugging and raping a young woman on her MySpace site, and Sollecito have already emerged. She is seen with a machine gun, while he is seen posing as a mad doctor wielding a meat cleaver."

The "mad doctor" photo that UK tabloids had great fun with was a shot of Raffaele swathed in white surgical gear and brandishing a lethal-looking meat cleaver, yet they must have known it was just a silly costume. He gave them little else to work with, never posing dressed in black leather, his foot on the kickstand of a Harley, or holding up a rifle even in jest.

"I'm very honest, peaceable, sweet but sometimes totally crazy," the computer science student wrote, not apparently realizing that "crazy" would be taken as a code for "cold, calculating killer."

An exasperated friend finally locked Raffaele's blog and ripped into the "cowards" online who "spit on him and make judgments." The friend wrote, "Hello, everyone, good and evil, I'm not the owner of this site, but I'm going to close this blog, because no one can fling mud at this same Sollecito unless he is a person who knows him as well as I do."

Which prompted an Italian student on a different site to write, "The press is throwing slingshots at Raffaele Sollecito's blog, finding, as always, sinister forebodings in words written by one who, had he not been involved in a murder, would sound like a typical boy, very ordinary, a little silly, a little emotional . . . a bit into soft drugs, joking around in some macabre pictures, socializing with friends."

* * *

THE Italian press, like police chief De Felice, placed Meredith's tragic death in some dark netherworld of foreign students, despite the fact that none of the three suspects was shiftless or purposeless. They were scholarly, with enviably strong family ties—as prosecutor Mignini would soon discover.

"God save me from my friends. I can protect myself from my enemies," said *TamTam*, one of many Italian publications to link the murder to two sensational cases in the *Bel Paese* in which disco-age children had killed their parents with the help of friends. *TamTam* claimed that such crimes were happening more frequently, blaming loosened family ties and violence "ripening in an environment which, if not the home, is surely that of friends and acquaintances."

Yet Mignini's group murder theory was causing worldwide controversy, because the particulars were so unusual. Not only did most murders involve a single assailant, but most were committed by men. Women seldom killed each other. Orgies rarely featured knives.

Even so, around the globe, the guilt of all three suspects was presented as established fact.

"It appears that the young English woman died at the hands of her friends," stated one American news show not long after the arrests. "That she—the victim—refused to play along in their high-voltage game of drugs and group sex and as a consequence was tortured, sexually assaulted, stabbed and left to die."

When asked how she thought Meredith died, one strikingly beautiful Italian reporter in a white trench coat and very high heels, shrugged her shoulders and uttered the three words that seemed to explain so much.

"*Sesso, bugie, droga*." Sex, lies, drugs. Reporters would run endless riffs on those three words, playing off the film title *Sex, Lies, and Videotape*. It gave a convenient answer to why Amanda would want to hurt Meredith, why Patrick would enter the bedroom, why Raffaele carried a flick knife.

Even in Seattle, where people who knew Amanda could

not believe the charges, strangers wondered if perhaps the Seattle Prep graduate had fallen in with a bad crowd over there in Europe, where she didn't have family around. Maybe she just trusted the wrong people, the kinder ones would say, trying hard not to be judgmental.

The blogosphere attracted people who felt immediately that they knew the suspects were guilty and who were suspicious of their every move, some even saying that Amanda should be strung up, that it was too bad that Italy didn't have the death penalty.

La Stampa offended many Seattle residents, though, when it dubbed Amanda "the dark lady from Seattle," and *Corriere della Sera* offended even more with its portrayal of the Emerald City as a breeding ground for serial killers. The prestigious newspaper linked Meredith's murder to Kurt Cobain's suicide in a Seattle mansion (neglecting to mention how he'd made his first suicide attempt in Rome), the crimes of serial killer Ted Bundy (a lone-wolf killer, actually from Tacoma), the overcast Seattle winters (more temperate than Rome or Perugia), and even TV shows set in Seattle, like David Lynch's tongue-in-cheek horror series *Twin Peaks* (fiction, pure fiction).

Corriere della Sera later lightened up on Seattle, calling it instead "*la citta magica*," the magical city, and giving the beleaguered Amanda a backhanded compliment: "If Amanda Knox were released on remand or because the charges have been dropped—it doesn't matter—she'd have Italy at her feet. She's got the fame, the face, the story and the right age. The frenzied attention that surrounds her today would turn into stardom. It's up to Amanda but if she is so inclined, Italian public opinion is primed to put her on the A-list."

CHAPTER TWELVE

DEAR DIARIES

Wednesday, November 7, 2007

"Even though I'm here, it's like I'm not, because I know I'm a special case."

—Amanda Knox, in her prison diary

"I do not know if it is right that I must pay such a price for not being able to focus on each moment of time on the first of November, but after this experience, believe me, I would never touch the pipe again in my life."

—Raffaele Sollecito, in a letter to his father

AT Capanne, prison guards in chic berets, royal blue uniforms, and white gun holsters chatted with the infamous American prisoner, leaning against the bars of her twelve-by-eight-foot isolation cell. They were happy to offer all the paper and ink that she desired.

Amanda, you are a writer, they told her. You should write everything down.

The Seattle girl didn't question why prison guards were so happy to provide her with paper while forbidding nearly everything else. Until her hearing on November 8, 2007, she wasn't allowed to watch TV, talk to other prisoners, or use a computer. Guards provided her with a reading lamp but wouldn't allow her to have books.

"Go figure," she wrote in her diary.

Really, Amanda could do nothing but eat and sleep and write. She didn't want to cry anymore, she wrote. On loose sheets of notebook paper, the Seattle girl began a jailhouse diary in clear, neat printing—with few of the misspellings and punctuation errors that marred her long e-mails.

With the grandiosity of youth, Amanda printed in big block letters on the title page: "*My PRISON DIARY *Il mio diaro del prigione*"

Then she recorded her thoughts in English with a certain detachment, a fascination even. She was so sure she'd be back in Perugia soon.

> I'm writing this because I want to remember. I want to remember because this is an experience not many people would ever have. I am not saying I am glad everything that has happened has happened. If it were up to me, my friend would never have been killed and we would all still be living together in our home.
>
> We were really good together. We all had our part in the house. I looked up to Laura. She is a very opinionated and strong woman who plays guitar and listens to music. Filomena, she is definitely the most loved. I think because she sings and is very funny. She gives advice to everyone and is always happy. Meredith was the most studious and she also went to discotecas with her friends and to have dinner. She was very smart. To me she was always a good friend. She gave me good advice and protected me when she knew I was in an uncomfortable situation. She was the most solitary of us all, but only because at home she liked to be at peace and read her mysteries, but at the same time she also joined us to watch silly game shows on TV together. Then there was me, the littlest one, young, but also very particular. I do things like sing and play the guitar and stretch. Laura really liked me because she told me I was a free spirit.

Shielded from the media storm, Amanda wondered if her roommates knew what had happened to her. "I want to tell them and I want to see them," she wrote, "and of course I want my mom to meet them. They are the best friends I have here in Perugia."

Only two days had passed since Amanda had called Filomena from the police station to discuss living together again. The Italian girl had addressed Amanda as "*bella*" and exclaimed "*Madonna!*" in sympathy when she heard that the American girl was back at the *questura*.

Yet Filomena's parents had already called reporters to paint Amanda in a harsh light. The American was a cold person with "icicle eyes," they told *Il Messaggero*, reinforcing Amanda's new ice queen image in the press.

"The murdered girl was always very friendly with our daughter and the other Italian girl who lived in the flat," said Filomena's parents, "while the American arrested for murder lived in her own world and was far more cool and detached."

Filomena's parents didn't say how they could take the temperature of the two foreign girls while living more than four hundred miles south, but perhaps they were simply protecting their own daughter, putting distance between her and any criminal entanglements. And in the Italian way of thinking, Amanda was neither a childhood friend nor a relative, but a joint tenant, an acquaintance of six weeks, and a foreigner to boot.

Indeed, the parents stressed that their Calabrese daughter was a local, having lived in Perugia since her university days. "Our daughter has returned to everyday life despite the shock of Meredith's death," they added, saying that she had not missed work because of it. She was all right, in other words.

The truth was that whoever shattered Filomena's window had also destroyed the cottage household. Filomena had moved in with Marco; Laura went elsewhere. Neither Italian roommate would ever visit the American in jail. The only enduring reminder of their friendship would be a photo that Deanna Knox had taken on September 2, 2007, the day that Amanda had first seen the pretty cottage with the wilderness all around. The soon-to-be roommates stood by the front door, with their arms wrapped around one another, Amanda in the center, looking sunburned but radiantly happy in shorts and a flowered top with puff sleeves; frizzy-haired Filomena posed in a tight pink blouse and black miniskirt; and deeply tanned Laura in a yellow tank top over jean shorts.

Everybody was smiling, squinting into the sun. Only Meredith was missing. They did not even know her yet.

Now, only two months later, everything was topsy-turvy. The outgoing, cheerful American that the Italian roommates described in the witness reports was behind bars. Nobody

knew whom to trust. Filomena and Laura would spend a
great deal of time in prosecutor Mignini's office. When they
next saw the American girl, it would be under the bitterest of
circumstances.

IN her diary, Amanda said that the prison guards at Capanne
were kind to her and checked often to make sure that she was
okay. "I don't like the police as much, but they were nice to
me in the end, but only because I named someone for them,
when I was very scared and confused."

Above all, she wanted to see her mother. She knew that she
had arrived but hadn't been allowed to talk to her. "She's most
certainly freaking out, but after I'm interrogated, either today
or tomorrow, I'll be able to talk to her and hopefully soon I'll
be able to go free."

Like Patrick and Raffaele, Amanda found herself in a
prison too new to have a fearsome reputation. Capanne was
chilly in winter and sweltering in summer, no paradise, but
it was neither Attica nor Sing Sing, and certainly a big step
up from Rome's teeming, grossly understaffed Rebibbia,
once described as "pure horror." The big Capanne compound
had concrete everything, from watch towers to pearl-colored
buildings. There was an exercise yard where prisoners could
spend one hour per day outdoors. Amanda at least had a
view.

> It's a sunny day outside my barred window. . . . I can
> see a walled-in area that's outside next to a fenced play-
> ground, for those prisoners who have children. Beyond
> the impounded area of my prison the trees are yellow and
> losing their leaves and beyond them are low hills, brown,
> with the swaying of the trees and the grass. My cell is at
> the end of the hall and there is another window there,
> from which I can see the outlines of another building not
> too far in the distance.

Amanda was in a cell meant for two women, which she
described as "a room attached with a shower, toilet, and two
sinks, one is the bathroom sink, and the other for washing

dishes. In my room, I have cabinets, although I wasn't allowed to bring in most of my things, just a pair of pants." The guards had presented her with a plate, two spoons, feminine pads, toilet paper, a toothbrush, toothpaste, cups, and a sponge. But they had also entered the prisoner's cell and removed possessions without explanation. They'd taken away, for instance, her hiking boots and nearly all her ear studs.

On November 7, Amanda had an important visitor, the jailhouse chaplain. Father Saulo Scarabattoli was a Roman Catholic priest, a tall, stooped-over man with rimless glasses, a kind face, and a slow, patient way of talking. Except for visits from this priest and a nun, Amanda was truly alone. The compound held fewer than fifty women, many of them recent immigrants who had been arrested on drug, theft, or prostitution charges. Amanda didn't have contact with any of them, not even at mealtimes, because Capanne had no mess hall. Guards brought the food on trays, passing them through the bars, offering a distraction. On Amanda's first night, they gave her spiced rice with peas and some cabbage.

"For breakfast I received milk with coffee, and a little while later, bread and two apples. They also gave me two dessert cakes, but I don't like them," Amanda wrote.

Although the press would report that the American prisoner asked for a guitar upon arrival, ate ravenously, and loved the view from her cell, her parents denied all those reports. They said that their daughter's chipper tone during the early part of her incarceration hid a grim reality. For one thing, Amanda continued to suffer from stomach problems, exacerbated by the acrid tap water and all-around stress she was under. She was also lonely and terrified. To her mother, she wrote, "Please don't leave me here. I need you to get me out. I don't belong here. I miss my life. I love you." An English tabloid later leaked a letter she wrote to DJ, part of her "diary." He never received it:

Dear DJ,

Right now I need you to hold me. I now have the hard thing in my chest and it feels like something really strong and cold is pressing the sides of my head together. Please, I can't be alone right now. I'm sorry for being weak, but I'm sick and so tired. I want to go home.

How can I continue like this for the next 14 days? How can they look at me, treat me like a murderer? They really think I am and it's not fair. This can't be my life. Please, this can't be my life. Please, hold me now.

As Amanda chronicled her new journey, her diary skipped back and forth in time, perplexing to a reader. She did seem oddly cheery at first, given the circumstances. It turned out that she was elated over a second *memoriale* she'd written the night before, after her arrest—not to be confused with the first *memoriale*, the one that she'd handed off in the morning right before her arrest, to Rita Ficarra.

In her diary, Amanda described how this second document had come about:

I was in my cell thinking and thinking, hoping I could remember, hoping I had done the right thing, worried that maybe the police are right, maybe I had seen Meredith's death and maybe I really was confused and couldn't remember anything so tragic and this just isn't so. In my cell I was waiting for an answer to come my head when a sister arrived at the door. She told me to be patient and that God knows everything and would give me the answer. I nodded along and finally the sister left and wished me good luck. Perhaps a minute later I sat down to write and try to remember and then it hit me.

She wrote that images of the night Meredith died came back to her "like a flood, one detail after another" and she saw herself at Raffaele's watching *Amélie*, eating, talking, putting her head down on the pillow and falling asleep—never going out. For her, this meant that she couldn't have played a role in Meredith's murder or seen Patrick in the cottage.

"I was so happy. I wrote down everything that I could remember. And an explanation for my confusion earlier."

Her new statement began:

So I guess now I'm supposed to do again what I've been doing since last Friday afternoon: recount what I know. In the last [illegible], I've been called a lot of things, a poor girl, a lier [sic], a good girl, a prisoner. People have talked sweetly to me, yelled at me, hit me, offered me help, and asked me a lot of questions. In this time I haven't known who to trust. Even in the dark I've feared even my own boyfriend just because I don't know what happened and I don't know who did this.

She then explained that since Meredith's death, she could manage to feel physically safe at times, but never mentally safe.

I only know I'm safe when I'm with the police or alone, although this is the only kind of safety I can feel for my body. Alone, and with the police, I fear my mind. Alone I imagine the horrors my friend must have gone through in her last moments.

I have to imagine what it must have felt like when she felt her blood flowing out of her. What must she have thought about. About her mom? Regret? Did she have time to come to any peace or did she only experience terror in the end? With the police I fear I would not remember something correctly, and the police would accuse me. I DID NOT KILL MY FRIEND. But I'm very confused, because the police tell me that they know I was at my house when she was murdered, which I don't remember. They tell me a lot of things I don't remember. Here is what I do remember. . . .

Then Amanda reverted back to her original story: I was not there.

GUARDS had also managed to turn Raffaele into a diarist, but his opus was bleak, starkly illuminating the differences in personality between the lovers. From the way Raffaele wrote, he could've been in a different prison entirely. Still, he had a fun-loving, childish side: mentioning that while he would love to have a computer in his cell, he had to admit that nothing would be better than a PlayStation or Nintendo for video games.

Like Amanda's work, what Raffaele composed wasn't a diary in the strictest sense, but loose sheets of papers on which he wrote various types of things. On November 7, he wrote a letter, translated below from the Italian:

> *Dear Papa and big sister, primarily, and all those who would read these lines.*
> *I write to you from an isolation cell, damp and cold, there are peepholes in every direction from which the guards can watch you even while you use the toilet. The bed is made of industrial sponge, the television cannot be used, the bath is dirty and I am requesting that they come and clean it. Today I had an extra blanket and therefore I am warm, at least while I sleep. Outside the window there is a guarded concrete pit and beyond that an enormous concrete mall, empty except for an armed guard atop the watchtower. Amid this sad and depressing view, on the horizon one can see a little mountain house. Good, that faraway little house in the middle of the plain wrests from me a timid smile of hope.*

He continued with noise complaints and a glimpse of his own interrogation.

> *While I write to you there is a pair of Moroccans (presumably) who speak an incomprehensible language and they knock on the wall of my cell. They continue to complain that they need a dose of heroin. I don't want to respond, I do not care.*
> *In police headquarters they tortured to me psychologically, put me in shackles, and made me strip in front of the scientifica, I was even barefoot.*

Raffaele then blamed pot smoking for his imprisonment,

saying that because of it he couldn't remember details about November 1 and he'd also been foolish enough to enter the *questura* carrying a knife, which he used to "notch tables and trees." He also laid out, for his father's benefit, his version of what he did the night Meredith died, promising to nail down every detail. Yet free-spirited Amanda, who boasted of never looking at a watch, still came across as the more precise of the two. Raffaele said that he'd woken up that morning at around ten, give or take an hour. Amanda left him to sleep some more, and went to the cottage, saying she'd wait there to have lunch with him.

"I joined her around 2 P.M. and Meredith, that poor girl, said she had already eaten," Raffaele wrote. He then made lunch for himself and his girlfriend while Amanda played the guitar and Meredith got ready to leave. The British girl left around 4 P.M., without saying where she was going. Around 6 P.M., Raffaele said, the lovers smoked a joint and then they left to return to his flat.

> *From this moment my problems begin, because I have confusing memories. The first thing is that Amanda and I went into the center from Piazza Grimana to Corso Vannucci, going behind the University for Foreigners and ending up in Piazza Morlacchi (we always take that route), then I don't remember but presumably we went grocery shopping. We returned to my place around 8 or 8:30 p.m. and there I rolled another joint, and since it was a holiday I took everything easy, without the least intention of going out again because it was cold.*

Raffaele got the time of his arrival at his own flat badly wrong, since Jovanna Popovic saw the couple there at 5:45 P.M. but the rest of his account more or less jibed with Amanda's. Like her, he could usually remember what he did, but not when he did what.

"I had dinner with Amanda," he said to his father in the letter, "but don't ask me what I ate or at what time. I remember the leaky pipe under the sink, that flooded the kitchen, but only because the Flying Squad nudged my memory. I probably surfed the Web, watched the film, and got a good night message from you, my father."

As for Amanda, now that he'd time to think, he couldn't remember her going out.

"I have strong doubts about whether she was ever absent," he finally concluded.

ONLY Patrick Lumumba felt no need to keep a diary. The international press showed much less interest in him anyway than in "Foxy Knoxy" and her "rich Italian boyfriend," that irresistible pairing. But the dawn raid on Patrick's home had appalled more than one resident. What did police mean, they said, by arresting a suspect without even checking his alibi? Without digging around for other evidence? Was it really necessary for them to have barged into his home and cuffed him in front of his wife and child? A man with no criminal record?

Getting arrested won no one friends in Italy, but many locals came forward to call Patrick Lumumba a good man. A group of black residents called for his release during a demonstration on Piazza Novembre. Customers came forward to offer him alibis, swearing that on the night of November 1, Patrick had been in his bar during the fatal hours. A Swiss professor, in fact, swore that Patrick had been there from roughly 10 P.M. to midnight. Police couldn't find anyone who remembered his having a crush on Meredith, a girl he apparently knew only as the roommate of his employee Amanda.

Esteban Garcia Pascual of La Tana Dell'Orso called the arrest a "hammer to the head." Certainly the Congolese immigrant was as fully integrated into Perugian society as any foreign-born person could be. He'd lived there for more than twenty years, since the early 1980s, he had a resident permit, many friends, a pleasant family life, and a cheerful if not lucrative bar. Many locals remembered him from his university days or from his time working in the clubs as a musician and a DJ. He still played in a reggae band and had just managed to buy his own house, a major accomplishment in costly Perugia.

"When I heard the news, I said if that man is a killer, then I know nothing of life," Esteban said later. "I have lived this long and I have understood nothing." Nor did he believe that Patrick would help the two students cover up a crime. "Patrick would never have helped them in any way. It is not possible. I would never believe such a thing."

Ivo Pioppi, the owner of a local music shop, told the *Times* that "Mr. Lumumba is a cultured, intelligent, respectful and respectable guy. I find the accusations hard to believe."

Indeed, the man whom the press called "the Congolese bar owner" was nearly as recognizable on the Corso as Pisco Alessi, the Merlin's co-owner. He would often stop to chat to this person or that one, eat in the kebab shops, invite students to come to his bar, or work on joint promotions with the other bartenders. He and his wife were a common sight on the Corso on Sundays, window-shopping while Patrick pushed the stroller for his little son.

Frank Sfarzo, who'd known the bar owner since their student days, wrote:

He introduced himself as the nephew of Patrice Lumumba, the anti-colonial leader, first elected prime minister of the newborn Republic of Congo and then imprisoned and assassinated under mysterious circumstances. . . . He knew many foreign students, including Erasmus scholars, through his connections at the Stranieri, where he helped organize entertainment. Patrick was always around, trying to involve the foreign students in his activities and had access to most of their houses. Often girls were hoping he'd select them for singing in a concert or to work in a bar. He'd always been a referee point for the African community, showed a certain degree of wisdom, was never involved in violent episodes. He always had a gentle attitude and was often seen cooling down other Africans who were maybe creating problems under the effects of alcohol.

Although Patrick would escape most of the mudslinging, he did suffer one supreme moment of embarrassment. Even in the Congo, residents followed the Meredith mystery. François

Lumumba, a nephew of the slain Congolese prime minister, told *La Repubblica*:

"I do not know Patrick Lumumba; he has no relationship with my family. None of our friends, all of whom live in the Congo, know him. If he is a person who has killed [somebody], then he must go to jail."

CHAPTER THIRTEEN

FIRST HEARING, NEW SUSPECT EMERGES

Thursday, November 8, 2007

"They are young people who moved to Perugia to study, live away from their families, and appear not to have any rules. They live by night, wandering from one party to another, often get drunk and smoke themselves into a stupor on hashish."

—Fiorenza Sarzanini, *Corriere della Sera*

TWO days after police chief Arturo De Felice declared *caso chiuso*, the Kercher murder case broke wide open. Detectives uncovered a new suspect, dubbed the "fourth man." They unmasked him through old-fashioned police work, not *CSI* forensics or psychoanalysis from Edgardo Giobbi's Rome-based SCO. They simply compared the bloody handprint found on Meredith's pillowcase to the prints provided by the three suspects. None of them matched.

The Italian press placed the "fourth man" story way down in the coverage, where few readers noticed it. Once reporters got a name, though, once they knew who'd laid that bloody hand on Meredith's pillow, then their coverage would explode.

On that overcast fall day, a hardy band of journalists and photographers, mostly Italians, hung around in Capanne Prison's stadium-size parking lot, smoking cigarettes and waiting to discover what Judge Claudia Matteini would make of Amanda Knox, Raffaele Sollecito, and Patrick Lumumba. A middle-aged brunette with a no-nonsense style, Matteini

was the GIP, the investigative judge for the preliminary
hearing. She would work in close consultation with Giuliano
Mignini, the public minister, drawing from his report and
interrogating the suspects alongside him.

Matteini had close ties to Mignini, as could be said of any
judge in tiny, clubby Perugia. Under Italian law, prosecutors
were part of the judiciary; whereas in the United States, these
officials play very separate roles. As Mignini was fond of
reminding reporters, Italian law *required* a prosecutor who
saw wrongdoing to conduct an investigation, a role reserved
in the U.S. for police chiefs. Prosecutors were also required
to submit to the judge any exculpatory evidence that would
benefit the defense and, finally, to suggest further courses of
action.

Since defense attorneys hadn't been permitted even to meet
their clients, Matteini had no defense briefs to assist her, only
Mignini's report and the responses of the suspects as they
came before her. Using this evidence, she'd decide whether
Mignini could hold them behind bars for a year, without
charges, while the prosecutor continued the investigation.

Since the hearing was closed, the bundled-up reporters
could only stand around in the cold, hoping to get a sound
bite when the suspects' lawyers showed up. Still, nobody was
feeling the chill. The Kercher case delivered Vesuvius-size
fireworks. One day reporters were feasting on Facebook and
MySpace; the next day, they got to pillage the witness reports.

"It is always like this in Italy," said one reporter, fresh
from another celebrated Italian murder case. "Everything is
supposed to be secret, locked down, but then everything is
opened up. It's really bad for the suspects, terrible in fact, but
you can get anything."

Corriere della Sera used the witness reports to weave a
tale about Meredith's social set, skillfully leaking the colorful
documents, even translating them helpfully from Italian into
English.

"The picture that emerges from the statements of the men
and women who knew Meredith and her friends is one of an
extended group," scolded *Corriere*'s Fiorenza Sarzanini, who
would later write *Amanda e Gli Altri: Vite Perdute Intorno
al Delitto di Perugia* (Amanda and the Others: Lives Lost

Around the Murder in Perugia), an Italian bestseller published in January 2009 that drew on witness reports and never-before-published excerpts from Amanda's "green diary," seized from her purse at the time of arrest.

In that November 2007 *Corriere* article, Sarzanini took readers into the world of foreign students in Piazza Grimana, telling them about a British girl, Meredith, who had an Italian boyfriend named Giacomo. She said the couple smoked hashish that the men bought on the church steps. The women "often came home drunk."

Under the subheading "MEN, MEN, MEN," Sarzanini ripped into Amanda for her *avventura della notte* (one-night stand) with Daniel de Luna. Yet Zach Nowak called Perugia a "pressure cooker for dreams, lust, hustle and romance" in *The Little Blue Book*, a guide for living in the hilltop town. He explained that as most students stayed in Perugia for only a few months, the romantic spectrum skewed away from lasting love and toward one-night stands and *la storia*, a semi-clandestine, nonexclusive sexual relationship.

Once Sarzanini stopped scolding, however, she raised good questions about Amanda's "partial confession." In fact, she was one of the first reporters to notice that it didn't make sense. But her story also presented police theory as fact, perhaps because reporters didn't yet have access yet to forensics reports and crime scene videos.

"If Patrick really did kill Meredith, what did they do afterwards?" Sarzanini wrote in *Corriere*. "Someone certainly tried to clean up the blood. Someone smashed a window in an attempt to simulate a burglary. But who? Did none of them get their clothes dirty? What happened to the clothes?"

Well, police believed the couple had spent the night of the murder in the cottage, vigorously removing traces from the crime scene. Investigators boasted of finding bleach receipts in Raffaele's flat, implying that he'd purchased the goods in order to carry out a massive cleanup. Yet the receipts were old; the bleach had been sought by Raffaele's previous maid, and there was plenty left over. So why would he have needed to buy more?

As for the lack of dirty clothes, a witness had come to the *questura* shortly after Meredith's body was found and told police that a North African man (meaning an Arab) and a foreign girl had been in a Perugia Laundromat that very day, acting suspiciously. The man had thrown all of his clothes in the washer, even his blue athletic shoes. The rumor was that Amanda was the foreign girl and Patrick the shoe washer.

On November 11, Raffaele mentioned this rumor in his diary. He said he had been having a pretty good day, because his father, uncle, and stepmother had come to see him, bringing clean clothes. But then they informed him that on the morning of November 2, when Amanda had told him she was going to the cottage to shower while he slept, she'd actually gone to a Laundromat with a man who wedged a pair of blue Nikes into the washing machine.

Yet Amanda didn't need the perfect alibi for the Laundromat incident. Police later revealed that Meredith was alive when it happened. Eventually Raffaele would learn not to believe any of the Amanda rumors and they would manage to achieve some kind of friendship.

Although the prosecution's group sex theory sold many newspapers, reporters did wonder, for instance, why a couple who'd been dating less than a week would want to bring in a third partner, especially the much older Patrick, an employer no less. And how could four people possibly have struggled, let alone staged an orgy, in a room barely larger than an ironing board? Shouldn't the furniture have been knocked topsy-turvy, the letters on the nightstand knocked to the ground, the pictures on the wall be askew? Giacinto Profazio, head of the Flying Squad, had complained that he'd "worked poorly" in that room, with two other investigators wedged in, and they hadn't been locked in mortal combat. And if four people had struggled, why had only one person in Nike shoes made all the bloody shoeprints? Why weren't there traces of Amanda in the murder room, if she struggled with Meredith, as the prosecutor believed?

Ever more interesting: Who orchestrated the press leaks, as irresistible as the Corso in spring? Who fibbed to reporters, claiming police found a clump of marijuana plants growing in the cottage garden, where not even a turnip poked through the soil? As detectives well knew, Giacomo cultivated his marijuana plants in a special room to which only he had the key.

Not only would an outdoor marijuana bed be a horticultural miracle in wintery Perugia, but it would also offer an irresistible invitation to passing drug addicts to roll some free joints.

"Both Ms. Knox and Mr. Sollecito admitted smoking the drug that evening," noted the *Times*, echoing the prosecutor's ominous tone. Supposedly, marijuana had fueled this one couple's depravity, a theory which might work for a drug such as meth or amphetamine, but was a tougher fit for marijuana, a drug that soothed most users, making them drowsy rather than energized, passive rather than violent.

THE reporters cooling their heels in Capanne's parking lot finally got their payoff. The lawyers for the three suspects arrived, climbed out of their shiny sedans, and headed for the prison hearing room. Their clients faced a year behind bars before charges even had to be filed, but because of the prosecutor's mandate, none of them had even met their lawyers yet.

"You're just voyeurs," Tiziano Tedeschi, Raffaele's new lawyer, said to the journalists when they rushed him for quotes. He was disgusted because he'd been trying to see Raffaele for several days, but the guards blocked the door. Meanwhile the media was distorting Raffaele's image and painting him as a killer.

"The press is blaming our client," complained Tedeschi. "It's doing a bad job, you are not giving honor to your profession."

Swinging a briefcase, he hurried across the parking lot as reporters dashed after him, waving microphones and cameras in his face. He scurried up a concrete ramp and entered a low-slung, faintly pink concrete building through a metal side door.

"No comment. No comment," said Amanda's lawyers when they arrived. Edda Mellas had hired two of them; later on, the smooth, preppy-looking Carlo Dalla Vedova of Rome would always shun the press, while the folksy, silver-haired Luciano Ghirga of Perugia would often end up saying things that he perhaps he shouldn't have. In an off-guard moment that day, he said that while his client had given conflicting stories, he had impressed upon her the importance of telling the truth—of having just one story and sticking to it.

Patrick also had two lawyers, the bullish Carlo Pacelli and Giuseppe Sereni. They smiled and nodded as they glided toward the hearing room. Just before they reached the bunker, Sereni threw out a cliché, like a football coach before a game: "We hope to find the truth and the justice about this case."

Reporters worked the phones during the hearing, swiftly gathering tidbits from the supposedly secret proceedings. The big news was that Amanda had finally stopped talking, on the advice of her new lawyers, but not before she had scribbled pages and pages of new testimony, telling investigators, "Oh, now I remember everything."

Meanwhile both Raffaele and Patrick had responded to the investigators, and when their lawyers emerged in late afternoon, they created a spin room in the Capanne parking lot. Their lawyers' chief talking point: Amanda Knox did my client wrong.

Patrick's lawyers called the Seattle girl "an absolute liar," insisting that her statements were "slanderous." Not only was their client innocent, they said, but he'd never even been in the "house of horrors," not a single time. Moreover he had a solid alibi for the night of the murder. His customers would swear that he had been tending bar all night. He'd then gone home around midnight or 1 A.M., and had slept with his wife.

"And she'll tell you that," Patrick had informed Judge Claudia Matteini. She and Giuliano Mignini made an intimidating team for any suspect to face, but Patrick was unflappable, giving neat, precise answers, never wavering from his claim of innocence. Sure, he knew Meredith, but barely, just as a friend of his employee Amanda. He'd seen the British girl maybe four times.

As for Amanda, yes, he'd texted her on the night of the murder, but only to tell her not to come to work. Yes, he understood Americans say "see you later" and it doesn't mean "hey, let's get together." And what did it matter, since he never went to meet her? As for Raffaele, Patrick knew him only by sight. He was just the Italian guy who picked up Amanda after work. She was always asking Patrick when he was going to close down so she could take off with this new boyfriend. Before, she'd seemed crazy about DJ. It was confusing, but not his problem.

Then Judge Matteini and Mignini hammered Patrick about deleting Amanda's message the day after the murder. Matteini demanded to know why he'd also changed the SIM card on his phone.

For no particular reason, Patrick said. He just had. Again, what difference did it make; it was meaningless, because he'd never left his bar that fateful night.

Patrick became agitated only when Mignini asked if he'd told Amanda that he desired her roommate.

"Never," Patrick insisted.

"Listen, you never wanted Meredith?" Mignini asked.

"No."

"You never *tried* with her?" Mignini said, meaning, you never made a move on her?

"Never! God knows that!"

When it was Raffaele's turn, the judge also grilled him about Meredith.

"She was simply the friend of my girlfriend," he said. "I spoke to her a few times. Meredith usually talked to Amanda in English. A few times I asked if she wanted to eat with us, but she didn't want to, because she'd already eaten with the other girls."

As for Patrick, Raffaele had seen him in Le Chic when he went to pick up Amanda from work, but they'd never had an actual conversation.

"He would give me a Schweppes [beer] because usually I ordered Schweppes, but nothing more."

The judge then drilled Raffaele about the events of November 1, but there he was in a better position than the talkative Amanda. He'd given only one witness statement before he "crumbled," and even then he'd changed his story only on two points. First, he'd said that he called the cops after the Postal Police came, a statement he now took back. Secondly, he'd said Amanda had gone out, but now he thought that, too, was wrong. Once the police left him alone, he wasn't sure she ever left the building.

"So did she go out?" the judge asked.

"I am not certain."

"You can't remember if Amanda went out or not?"

"Seriously, Your Honor, she went out the night before and other nights, so I don't remember exactly."

"Answer me. I am not interested in other nights. I want to know if Amanda went out that night."

"*Non posso. Non posso.*" I can't. I can't.

"You have only three options," the exasperated judge told Raffaele: "Yes. No. I don't remember."

"I don't remember *exactly.*"

Then the judge asked the Italian student what he *did* remember, prompting a long, dull discussion about the broken pipe under the sink, which he had showed Amanda, discussing with her the probable cause of the leak, a perennial problem in that flat. He also remembered eating dinner with her, watching a movie, working on his computer, getting tired, and going to sleep. Yes, of course they slept together. He just couldn't remember what time they did each action, because he'd been stoned, in a holiday mood, and not punching a time clock.

"Did Amanda go out?" The judge tried one last time.

"I don't remember."

"Then why did you tell police she had?" the judge asked, a reference to Raffaele's heated questioning by high-ranking officers at the *questura* on November 5/6, during which he'd suddenly "crumbled" and said Amanda left him on the night that Meredith died, and had gone to meet her friends at Le Chic. His interrogation, like Amanda's, would always remain a he said/they said mystery, because Italian police would never provide audio or videotapes. However, both sides agreed police called in the two witnesses after 10 P.M. and interrogated them long into the night, until nearly 6 A.M. in Amanda's case. Besides sleep deprivation, the police subjected the college students to sensory overload. They said that officers crowded into the interrogation rooms, shouted the same questions hour after hour, and threatened the two witnesses with long years in prison if they stuck to their original stories. Neither student received lawyers, as required by law, when they went from "persons informed of the facts" to suspects. Raffaele said he asked to have the questioning halted so that he could speak to his father, but that also was refused.

All of this, he now explained to the judge, led to his saying things at the police station that he later remembered to be untrue.

"Precisely because on that night I was very, very agitated because I was under so much pressure," he told her, adding that police had interrogated him very forcefully, saying repeatedly, "don't give us shit" and "be careful what you say." Later, they'd written down that *he* said "sack of shit." It had all been a nightmare.

Raffaele said the Nike print couldn't be his, because he'd never stepped into Meredith's room. He admitted that he had "a passion for knives," even swords, but said the blades in his collection weren't sharp. Indeed, he'd been carrying a knife in his pocket since he was thirteen years old. As for why he'd lied about talking to his dad on his landline at 11 P.M. on the night of the murder, he said he'd gotten confused, since Francesco called him every day.

"I think it's well within the realm of possibility that he did simply forget whether or not his father called that particular night," said Zach Nowak, who did some reporting on the case for ABC News. "Or, what seems more likely from his subsequent interrogations, he simply lied to create an alibi. If he were guilty and knew it, he would know that this would be quite easy to check up on. I think he just fibbed to get off the hot seat, not because he was some sort of criminal mastermind—you know, the kind the prosecutor loves, the masterminds that are geniuses one minute and complete idiots the next as far as alibi creation, evidence disposal, murder scene cleanup, and so on."

AFTER Raffaele wrapped up his testimony on November 8, his lawyer came out to chat with reporters. He insisted police had no forensic evidence against his client. Raffaele's flick knife wasn't the murder weapon. The bloody shoe print didn't match his Nike shoes. Amanda was the source of the Italian boy's problems, the lawyer claimed, forgetting that it was his client, Raffaele, who had broken first and been the one to implicate her on November 5. Not only had Raffaele told detectives that she left his flat on the night of the murder, but he'd insisted that she asked him to lie for her.

"It was he who called the police," his lawyer pointed out. "And the girl has shown a penchant for outrageous lying."

For Frank Sfarzo at Perugia Shock, the leaked testimony solved a few mysteries. Why didn't Raffaele remember whether or not he'd had sex with Amanda on the night of the murder? Why did he take a knife to the *questura* on November 5? Because he'd smoked a *spinello* both nights.

Later that day, Francesco Sollecito told reporters that his son was "a bit perturbed at Amanda. He's reviewing his impressions of this girl."

Francesco dismissed any connection between his son's knife collection and the crime. "I, too, collect weapons. I collect rifles and other things," he said, pointing out that he'd never killed anyone.

Amanda's family finally spoke, if only through a brief press release. "The events that have unfolded in Perugia, Italy, over the last few days regarding our daughter, Amanda, have shocked and devastated our family," they said. Noting that Amanda was "no doubt scared and upset," they made a futile request. "We would ask the media to respect the privacy of the members of our families and friends, and refrain from putting further pressure on them for interviews and comment, especially our children."

CHAPTER FOURTEEN

SEX AS A GATEWAY CRIME TO MURDER

November 9–17, 2007

"You know what's interesting? I'm affectionally curious about how Raffaele is. Are they treating him well? He must be really scared. I also want to know why he lied about me. Is he still lying? What will happen to me if he keeps it up?"

—Amanda Knox, prison diary

THE next morning, on November 9, 2007, Judge Claudia Matteini delivered a nineteen-page judge's report as spellbinding as a crime thriller. She framed Meredith Kercher's murder as a morality tale, complete with a beautiful victim, heroic police officers, and depraved student killers. Concocted before police received the forensics results from Rome, based on scanty knowledge of the suspects, this page-turning tale of lust and betrayal would linger in the minds of conspiracy theorists, judges, and jurors like a perfectly cast film noir.

Judge Matteini could have dubbed her opus "The Mignini Report," so closely did it mirror the prosecutor's drug-fueled sex game (*gioco erotico*) crime theory. Bright, focused, complex, Giuliano Mignini was a middle-aged Perugino, bulky, with thinning hair and a long marriage. A lover of history books, he was a cross between "Kojak and Inspector Columbo," said one Italian reporter.

"The flimsy alibis are said to have infuriated officials, who are thought to have leaked Claudia Matteini's nineteen-page report," claimed the infamous British tabloid the *Sun*, which then published entire sections of the leaked report, as did media outlets everywhere.

Matteini's page-turner didn't begin with two pretty foreign girls left alone one weekend in an isolated cottage with a faulty front door and broken shutters, in a *brutta* neighborhood fraught with break-ins and drug dealing, where only days before the victim had spotted an intruder in the garden. Instead it opened with a couple of humble postal cops sent out on a routine errand. They traced two lost cell phones from a pricey villa to an impregnable student accommodation that could be breached only through the front door via a key held by Amanda Knox (even though her roommate Filomena Romanelli also had a key, was in town, and had pretty much the same alibi: I was with my boyfriend all night).

When the plainclothes cops reached the whitewashed cottage on a hillside, they encountered Amanda and Raffaele hovering near the garden. The couple was acting suspiciously, they thought, because they stood near each other, whispering, looking affectionate. These students—one American, one Italian—claimed to be waiting for the Carabinieri, having called them to report a broken window and a suspected theft.

> In the meantime, at 1 p.m. [Filomena] Romanelli, [Amanda] Knox's housemate, arrived and verified that nothing had been taken from the apartment. In the course of the search it was ascertained that the door of the room used by Meredith Kercher, the other girl living in the apartment, was closed and locked and it was decided therefore to break down the door because Romanelli said it was strange that her friend Kercher would have both of her telephones switched off. . . . With the door opened there was a chilling scene as the room was found in disorder with blood stains everywhere, on the floor and on the walls, and also under the duvet of the bed, a foot could be seen. The agents, in order to avoid any contamination of the crime scene, stopped everyone from entering the room.

The report de-sexed the romance between Giacomo and Meredith, quoting Filomena's remark about a "sentimental attachment" and implying that the couple merely discussed

Italian grammar together. Then, confusingly, the judge also identified Giacomo as the British girl's lover, stressing that Meredith never let any other man into her bedroom. From then on, the report focused entirely on Raffaele and Amanda as prime suspects, without considering other scenarios, such as the possibility that Meredith might have been sexually assaulted and killed during the course of a burglary, an everyday occurrence all over the world.

Matteini used Raffaele's call to the police to pin the two college students to the crime, insisting that the call occurred after the Postal Police supposedly surprised them in the garden. The judge implied that the two were up to no good in the shrubbery, hinting that they had emerged with mop and bucket following a long cleanup—of which there would never be any forensic proof, only theory and suspicion.

In fact, from our investigation it emerged that the Postal Police arrived at 12.35 while the call to 112 [to the Carabinieri] came at 12.51 and 12.54, circumstances that suggest that they wished to look as if they'd been surprised outside the building where the homicide was carried out. They wanted to justify their presence outside, considering the conditions in which they had found the flat, above all because of the blood stains on the floor and the wall [in Meredith's room].

The timing of the Postal Police would be the Kercher case's grassy knoll. In the end, even the prosecution would contend only five minutes of difference between the two sets of calls, while the defense would claim that Raffaele called the Carabinieri several minutes before the Postal Police arrived. In the end, court watchers would believe whatever fit their own particular theories of the crime.

The same confusion affected the time of death. Coroner Luca Lalli analyzed the contents of Meredith's stomach and said she'd died two to three hours after her last meal. He lamented that he couldn't nail down the time more accurately using temperature readings, because he hadn't had access to the body until it was too late.

Judge Matteini's report followed Lalli's reasoning, giving

the time of death (crucial to the suspects' alibis) as "between 9.30 P.M. and 11 P.M. on November 1, 2007, a timetable that tallied with the consumption of dinner an hour before 9 p.m.". The report said that Meredith had suffered a "relatively slow agony" because the knife hadn't hit the carotid artery in the neck. "Relatively slow" would become "slow and agonizing" on the blogosphere and even in the *Times* of London, even though the coroner's report made clear that Meredith died soon after the final blow and probably could not have been saved.

The judge also came down hard on Amanda for not scrubbing the crime scene (while Mignini would accuse her of spearheading a near-magical cleanup). Amanda, the judge complained, "was in one of the two bathrooms when she found traces of blood, which she did not worry about cleaning, and noticed that in the other bathroom the toilet water was full of feces that she was astonished to find but did not try to clean." This linking of sloppiness to viciousness would be made many times in the Perugia courthouse, whose odorous bathrooms were ironically never stocked with toilet paper or soap, forcing users to do without or bring their own.

The judge also cast a stern eye on Raffaele. She noted that he'd broken down during his interrogation on November 5, deciding that, yes, Amanda had gone out on the night of the murder and that maybe he did call the cops after the Postal Police arrived on November 1. Matteini was unconvinced by his return to his original story (Amanda was in all night; he called the cops before the Postal Police arrived). She noted that if he had always been with Amanda on November 1, then it followed that he was in the cottage when the girl heard Meredith scream. The judge didn't speculate on who held the murder weapon but claimed that Raffaele's black flick knife, with its 3.5-inch-long blade, delivered the fatal wound. She also insisted it was his Nike shoes that made the bloody shoeprint by the bed, although they would test negatively for blood.

Judge Matteini's report boldly stated, "It is possible to reconstruct what happened on the evening of November 1," although a few days earlier, Coroner Lalli had ended the autopsy report by explaining why that could never happen.

On the basis of the previously mentioned biological samples it is not possible to indicate, in a hypothetical reconstruction, if the aggression was perpetrated by one or more people nor is it possible to indicate with certainty the succession of the cuts nor the respective positions of the victim and aggressor.

Matteini claimed, in the judge's report, to know exactly what kind of sex the three suspects liked and in what combination. She said Raffaele and Amanda had smoked hashish for an entire afternoon, although they'd only admitted to sharing one joint. And what of Patrick? When had he become "drug-fueled"? Matteini's own report had him going to the cottage directly from work, as soon as he fired off the text to Amanda.

Raffaele's compliance was just assumed.

Raffaele Sollecito, bored with the same old evenings, and wanting to experience extreme sensations, intense sexual relations which break up the monotony of everyday life, went out with Amanda and met Lumumba at Piazza Grimana at 9 p.m. They went together to the apartment on Via della Pergola 7, to which only Amanda had the key. It was roughly at this time that both Sollecito and Knox switched off their mobile phones until the following morning. A short while later, Meredith returned, or she could have already been there. She went into her bedroom with Patrick, after which something went wrong, in the sense that Sollecito in all probability joined them and the two began to make advances, which the girl refused. She was then threatened with a knife, the knife which Sollecito generally carried with him and which was used to strike Meredith in the neck. The three, realizing what had happened, quickly left the house, creating a mess with the intention of simulating a break-in, spreading blood everywhere, and in an attempt to clean up drops of blood in the bath, on the ground and in the sink.

The motivation? Sex, sex, and more sex. Raffaele longed for "extreme sensations," a phrase ripped from his blog, while the American girl would apparently do anything with anyone in bed. Supposedly, she had brought both males to the house on November 1 because Patrick had a crush on Meredith, and Amanda wanted to hook them up. The prose took on a romance novel flavor when the judge described Patrick's supposed attraction to Meredith (despite the fact that, as he mentioned in court, he had a young, beautiful wife waiting at home). Matteini baldly stated that all three suspects were present in the cottage and then contended that we "must attribute" guilt to all three.

> For Patrick there was the desire to have sex with a girl who had turned him down. Confronted by the refusal of the victim he was unable to stop, but sought to persuade her with a knife which Sollecito always carried. The murder was carried out after the knife had twice wounded the neck of the victim. The third blow deeply penetrated and caused the fatal wound. All three suspects were present. We must attribute to them involvement in the crime.

Amanda did nothing to help her dying roommate, according to this scenario, since by her own account she was in the kitchen, blocking out the screams. At best, she callously returned to her boyfriend's studio afterward and nodded off to sleep; at worst, she held Meredith down while Patrick violated her, although the forensic evidence would show no such thing.

LA *Stampa* reacted to the judge's report by providing readers with brightly colored, completely imaginary drawings of the crime scene, showing Meredith reclining on a palatial bed in a spacious room, with Patrick leaning over her, brandishing a sort of machete. A naked Amanda stood nearby, patiently waiting her turn. Raffaele wasn't pictured, but then he would never be more than a bit player in what Italians would call "the Amanda show."

Beyond the lack of a motive for murder the biggest problem with the sex game theory was that no forensic evidence supported it. The supposed rapist and killer, Patrick Lumumba, had left no trace at the scene. Already, some reporters were saying, well, maybe he wasn't there. The judge's report claimed that the drink receipts at the bar didn't start until 11 P.M., but since Italians pay for their drinks upon leaving, the receipts weren't as damning as they might have sounded. On November 11, 2007, a Swiss professor confirmed Patrick's alibi, telling police that he'd been with the bar owner at Le Chic from 8 to 10 P.M., but police continued to hold Patrick in jail.

For the judge, the text message that Amanda sent to Patrick on the night of the crime was the smoking gun, but her report quoted it incorrectly as "see you later" without the "good evening." The *Times* and many other newspapers also got it wrong.

How could everybody botch such a simple message? According to Frank Sfarzo on Perugia Shock:

Mignini reported that the message Amanda sent to Patrick was "See you later." He forgot to include the last sentence of the text, which was "Good evening." Obviously, that "Good evening" changes the meaning of the "See you later" completely. The judge did not verify directly, so a second element apparently against Patrick was packaged. At least until the lawyers got that evidence and the truth came out.

Judge Matteini's report spoke of "serious" signs of guilt and put all three prisoners under suspicion for aggravated murder and sexual violence. Her confirmation of the arrests meant that Mignini could hold them for a year without bringing charges. The flip side of this system was that it did allow many suspects to remain free prior to a conviction, even for serious offenses. For example, Alberto Stasi, a rich Italian college student who had been accused of killing his girlfriend Chiara Poggi only a few months before Meredith died, was permitted to go about his normal life as he awaited trial. Indeed, photographers would capture Alberto hanging out in ski resorts as his case played out in court.

In contrast, Judge Matteini locked the prison doors firmly on the suspects in the Meredith Kercher case, claiming that all three could easily leave the country "to escape the investigation" because Patrick was from the Congo and Amanda was from the United States. As for Raffaele, according to the judge, his American girlfriend could help him make a getaway.

"**MEREDITH** killed after refusing orgy," the *Times* of London announced during the tidal wave of coverage that followed the judge's report. Buried within the stories were new, erroneous allegations against Amanda Knox. Police insisted that the striped sweater she'd worn on the night of the murder was missing, implying that she'd gotten rid of it to hide the bloodstains. Detectives would find it months later, on top of Amanda's bed in the cottage, where she'd left it after taking her infamous shower.

"Foxy Knoxy held down Meredith during deadly sex attack," the *Daily Mail* boldly proclaimed, kicking off the ugliest of the false Amanda allegations. It insisted that she had "pushed so hard on the 21-year-old's face that she left an imprint of her fingers on the skin."

Police had apparently gotten this rumor started on November 8, 2007, skillfully inserting the word "may" into assumptions that no one had confessed to and that they couldn't prove.

Amanda may have been responsible for holding the victim down while one of the male suspects cut her throat, they reportedly told the press.

The logic of holding a victim down by the face was never explained. Nor do many rapists require assistance, especially at knifepoint, nor would they desire eyewitnesses who could testify against them. Amanda also made a peculiar accomplice. Not only did she have no history of violence, but at five foot three, she was the smaller of the two girls. And Meredith, her parents later revealed, was skilled in karate and would have fought back very hard, given an opportunity. Yet the orderliness of her bedroom implied a surprise attack.

Still, the charge that Amanda held down Meredith spread like a virus across the Internet, where some commenters claimed that it must be true because Amanda was a rock climber, a sport that they imagined created super-strong hands (though it actually requires powerful legs). And in fact, as journalists learned when they finally saw the autopsy photos, Meredith had no such handprint on her face. Still, the allegation lived on in old news stories on the Internet. There, even well-meaning people new to the case would cite it, wondering how the apple-cheeked Amanda could have committed such an atrocity.

Coroner Lalli's report, as cited by Judge Matteini, described a more typical method of knifing, easily carried out by a single assailant. The coroner said that he'd found "bruises and lesions on the neck, suggesting that Meredith was held by the neck, leaving bruising compatible with the pressure of fingers, and subsequently threatened with a knife held to her throat."

ON November 10, 2007, Edda Mellas was finally allowed to see her daughter. The press captured Edda, a small, distressed figure in a hooded coat, walking slowly up a concrete ramp into a side door of the prison. "No comment," she kept saying softly, "no comment," and batting away reporters with a wave of her hand.

"We cried and held each other and Amanda told me that she never confessed to anything," Edda said later. "She told me that they asked her to suggest things and she'd say no, that didn't happen, but they were like oh, don't worry, just let us write that down."

The next day Edda told the press, "Amanda is innocent of this and is devastated by the death of her friend. She is completely distraught." She said that her daughter had explained that no, she hadn't heard Meredith's dying screams, because she wasn't in the cottage that night.

Actually, reporters already knew about their conversation, since the visitor's room was bugged.

"I said a lot of stupidity," Amanda supposedly told her mother. "I was not home that night. I do not know who killed Meredith, the truth is what I said when I was questioned for the first time."

"I wasn't there" was, of course, her first story, but without access to Amanda's *memoriale* or perhaps even her three witness statements, the press treated this statement as a complete turnaround. It became popular to say that Amanda had changed her story many times, first saying she was at the murder scene, and later saying she was not. But actually she'd told only two stories: first, "I was not there," then, "I was there with Patrick."

Curt Knox soon joined his former wife in Perugia. A blond man with Nordic features, rimless glasses, and a reserved manner, he looked like a typical Seattleite, always garbed in North Face fleeces or leather jackets over jeans or knit pants. During these early days, reporters had to chase him down the street if they wanted a quote, but later he became savvy in handling the press, as did Edda Mellas.

"My daughter is innocent" was the most he would say in the early days. "She doesn't understand why she is in prison for something she didn't do."

Later, Amanda's parents would be heavily criticized on the blogosphere for hiring David Marriott, a Seattle public relations professional specializing in crisis management, to handle the media, but Edda insisted that they'd done so only after the maelstrom of bad publicity that led up to Amanda's first major court appearance on November 30, 2007.

"At first the only thing we told Dave Marriott was to tell the press that we didn't want to talk to them. In other words, his job was to say no," Edda said.

FOR reporters, November was a fabulous month. They enjoyed near-daily leaks from the investigation, which they lapped up like Torgiano Rosso, the celebrated Umbrian red wine. The leaks would continue throughout the course of the case, arriving with exquisite timing, often coming just before or after a court appearance or following a rare bit of good news for the suspects. At key moments, newspapers and TV stations all over the world would run essentially the same story, echo the same spin, and even share strikingly similar headlines. Often the information would turn out to be incorrect or garbled, but once it was out there, it could not be erased. For Amanda, every news cycle delivered another dose of poison.

"Amanda Knox caught on film" headlines appeared everywhere on November 12, 2007. The press reported that CCTV cameras had captured her arriving home on the night of the crime. These cameras, mounted on the parking garage across the street, did show a girl, presumably Amanda, in a light-colored skirt and blouse emerging from the garage around 8:43 P.M. That would have contradicted her claim of having spent the entire night with Raffaele, if the girl had actually been her.

"It will be interesting to see what she has to say when we show her the footage," said a widely quoted "police source," even though Amanda had no car and thus no need to enter or leave the garage. She was also much shorter and curvier than the girl caught on film.

"The film showed a girl, but it wasn't Amanda," said Frank Sfarzo, who actually walked around the parking area and discovered that the cameras weren't even turned in the right direction to catch anyone entering the cottage. Besides, as the Italian press later pointed out, why wouldn't the same cameras have therefore shown the victim entering her house that night, not to mention the other two suspects? For all those reasons, the grainy CCTV footage never made it into court.

On November 14, the press began leaking a highly prejudicial witness statement made by Meredith's friend Robyn Butterworth, which she'd given to police in the UK. She claimed that Amanda had bragged about having found Meredith's body, the night that the American girl had been flung together with the English girls at the *questura*. Robyn also found Amanda's loud singing and lack of toilet flushing to be suspicious. As an example of where mere intuition can lead, she also fingered Juve, Amanda's coworker at Le Chic. She compared him unfavorably to Hicham Khiri ("Shaky"), a man whom Amanda, in turn, had described as strange and doubtful. Robyn also pointed police toward Pietro Campolongo, aka D. J. Naf, the Merlin's bartender and wearer of the "*Scream* mask," saying he hadn't known Meredith that well but was doing interviews everywhere. Yet not only had he appeared very upset when he spoke to a *Corriere* reporter on the day the slashing was discovered, but he'd also attended the candlelight vigil with Pisco, the Merlin's co-owner, whom the British girls adored.

ON November 15, Amanda Knox hand-on-the-murder-weapon stories swept the media. Police announced that they'd found a kitchen knife in Raffaele's flat that had a speck of Amanda's DNA on the handle and a speck of Meredith's near the tip. Since Amanda had used the knife for cooking, her DNA wasn't an issue. But Meredith had never been to Raffaele's flat, so that evidence would be damning, if true.

Police hadn't found any blood on the knife, but they dismissed that by saying the suspects had scrubbed the blade and bleached it before tossing it back into the drawer. How did they know this? Because Armando Finzi, an assistant in the Perugia Police Department, had insisted that the scent of bleach had practically knocked him over when he'd entered Raffaele's flat on November 6 and found the knife in the cutlery drawer. How had he chosen that particular blade? By instinct, he boasted, saying it had looked big and shiny.

Later, during cross-examination, the defense would suggest that the flat merely "smelled clean," not surprising given that Raffaele's maid had scoured it with Lysoform a day earlier. Finzi also admitted that he'd handed the knife off to another officer, Stefano Gubbiotti. Not only had the latter been at the cottage that day, where Meredith's DNA was everywhere, but he then broke the chain of evidence by storing the knife in a Renato Balestra calendar box, repacking it, leaving it in a closet and then not being clear about how it got to the Rome lab.

The knife was problematic on other fronts. First, it didn't match the bloody outline on the bed. Secondly, it was too large to have made the two small knife cuts on Meredith's throat. Mignini got around this problem with typical nimbleness. The suspects must have used *two* knives, he said.

He did not explain how the big kitchen knife could be compatible with the wounds when the judge's report said that Raffaele's little flick knife matched them. As an Italian lawyer later said: "The term 'compatibility' can be confusing for those not familiar with Italian terms. It means the knife is sharp and it can cut."

Likewise, the Italian crime reporter Mario Spezi, coauthor of *The Monster of Florence*, remarked in the book that "compatible, not compatible, and incompatible are merely the baroque inventions of Italian experts who don't want to take responsibility," claiming that detectives used the term to avoid admitting that they couldn't figure out something. "Was that laryngeal break inflicted by someone who intended to kill? 'It is compatible.' Was that painting done by a monstrous psychopath? 'It is compatible.'"

However, the kitchen knife would prove to be most controversial for the way the DNA results on the blade had been analyzed and reported. Patrizia Stefanoni, working in the uncertified Rome lab, reported the knife blade sample to be "compatible" with the DNA profile of Meredith Kercher. It was a LCN (Low Copy Number) DNA sample (now also referred to as Low Template DNA), and may have yielded results not relevant to the case. Scientists can extract a DNA profile from minute bits of matter, even from a few cells. Low copy samples should be run two to three times and a consensus profile developed following more cautious data interpretation rules. A very sterile environment is necessary, as the chances for contamination are higher in low copy work, and the Rome lab had processed abundant DNA from Meredith Kercher. Dr. Stefanoni had used part of the sample to test for blood, which was negative, and to see if the sample was of human origin; then she used the rest of the sample to find the quantity of DNA, to amplify it, and to get a profile. It would be revealed much later that the machine she had used to detect Meredith's DNA had warned her that the sample readings were "too low," at which point she used the readings anyway. The Rome police forensic lab did not provide complete information to the defense, the lawyers said, regarding the DNA testing.

Nevertheless, Stefanoni's tests would have great force in Italy, where residents would often say that the suspects were guilty "because of the DNA evidence." In fact, DNA had become the gold standard in criminal investigations everywhere, partly because of what lawyers worldwide were calling the "*CSI* effect," named for the popularity of the American TV show *CSI*, which celebrated the work of crime scene investigators. Lawyers complained that the show often took creative license with actual procedures, giving jurors unrealistic expectations of what a case should look like. Often, lawyers had no DNA evidence, fingerprints, or smoking gun to show a jury, just one person's word against the other. Also, attorneys point out, evidence is fragile and easily destroyed. Tests can lie where there are issues of contamination or incompetence.

"The fact that Meredith's DNA is on my kitchen knife is because once, when we were all cooking together, I accidentally pricked her hand," Raffaele wrote when he learned about the knife. This was, of course, another fib, since Meredith had never been to his place.

Amanda, meanwhile, made no public comment. She said she had been trying to avoid watching TV newscasts, because she found them depressing. She now did jumping jacks and sang Beatles songs during her one hour of daily exercise, in a sad little garden. In her diary, she said the worst thing about prison life was the boredom. She wrote about her longing to see her family, DJ, and her other friends, about the visits from the priest and a psychologist, and the horror of being considered a murderer.

> I know that I'm not writing to anyone, but you who are reading, listen. Do you know what it feels like to look across at the person in front of you and see them looking at you like you are a monster? Do you know what it feels like to have somebody call you a liar right to your face? When you are telling the truth? Stupid liar! Then hit you.

Now, she complained, prison officials had started hassling her about the knife. ("YOUR fingerprints. HER DNA.") She insisted that she wasn't worried because she'd never taken that knife anywhere, nor had she killed Meredith. She said she didn't know what to think about it, because she knew she'd never taken a knife from Raffaele's flat to the cottage.

Then, on November 17, she got more bad news. The police insisted that she'd told her parents, during a bugged visit in Capanne, that she hadn't been in Raffaele's flat on the night of Meredith's slashing.

"I cannot lie, I was there," she'd said. The press ran with this story, even though the police had leaked it out of context, so that the antecedent for "there" wasn't apparent. And in fact, when police had to produce the entire intercept in court, even Judge Paolo Micheli, no friend to Amanda, would accept that she'd meant "I cannot lie. I was at Raffaele's when my roommate's throat was slashed."

Meanwhile, police officers came into her jail cell to look through her things.

> *The police had come to search through my bags to see how guilty my schoolbooks were and one police officer asked me if I had seen the news, about the knife. Wanted to know if I had anything to say. I repeated my story, that I wasn't anywhere near Meredith when she was murdered. Then he laughed and said, "Another story? Another lie?" He stared right at me as if I was no better than gum he wiped off the bottom of his shoe. It was the first time that anybody has looked at me like that before. So when I went back to my cell, I cried at the ugliness of it all, my being in prison, my friend dead, the police following a cold and irrational trail because they have nothing better.*

"Amanda accuses Raffaele of murder" stories soon swept the globe, based on a brief moment in her diary where she speculated about the knife. For Sky News, this was proof that "Amanda had changed her story once again." In a story called "Murder Suspect 'Accuses Lover in Jail Diary'" the Sky reporter offered a leaked selection that appears to be a bad translation from English into Italian and then back into English, with key words left out:

> *That night I smoked a lot of marijuana and I fell asleep at my boyfriend's house. I don't remember anything. But I think it's possible that Raffaele went to Meredith's house, raped her and then killed her. And then when he got home,*

while I was sleeping, he put my fingerprints on the knife.
But I don't understand why Raffaele would do that.

In their defense, the reporters who repeated this incriminating statement didn't have the original document to check
the words against, which actually read:

Raffaele and I have used this knife to cook, and it's impos-
sible that Meredith's DNA is on the knife because she's
never been to Raffaele's apartment before. So unless Raf-
faele decided to get up after I fell asleep, grabbed said
knife, went over to my house, used it to kill Meredith,
came home, cleaned the blood off, rubbed my fingerprints
all over it, put it away, then tucked himself back into bed,
and then pretended really well the next couple of days,
well, I just highly doubt all of that.

CHAPTER FIFTEEN

WHERE IS RUDY GUEDE?

AMANDA FACES MIGNINI
November 18-30, 2007

"In town there is a growing feeling that Patrick Lumumba is not the bogeyman of Mez's ugly story."

—Detective Martina on brividogiallo.it

MEANWHILE, twenty-one-year-old Rudy Guede was still in Germany, away from his little flat, the dance clubs, and everyone he knew. His friend Gabriele Mancini, the son of one of his childhood teachers, was concerned because Rudy hadn't touched base in two weeks. When Gabriele checked the Internet in mid-November, he noticed that Rudy's Instant Messenger account was active. He tried to reach him just to say hello. He was worried that Rudy might have run away, a habit of his from childhood.

As Rudy's friends knew, he was fresh out of family. In fact, he'd been at loose ends for much of October, depressed, drinking a bit more than usual. Certainly, he'd never had it easy. His mother had abandoned him at birth in the Ivory Coast and he'd immigrated to Italy—with his father, Roger Guede—from Abidjan when he was five. They could have settled in Lecco, near Milan, where Rudy had an aunt, but Roger found a job as a laborer in Perugia and they went there instead. They lived in Ponte San Giovanni, outside the city walls, where Rudy went to the local schools. His teachers knew he had no one to care for him, so they took him home after school each day and let him stay with them until his father could pick him up.

Then in 2002, when Rudy was sixteen, his father turned his world upside down. Roger decided to move back to the Ivory Coast. Incredibly, Paolo Caporali, a wealthy Perugian businessman, then informally adopted the twice-abandoned boy, having met Rudy when the teenager played on a local basketball team that the Caporali family sponsored. His coaches remembered Rudy as talented and well behaved, but not tall enough for superstardom.

Eventually, Rudy accepted a gardening job on a Caporali estate, but the work didn't suit the nocturnal party lover. He had to rise early to catch a bus to the countryside and work in the soil all day, returning home tired, dirty, and dispirited. Meanwhile his childhood friends were going to college, getting on with their lives. Rudy himself was not without cleverness. He had a gift for gab; he spoke fluent Italian with a heavy Umbrian accent, knew a smattering of English, and had studied both hotel-keeping and accounting sporadically. But, as his adoptive father complained, he loved the nightlife, spending more and more time in Milan or with his aunt in Lecco, skipping out on his gardening job.

Caporali sacked Rudy at the end of August 2007, about the same time Meredith arrived in Perugia, eager to live out an Italian dream. The magnate also ousted him from the family's home, saying that Rudy was a tremdous liar who preferred video games to work.

"He was like another son to us," Caporali said later. "I cannot hide the fact that he disappointed me. I thought I could help him build a future, but with the passing of time, I realized I had made a mistake."

Now, in mid-November, Rudy had been incommunicado for two weeks, which was strange since he was the kind of guy who liked to stay in touch. Gabriele finally got a cryptic Instant Messenger response:

RUDY: I can't.
GABRIELE: What can't you?
RUDY: You know.

GABRIELE: What am I supposed to know?
(Rudy disconnected.)

On November 18, 2007, Italian police announced a worldwide manhunt for "the fourth man." They described him as a North African (Arab) involved in the drug trade. Even though the description didn't quite fit Rudy, Gabriele paid a visit to the Flying Squad office in Perugia and told the officers about his missing friend.

On November 19, police made it official: Rudy Guede was the fourth man. The Rome forensics lab, whose results had finally come in, was able to identify him through the bloody imprint of his hand on Meredith's pillow. They'd also lifted his DNA off a toothbrush in his flat, which would eventually allow them to identify his "papillary fragments" found on toilet paper in the larger bathroom, and the cells he'd left inside the victim "during the sexual act," which he himself later described as consensual "petting."

Rudy awoke in Germany to see his face flashed on TV screens everywhere. Police had given the stations everything from his residency ID card to mug shots snapped in Perugia and Milan. Reporters quickly raided his Facebook page, uncovering such gems as a photo of Rudy posing with Giorgio Armani in the fashion designer's Armani bar in Milan. Rudy had been so fond of this photo that he'd even used it as a screen saver on his computer. The famous man's public relations staff quickly disavowed all knowledge of the Perugia fugitive, saying Mr. Armani was a friendly person who often posed for pictures with people he didn't actually know.

Rudy's vampire video, which he'd made just to amuse friends, quickly made its way to YouTube. Now anyone in the world could see him baring his teeth and saying in lurid English:

"I'm Count Dracula. I'm going to suck your blooooooooood."

Meanwhile police were looking for a friend who'd help them bring Rudy in. Because he'd kept his Facebook page open, this task was a breeze for cops. After they grabbed the names off the Web, they simply asked around until they found a friend willing to help them nab the fugitive.

Giacomo Benedetti, a longtime buddy of Rudy's who

played in a local band, agreed to keep an eye on his Instant Messenger account. On the 19th he saw activity, so he went to the police station and connected with Rudy there. They chatted first on Messenger and then Giacomo casually suggested a switch to Skype, telling Rudy that he'd cover the cost if Rudy would go to an Internet Point and make the connection.

Later, audio of this three-hour call was posted on the Web, Rudy speaking with a thick, unmistakable Umbrian accent. Giacomo asked him how he was. Not too well, Rudy replied, saying he'd been sleeping on trains and barges on the Rhine. Giacomo asked him what the problem was.

RUDY: I'm in Dusseldorf and I have no money.

GIACOMO: Would you like me to send money?

RUDY: Well, that would be useful.

GIACOMO: OK, look, I'll send you 50 Euros through Western Union, then you can pick it up.

RUDY: Thanks, but it's already late in the evening.

GIACOMO: They're talking about you here [in Perugia].

RUDY: I know what happened in Perugia, but they're making a mistake. I am not "The Baron," I'm called Byron after Byron Scott, the famous basketball player.

GIACOMO: But they are saying other things.

RUDY: Listen, you know I knew those girls, I knew them both, Meredith and Amanda, but nothing more, you know that. I've been to their house twice, the last time a few days before all this business, but I didn't do anything. I have nothing to do with this business. I wasn't there that evening. If they have found my fingerprints it means I must have left them there before.

GIACOMO: But your photo is everywhere.

RUDY: I've seen it, the police were wrong to put my photo around like that. I'm not how they describe me. I have nothing to do with that night.

GIACOMO: But if you have nothing to do with it why don't you come back? I'll help you to find a good lawyer who can clear things up.

RUDY: I'm afraid. But I don't want to stay in Germany,
I'm black and if the police catch me I don't know
what they might do to me. I prefer Italian jails.

Even more bizarre than the Skype call was that Rudy responded that same day to a reporter for the *Telegraph* who'd left a message for him on Facebook.

"He was allegedly on his way back to Italy to turn himself in to police," wrote Malcolm Moore, in a *Telegraph* story called "Meredith Suspect Caught After Sleeping Rough." Moore said that Rudy knew he was the target of a manhunt and claimed that he wanted to talk to police to clear his name. The fugitive wrote, apparently in English, "I know that [I am a suspect]," adding, "The reson [sic] I want to talk with police man, cause the news give at me a wrong profile."

During the Skype call with Giacomo, Rudy eventually sketched out his first alibi. He told his friend a story about seeing Meredith at a Halloween party, flirting, and then setting up a date with her for the next night. He showed up, they fooled around, but then had to stop because he didn't have a condom. He went into the bathroom and sat on the toilet. Then he heard a buzzer and came out of the bathroom with his pants down, tripping, falling over. Which was why he couldn't do anything when he spotted an intruder who murdered Meredith. As Rudy said of this mystery man during the Skype call:

I couldn't stop him while he escaped. I couldn't see him well. He had brown hair. Maybe chestnut. I know he's Italian because we insulted each other.
Then I tried to aid Meredith by putting a towel on the wound. I don't know why I didn't call the ambulance.

Rudy said that when he left, the window wasn't broken and Meredith was dressed. He didn't mention either Raffaele or Amanda.

PERUGIA police planned to rush off to Germany and spring a trap, but the very next day, German cops nabbed Rudy Guede on a train near Mainz, where he was riding without a ticket. He told the German police that he'd left Perugia because he'd "had trouble with a girl," but they didn't buy that story. They arrested him, took him to Koblenz, and put him behind bars.

On November 21, he delivered the first of his colorful stories to German police. Regarding Amanda Knox, he said he knew her from Le Chic and added, "Sometime later I met Meredith. She was with two guys that I know from playing basketball together. I don't know their names."

Although prosecutor Mignini insisted Rudy had a powerful crush on Amanda, in his own statements Rudy fixated on the British girl, whom he found sweet and beautiful. He mentioned Amanda as a troublesome roommate, a pot smoker, and a girl of loose morals (based, evidently, on his reading of the Foxy Knoxy stories). He told police the story about meeting Meredith on Halloween, while he'd been out with his Spanish friends. Supposedly, she'd set up a date with him for 8:30 the next night. He said he'd arrived at the cottage around 7:30 or 7:45 P.M. He couldn't say exactly when, because he didn't wear a watch. Meredith wasn't home, nor were the boys downstairs. So he went back into the town center, ate in the kebab shop near La Tana Dell'Orso, and then returned to the still-empty house. He waited around for a few minutes and then Meredith showed up and let him in. They went inside, flirted and kissed, but he claimed he didn't have sex with the victim, nor did he violate her in any way.

"And I would be willing to take a medical exam to prove this," he said.

Rudy interrupted his narrative at that point to say he needed to tell police something very important. When he and Meredith first went inside, she had opened the little drawer in her nightstand and discovered her cash was missing. He said that she immediately suspected Amanda, saying she was always smoking marijuana, and she went into the American girl's room to look for her money.

Amanda wasn't there, Rudy said.

He then described going into the bathroom near Amanda's room, where he said he sat on the toilet long enough to hear three hip-hop songs on his iPod.

Then, he said, he heard a loud scream, over the music. He ran out of the bathroom, without time to zip up his pants, and encountered an Italian man. Rudy said he called out, "What are you doing here?" and the man said, "*Negro trovato, colpevole trovato.*" Black man found, guilty man found. After some altercation, the intruder left, and Rudy rushed into Meredith's bedroom, where she lay bleeding to death on the floor. He grabbed some towels from the bathroom to staunch her bleeding. She tried to name her killer with her dying breath, either by choking out the initials "A.F." or the sound "af."

Rudy said he was extremely upset and couldn't remember what he did after that, but maybe he touched a few things in his panic, yes, perhaps even the bed. He was "shocked to death," he said, because he'd "never had a similar experience." He thought he heard some noises in the downstairs flat, so he fled. He claimed Meredith was still alive when he left, and in all his alibis, he blamed himself for being too frightened to do anything to save her.

Rudy attached a number of fascinating addendums to this tale. He said he'd worn jeans on the night of the murder and took them to Düsseldorf "for washing," but assured officers they'd find the rest of his clothes in his flat. He knew there'd been a robbery, because he'd followed the case in the newspapers, and for that reason he wanted police to know that the window wasn't broken at the time he was there. Also, he left Meredith's bedroom door open and hadn't locked the front door after himself, which would have required using Meredith's key.

He confirmed that he'd been in Germany for two weeks, and mentioned his two run-ins with the police in Stuttgart and in the Bavarian town of Monaco, in the Alps, but in both cases the officers had released him. Indeed, Rudy appeared to have been skillful at sweet-talking the police.

While awaiting extradition, Rudy, too, composed a diary, adding more details to his alibi, a habit he would continue over the next two years. The start of the story remained the same: he encountered Meredith on Halloween, went to her house the next night, and then they made out in her room. But this time he went into the bathroom because the kebab he'd eaten earlier had upset his stomach. He strapped on his iPod and listened to some tunes, then heard Meredith give a very loud scream. He rushed out of the bathroom, his pants around his knees, to find Meredith lying on the floor of her room bleeding while an Italian guy with a knife stood over her. Rudy said he fended him off with a chair. The left-handed intruder told him he'd better flee because he was black and would get blamed for the crime, so Rudy took off, always without saving Meredith.

The Monster of Florence coauthor Douglas Preston found Rudy's alibi unconvincing. "The rapist's most common defense is 'The victim and I had consensual sex. I left, somebody else came in and murdered the victim. I came back, saw what had happened, got scared, and ran.' Let me tell you, this is the pathetic lie they all tell. When Rudy Guede finds her, does he help her, call the police, or call an ambulance, like any normal person would? No. He flees the country. Because, he says, he was afraid the police would think he did it. His entire story is, in my opinion, an obvious lie.

"Look, I write thrillers for a living," Preston added. "And in my thrillers the person you least expect is the guilty party. But in real life, it doesn't work like that. There is no conspiracy here. In real life, murders are banal and obvious. This case is no different than any other. I have seen the photos. This was a typical rape and murder scene. Sure, there will be loose ends. Even the most banal crimes have a puzzling element to them. No case ever adds up completely. People cannot expect that."

WHEN Rudy Guede's photo hit the TV screens, Zach Nowak immediately recognized him.

"I used to see him in the pubs. He's the classic Italian girl botherer. The kind of guy who goes up to a girl in a bar whom he doesn't know and he makes a move. She lets him know that she's not interested. He makes another move. She lets him know again. And he still keeps trying. At that point you're not just hitting on a girl, you're bothering a girl. Some guys are just too persistent. This is not an African trait. It's an Italian guy trait. He was raised here, remember?"

As for Raffaele and Rudy knowing each other, Zach doubted that, given Perugia's class system.

"Even though Rudy and Raffaele lived on the same street, they could've walked by each other a hundred times and likely Raffaele would never have noticed him. Raffaele is Mr. Spit and Polish, and Rudy is the layabout, do-nothing guy in the neighborhood. As for Raffaele organizing a sex party and including Rudy Guede, give me a break. It would never happen."

In fact, Zach thought it was unlikely that *anybody* would be partying that night, because the foreign students were exhausted from Halloween night, and many Italians had left town for All Souls' Weekend.

Rudy was often seen in the Corso Garibaldi neighborhood, grabbing a slice of pizza, using the Internet Point, doing normal things. Up the hill at La Tana Dell'Orso, owners Lucy Rigby and Esteban Pascual had gotten a bad impression of Rudy the first time he came in, because he claimed to be American. They'd both lived in the U.S., so the lie was apparent. But the second time, Rudy told Esteban that he was interested in wines and hoped to learn from him, and they had an enjoyable conversation.

Pisco Alessi, the Merlin's co-owner, remembered Rudy as a guy who hung around with a bad crowd on the church steps at night. "If you hang out on the steps like that, then you are either taking drugs or you are selling them," he said.

But Zach Nowak doubted Rudy was up to anything major. "I never saw him dealing and have never heard anybody say he was dealing," Zach said. "I think he was just a small-time crook."

RUDY'S arrest was a godsend for Patrick Lumumba, freed by prosecutor Mignini on November 20. The bartender emerged from prison wearing the same brown sweater in which he'd been arrested, kissed his wife and son in front of the cameras, and flashed a radiant smile.

Patrick announced that he would never forgive Amanda. Indeed, he would later become a vocal critic of hers, often appearing on Italian television shows such as *Porta a Porta* to characterize her as a skillful actress, a queen bee, and a crier of crocodile tears. He announced that as soon as Judge Matteini officially released him from any connection to the Kercher case, he intended to sue Amanda for slander.

He was not the only one to file a civil suit. The Kerchers filed civil claims against all the suspects, as did the owner of the cottage.

After many months, police allowed Patrick to reopen Le Chic, but the struggling club remained near empty many nights and eventually it closed down.

WHEN Raffaele learned of Rudy's arrest, he wrote to his father, saying that it sounded like a good development, but he was worried about what this new person might claim.

An officer came to Amanda's cell to tell her about Rudy's arrest. In her diary, she described this exchange:

ME: *"Rudy? The fourth person?"*
THE POLICEMAN: *"Yes, Rudy, so you know him?"*
ME: *"Vaguely."*
THE POLICEMAN: *"Vaguely, huh? We'll see what he says about that." Scowl.*
ME: *"Okay." Have fun hating me, buddy. I haven't done anything wrong.*

Amanda was thrilled, on the other hand, when she heard that Mignini had released Patrick. "Patrick got out today!" she wrote in her diary. "Finally! Something is going right! Maybe I'll be next. Well, most likely Raffaele before me, but soon. I'm so happy!"

AMANDA'S lawyers predicted she'd be out in two weeks, if only on house arrest, but they couldn't protect her from the British tabloids, which began offering money for "exclusive interviews," creating what one Italian journalist called "the supermarket of horrors." The rumor was the leading figures in the Kercher case could sell their stories twice—once in

Britain for six figures and once in Italy, though for considerably less.

"Meredith's boyfriend reveals the moment he suspected Foxy Knoxy killed his lover" announced England's *Daily Mail* in a November 18 "exclusive" with Giacomo Silenzi, pictured with a beard, shaved head, and black ear studs. He said Meredith was "beautiful and innocent," but Amanda, well, he'd wondered if she was a killer the second he saw her at the *questura* hours after Meredith's body was found. Yes, she'd hugged him and said "how sorry she was" about her roommate's death, but right afterward a chill ran down his spine.

A clue that the writer might have taken dramatic license was that Giacomo supposedly said "the girls were 'as different as chalk and cheese,'" a decidedly British phrase. Indeed, when he had a chance to trash Amanda in court, Giacomo instead described her in warm tones, just as he had in his witness reports.

Then on November 24 Amanda and Raffaele became the "couple who bought lingerie one day after a throat slashing." Photos of the suspected murderers sorting through panties in Bubble caused a media blitz. The store owner testified that Amanda bought some thongs (erroneously described as G-strings) and that Raffaele leaned over to her and said, in his ungrammatical English, "We go home and have hot sex." In the courtroom, the lawyers would debate whether the sex was wild or hot, since in Italy "hot sex" was interpreted as violent sex.

"We only went to buy Amanda underwear because her things were locked up," Raffaele later said. "Everything written about us is wrong. I was only joking."

The lovers did exchange one little kiss, but nobody paid attention to them. In fact, in the still photos the store owner looked about to keel over from boredom. The incident ended unromantically, when Amanda hauled out her own wallet to pay the bill. Had the couple wanted erotica, they would've gone next door, where a real lingerie store offered black lace garments splashed over nude mannequins in the window. Bubble stocked girlish dresses, jackets, and pastel undies stamped with flowers and berries.

If Amanda expected a torrid evening, she must've been disappointed. Afterward, they grabbed a pizza and headed off for the meeting with the two Italian roommates that Amanda called "a hurricane of emotions and stress" in her e-mail.

"I Fired Foxy Knoxy for Hitting on Customers" appeared on November 25. In this Patrick Lumumba "exclusive" to the *Daily Mail*, he claimed he'd canned Amanda for flirting with customers. He also psychoanalyzed his former employee as an exhibitionist and pathological liar, insisting that she was a vengeful college student who'd struck back at him because he'd taken away her part-time job, for which he paid 5 euro an hour.

"She was angry I was firing her and wanted revenge," Patrick said, even though he admitted in court that she quit on November 5. "By the end, she hated me. But I don't even think she's evil. To be evil you have to have a soul. Amanda doesn't. She's empty; dead inside."

Patrick also claimed that police screamed at him when they arrested him, hit him over the head, yelled racial epithets, and kicked him. As Frank Sfarzo pointed out, these details dovetailed with the kind of conduct described in Amanda's *memoriale*, "confirming the behavior of our police. Beyond this, it offers a portrait of Amanda that could not be worse; evil personified."

A few days later, during a dramatic appearance on *Matrix*, an Italian TV show, Patrick claimed to have been misquoted. The police had humiliated him, he explained, and it had been terrifying. They'd come to his door and taken him away without explanation. But he hadn't actually been hit.

He didn't take back the parts about Amanda, however, and never explained why he texted her on November 1 and told her not to come to work if she'd no longer had a job.

The most damaging allegation that Patrick made, though, was to claim that Amanda had been jealous of her roommate, a rivalry he could scarcely have witnessed, since he'd told Judge Matteini that he had only one conversation with the English girl and that was about Polish vodka.

"Meredith was sparkly and she lifted your spirits . . . Amanda was jealous," he now claimed.

Prosecutor Mignini had a genius for weaving every juicy tidbit into his crime theories. Now he added jealousy to his list of motives, along with robbery and orgies. Incredibly, Mignini hadn't altered his theory in the least when Rudy appeared. He simply took out one black man, Patrick, and subbed in another black man, Rudy. Police followed his lead.

"In Italy, prosecutors are firmly in charge," Douglas Preston explained. "They tell the police what to look for, where to go, what evidence to analyze, what evidence not to analyze. In America, the police work independently and are specifically trained in evidence gathering and criminal investigation.

"In Italy, the police must do what the prosecutor tells them. As a result, many criminal investigations in Italy are botched by prosecutors who are judges, trained in the law, but who have no background in criminal investigation, police work, or forensic science."

AMANDA had far worse things to worry over than her portrayal in British tabloids. In fact, she was feeling very frightened, as she described in her diary on November 22:

> Last night before I went to bed I was taken down to see yet another doctor who I haven't yet met before. He had my results from a test they took—which says I'm positive for HIV. First of all the guy told me not to worry, it could be a mistake, they're going to take a second test next week.
>
> I don't want to die. I want to get married and have children. I want to create something good. I want to get old. I want my time. I want my life. Why why why? I can't believe this.

She then dutifully made a list of everyone she'd ever had sex with, describing the birth control method used with each. Then a week later, a prison official told her not to worry, that she didn't have HIV after all. When the English tabloids leaked that page of her diary in June 2008, they claimed, erroneously, that she'd boasted of her sexual conquests and had had "seven lovers in sixty days in Italy," even though the diary stated that seven was her lifetime total of lovers.

With perfect timing, the police announced right before Amanda's November 30 court date that they'd found a drop of Amanda's blood in the small bathroom she'd shared with Meredith. Since forensics scientists have no accurate way to date blood or DNA, prosecutor Mignini argued that the stain was highly visible and therefore couldn't have been left before the crime, since it "surely would have been washed."

Then he took another imaginative leap. He claimed that Amanda had fought with Meredith on the night of the crime and had sustained a nosebleed, thereby accounting for the blood drop (while failing to explain why her nose dripped only once and not in the murder room).

Not coincidentally, Mignini also began pushing a robbery motive against Amanda, salting in details spilled from Rudy's German statement. Meredith's money was missing from the little drawer of her nightstand, investigators assumed, although they had no proof that the English girl even kept her cash there. Police implied that Amanda had stolen Meredith's rent money by noting that Amanda had a couple hundred euro in her purse (which was, of course, her own rent money).

Later, they would find Rudy's DNA on Meredith's handbag, yet he would nevertheless escape a theft charge.

Police entered Amanda's cell on November 29 and seized her prison diary. She'd just finished writing, in her maddeningly optimistic manner, that she had three goals for her court appearance the next day: She wanted to confirm the *memoriale* that she wrote on November 6, expressing doubt about the Patrick story; to tell judges that she was "SURE" she wasn't there when Meredith died; and to assure them she'd only named Patrick because "I was stressed and pressured by the police. They brainwashed me."

Amanda drew rainbows and sunbeams on another page. She listed things that she liked, from Beatles movies to songs by Jennifer Lopez, Alicia Keys, and Foo Fighters. She also devoted a page to Italian swear words, saying she would need them in Capanne.

"I don't know whether to be optimistic or not," she wrote of her second court hearing. "Either way, though, I have to accept the decision of the judges, and whether or not I'm freed tomorrow or later, I just have to know that I will be free sometime in the near future, maybe not before, but at least when the investigation is over. I don't have to be afraid. I just want to go home as soon as possible."

ON November 30 Amanda and Raffaele traveled in separate, shiny blue police vans to the courthouse in Perugia, just down the street from Bubble. They'd been in jail now for twenty-four days and had returned to the old town to ask a three-judge panel to free them. They would have created a paparazzi frenzy if the hearing hadn't been closed, because they hadn't been seen out in public since the perp walk—and even then Raffaele's face had been concealed under the hood of his jacket and Amanda's under a wool hat. All photographers captured this time, all their friends back home would see, was the back of their heads. Raffaele came across as a blur, while Amanda was just a small girl with her hair twisted into a French braid, guards hovering all around her.

"Amanda was presented with her hair in a braid, like a proper schoolgirl," wrote Frank Sfarzo on Perugia Shock. He was one of many to characterize the Seattle girl as an actress, the inevitable result of her having recanted her confession.

She proclaimed her innocence and to convince the court, she used tears, the weapon of talent. She claimed she'd spent the night at Raffaele's place. She also apologized to Patrick. The scene was beautiful, but the judges didn't burst into applause.

Since locals in Perugia hadn't taken an interest in Frank Sfarzo's blog, he started writing his dispatches in English, resulting in the blog finding an audience in the United Kingdom and the U.S., where case followers needed a guide through the labyrinth of the Italian legal system. Through all the twists and turns the case took, he covered every court date.

Now he explained that Amanda and Raffaele could actually

be set free at this point, if the judges decided there wasn't enough evidence. But on December 5, 2007, in a scathing fourteen-page report, the judges threw the book at them. Meredith's injuries indicated more than one attacker, they said, and the lack of forced entry "strengthens the theory that she was killed by someone she knew." Amanda, they kept saying, had a key to the front door. No one pointed out that the front door lock often did not latch properly. Like prosecutor Giuliano Mignini, they refused to believe that anybody could have entered the cottage via Filomena's window.

Judge Massimo Riccarelli described the UW honor student as "crafty and cunning," saying her role in the murder was by no means secondary. Amanda was "a multi-faced personality, unattached to reality with an elevated, one would say fatal, capacity" to kill again. As for Raffaele, the judges didn't believe he was on the computer when Meredith died, and they pointed to the bloody shoe print by Meredith's bed as a serious clue against him. They said he'd lied when he claimed to have called the Carabinieri before the Postal Police.

Frank Sfarzo struck a cautionary note. Even though he suspected the two might be guilty, he took Judge Claudia Matteini to task for the judge's report, still accepted as gospel, even with Rudy now standing in for Patrick.

> Nobody's perfect. Did we already forget Claudia Matteini's description? How she described the meeting of the two with Patrick at the basketball court. Then she even knew the sexual tastes of Patrick. She knew he was lost for Meredith. Not only facts, she described, but even internal feelings of the suspects. Didn't I define her version, the day it came out, as naïve? Indeed it was all wrong. She lacked precision. About Patrick's text to Amanda, she said it was sent "about 20:30." We are talking of a murder and she talks 'about.' She wasn't able to give an exact time!

Frank also wondered how the Postal Police *knew* they'd arrived at precisely 12:35 P.M. Unlike Raffaele, they didn't have anything concrete, like phone records, to back up their recollections.

What if the officers don't remember well and they arrived, let's say, at 12:45? After all, they didn't go there for a murder. They went there only to deliver two cell phones, there wasn't a reason to memorize the time exactly. That's what we need now. We need people to be precise and without bias.

JUDGE Matteini and prosecutor Mignini got a crack at Rudy Guede on December 7. After a seven-hour interrogation, Mignini called Rudy's story "ludicrous," especially the part where he ran for the bathroom after eating a spicy kebab. Rudy's lawyer, Valter Biscotti, told reporters his client couldn't name the real murderer because he hadn't gotten a good look at the man's face. He said Rudy knew Amanda only by sight and had never met Raffaele.

Rudy's other lawyer, Nicodemo Gentile, had the thankless task of explaining why his client went dancing at the Domus after leaving Meredith bleeding to death on the floor. "If he had gone home he would have gone mad," Gentile insisted, "so he went out and circulated, and met some foreign girls."

MEANWHILE, Meredith's family had been pleading with Italian police to let them bury their daughter. Finally on December 15, 2007, they got their wish. Four hundred mourners attended a private service at St. John the Baptist, her parish church in Croydon. They listened to Meredith's favorite song, U2's "With or Without You," and her sister Stephanie read a poem she'd written for Meredith called "Don't Say Good-bye." Among the many bouquets was one purchased by Meredith's family, spelling out "Mez" in yellow flowers. Her brother Lyle, recalling her delightful sense of humor, said his sister would be "looking down smiling," joking that they'd kept the cost for the flowers down by only paying for three letters instead of her full name. He said the family wanted to remember the good things that had happened in Meredith's life—and not dwell on the bad.

* * *

AMANDA made one more attempt to tell her story to Mignini on December 17, an opportunity Raffaele had also sought but then rejected. She faced a daunting task, since Mignini would question her in the presence of two very high-ranking officers who'd helped orchestrate the all-night interrogation back in November: Flying Squad director Domenico Giacinto Profazio and homicide head Monica Napoleoni.

No one doubted Mignini was a skilled questioner. Douglas Preston, in *The Monster of Florence*, freely admitted that he'd been terrified when Mignini interrogated him. "Behind the desk sat the public minister of Perugia himself, Judge Giuliano Mignini," Preston wrote in that book. "His fleshy face carefully shaved and patted. He wore a blue suit and carried himself like a well-bred Italian with a large sense of personal dignity, his movements smooth and precise, his voice calm and pleasant."

Mignini told Preston that he had a right to an interpreter, but said that finding one might take many hours, and in his opinion, Preston spoke fluent Italian. "I asked if I needed a lawyer and he said that, although it was of course my right, it wasn't necessary, as they merely wanted to ask a few questions of a routine nature."

Preston's ordeal began with an hour of genteel questioning, in the presence of Mignini and several police officers, followed by an abrupt shift into a dark, accusatory tone.

"Despite answering their questions fully and truthfully, in the end they charged me with '*reticenza*' and '*falsa testimonianza*,'" Preston wrote afterward in a widely circulated e-mail, "two serious crimes of perjury—but said the charges would be suspended to allow me to leave Italy, to be reinstated later. In other words, it seems their goal was to get me out of Italy, never to return."

Preston was not shy about saying, in essays and on American TV, that he believed the deeply religious Mignini was under the thrall of a radical blogger who "saw" the devil at work both in the Monster case and in the Kercher case, acting through Amanda and Raffaele. This explained, he believed,

Mignini's decision to pursue the two college students with single-minded intent.

Mignini, for his part, would make a point of telling American journalists that he never told Preston he had to leave the country. He put that misunderstanding down to Preston's poor grasp of Italian, saying he had not realized the American was so hampered. He also denied being under the thrall of anyone.

THE first time Amanda had faced Mignini, she had been lawyer-less. That was during the all-night session at the *questura* when she named Patrick and placed herself at the murder scene. Mignini had come into her interrogation room at some undisclosed time (perhaps 2 A.M., perhaps 3 A.M.) and left at 5:45 A.M., a long time period that he'd never accounted for. Someone offered "suggestions," Amanda said, about where she could have been and what she might have witnessed on the night that Meredith's throat was cut. Suggestions like "Maybe you heard a scream."

Once she signed the statement, Mignini drew up her arrest warrant.

Now Amanda had two lawyers and a translator, helping her to face down Mignini in a hearing room at Capanne. He began by questioning her about the nickname Foxy Knoxy, which the translator proceeded to mistranslate as *Volpe Cattiva*, "Evil Fox." Amanda said that her soccer squad had given her the nickname for acting foxlike on the field. They went back and forth, Mignini asking if the moniker might have other meanings. She kept returning to the soccer. Then the prosecutor turned almost courtly, asking how the America girl had found the house in Perugia, where she traveled in Germany, why she called her aunt Dorothy "Dolly." Then he swung abruptly into questions about her drug use. Amanda admitted she'd used marijuana at times, and also hashish. Yes, she had shared a *spinello* on November 1 with Raffaele. She didn't know where he got it.

"Who do you buy it from?" Mignini asked in six different ways.

"I would smoke it with my friends, but I never bought it from them. . . . I didn't buy it because, for example, I would give ten euro to Laura and she would buy it for me."

Under repeated questioning, Amanda also said that Meredith shared joints with the roommates, but not often. The British girl was a serious student.

Mignini then asked how Amanda happened to work for Patrick, and she explained that sequence of events. She said she'd started in October, but couldn't remember the exact day. They discussed her rent, 300 euro a month (about $450), and Amanda said she had withdrawn that amount before Meredith's death in order to pay the landlord.

As for Rudy, she knew him vaguely, he might have come into Le Chic once, and perhaps she walked by when he was on the basketball court. No, she didn't think Patrick knew him.

Mignini then asked about Spyros Gatsios, and she said he was a good friend and she'd hung out with him on Halloween. The prosecutor then asked if she had any Spanish friends, an obvious reference to the two Spanish Erasmus students who lived in the flat above Rudy's.

Amanda said she did not know any Spanish people in Perugia.

Then they discussed the night Meredith was murdered. Amanda said she'd read a Harry Potter book in German, then watched *Amélie* and done other things at Raffaele's. She was not able to tell him exactly what time she did what, but she did recall many details of the evening. Then they had the usual discussion about the text message, and Amanda insisted she'd said "good night" after "see you later."

Mignini was particularly interested in how Amanda had learned Meredith had died; since the English girls had told him that she knew details "only the killer would know." She said Raffaele had told her what Paola and Luca said in the car going to the *questura* on November 2. She also remembered Filomena saying, "Oh God, Meredith," but she didn't learn much from her. The police had also supplied a few details while she was giving her witness statement. As for the finding-Meredith-in-the-wardrobe story, Amanda said she was merely repeating what she'd heard, perhaps in garbled form, given the language barrier.

Amanda had been answering questions for about nearly six hours by this point. Then Mignini asked why she had named Patrick. He peppered her with questions. She answered him calmly at first, saying the police had asked her to make suggestions. And in her state of mind, in her imagination, after many hours, she thought the vision she was seeing might be true. She had been under great stress, she said, because the police kept insisting she was guilty.

Mignini stepped up the questioning. He raised his voice, increasing the pace. He wanted to know exactly *why* she'd named Patrick. He insisted that police hadn't known about Patrick until she brought up his name, which seemed unlikely since they knew she worked at Le Chic and they had boasted of startling her by showing her the now-famous text, which had still been on Amanda's cell phone when her November 5–6 interrogation began. As Amanda now told Mignini, the police were very suspicious about the message and she began to believe that Patrick was involved. They kept asking her to imagine things. When they asked, "Did you hear a scream?" she answered, "Well, I must have covered my ears," and that got written into the declarations.

"Why is it only at a certain point that Patrick appears?" Mignini kept asking, although he must have known the answer since he had led the investigation. Moreover, high-ranking police officers had supervised the proceedings from the control room. Despite Mignini himself having been in Amanda's interrogation chamber from roughly 2 or 3 A.M. (the story varied) until 5:45 A.M., he seemed mystified by the very statement he'd watched her sign, without a lawyer to advise her. Now she had two. Here's an exchange about why she accused Patrick of killing Meredith:

> MIGNINI: In the subsequent *memoriale*, that was
> written before going to prison, you have not
> substantially denied this accusation. It was however
> in terms, always in terms, let's say, of uncertainty
> between the image . . . between the dream and the
> reality, in sum in manner . . . however you have
> not . . . it seems that you say in this *memoriale* "I

see still before me this image" and then you see
while you hear, you say it in that first *memoriale*
that you made, "I hear Meredith's scream" and you
covered your ears. Why do you have these images?
The ears . . . the scream . . . however it is not that it
changes very much, eh?

LAWYER: No, however she says that she was very
confused . . . she was under a lot of stress.

Then Mignini continued hammering Amanda about the
text message, saying it was normal for police to wonder when
they see a series of messages between two people "not long
before the hour of a crime," but he couldn't manage to express
his thoughts succinctly. Finally, Amanda answered one question
out of all of this verbiage, about why she'd named Patrick
as the killer:

Because I was thinking that it might be true.

Then she burst into tears and, on the advice of her lawyers,
said no more. Nobody was listening, she said later; it
was more of the same, the yelling, the repeating of questions,
the disbelief—more of what she'd gone through during the
undocumented hours of November 2007.

RUDY'S increasingly detailed alibi did not impress a three-judge
panel on December 20, 2007. They refused to grant his
release, saying his testimony was so riddled with lies that it
couldn't provide "even a minimal or partial account of what
happened."

Judge Andrea Battistacci said she was baffled as to
motive, not understanding how "young people of the same
age who are also acquaintances of the victim, could take
their thoughtlessness to such an extreme as to commit such
a cruel crime without a strong conflict or an extreme state of
alteration."

Yet she had no doubt that the trio had done the deed while
engaged in a sex game. The judges placed great reliance
on the confused testimony of Nara Capezzali, the woman
who'd heard a scream and people running on November 1

but didn't see who the people were and hadn't looked at her watch.

Nevertheless, for the judges, her testimony was "the confirmation of a group participation in the ferocious criminal act that cannot be considered in passive terms for any of those present."

PART THREE

TRIAL AND PUNISHMENT

CHAPTER SIXTEEN

THE SUPREME COURT: LAST CHANCE TO AVOID TRIAL

January 1–April 1, 2008

"He's innocent because he's just like I am: unable to hurt anyone, sincere, altruistic and generous, exactly like me. He's not able to lie, as I'm not able to lie."

—Francesco Sollecito, speaking of his son, Raffaele, to reporters

"Meredith was a girl full of life and enthusiasm, who—for the sole purpose of having some pleasure and sensation during a boring day spent smoking joints—was subject to acts of brutality and cruelty that are disgusting to any normal person."

—Judge Claudia Matteini

JANUARY 2008 began with hand-to-hand combat between the defense and the prosecution, leading up to April 1, when the trio of suspects would appeal their detentions in front of the Supreme Court of Cassazione, the equivalent of the U.S. Supreme Court. In a marble monstrosity on the banks of the Tiber, the red-robed judges would conduct a one-day hearing. They couldn't launch their own investigations or look at new evidence, but they did have the power to strike Judge Claudia Matteini's ruling and free all three suspects if they chose. Both defense and prosecution used the four months before the court date to strengthen their hands.

Investigators delivered a devastating blow to Raffaele Sollecito right before the New Year. They'd found his DNA on a bra clasp belonging to Meredith Kercher, collected from her bedroom forty-seven days after her death. The microscopic speck of DNA was Raffaele's for sure. The question was, how had it gotten on the clasp, which was still attached to a ripped bit of white cloth? Contamination was a distinct possibility, given that investigators had also found the DNA of three other unidentified people on the same tiny metal clasp. Also, while early crime scene footage showed the clasp near the victim's body, investigators had either accidentally kicked or swept it across the room, where it had ended up under a dirty rug.

"These girls lived in the same house," said Raffaele's father, Francesco Sollecito, who claimed that perhaps Amanda and Meredith had shared bras, and that might have accounted for his son's DNA ending up on Meredith's bra clasp.

"Amanda was very casual," he pointed out. "I don't think she'd have any trouble borrowing her friend's bra."

After that bizarre remark, Raffaele's lawyers either muzzled Francesco or he learned not to express his every thought in public.

Raffaele created a stir on January 17, 2008, when he came to the Palazzo di Giustizia, the Hall of Justice, in Perugia for a preliminary examination of the case computers. Investigators had announced with great fanfare that they had cloned the hard drives of the computers owned by Raffaele, Meredith, and Amanda—and would allow experts on both sides to examine them.

A boisterous throng of photographers and journalists glimpsed a small, handcuffed figure in a dark jacket emerging from a police van and gripped by two blue-clad officers. Since the three prisoners were now hidden from public view most of the time, their every appearance created a circus atmosphere.

Judge Claudia Matteini had appointed an independent expert to look into the workings of all the hard drives. The idea was to create backup copies of all of the hard drives and then to retrieve the data, but instead the experts managed somehow to destroy Meredith and Amanda's drives. Only the computer that Raffaele had used on the night of the murder could be read. Dueling experts never would agree on what his hard drive showed. The prosecution claimed he wasn't on the computer during the hours for which he needed an alibi, roughly 9 P.M. to 11 P.M. on November 1. For defense experts, the evidence showed the exact opposite. Many battles would be waged over the downloading of Manga cartoons, the starting and stopping of *Amélie* on Raffaele's computer.

The destruction of Amanda's Toshiba, and specifically the photos stored on it, greatly upset her parents. Edda said they'd planned to show photos of Meredith and Amanda together, out having fun at the Eurochocolate Festival and other places, to prove the girls were friends.

Conversely, prosecutor Mignini, naturally enough, was doing everything he could to create a picture of acrimony. In February 2008, he headed to Northern Italy, where Robyn Butterworth and Amy Frost were then studying, to re-question six of Meredith's friends, who had all gathered there in Bergamo. He grilled them not only about their last evening with Meredith, but also about what Raffaele and Amanda had said about the slashing while at the *questura* on November 2.

Had the couple really known things "only the killer would know"? That was the question. The few details Amanda had supplied so far had turned out to be wrong. Meredith's death was certainly tragic, painful, brutal, and senseless, but the coroner had not said it dragged out over many hours (thereby forcing the suspects to lengthen their alibis). Nor had the victim been found in the wardrobe, as Amanda had initially told the others.

While some bloggers boasted that the English girls were "about to nail Amanda," for Frank Sfarzo, the strong reliance on circumstantial evidence was troubling:

> The case is complicated; it certainly can't be solved by taking into account what Meredith's girlfriends and housemates had been chatting about in the *questura* waiting room or in Perugia's piazzas. We'd better count on the electronic microscope. That one is reliable. And it doesn't have opinions nor memory problems.

Yet in the Kercher case, no one could count even on microscopes to tell a clear story.

*   *   *

THE Kercher family was not spared further anguish in the run-up to the Supreme Court appearance. On January 16, 2008, the *Daily Mail* posted chilling crime scene photos on its Website. These new photos were even more disturbing than the black-and-white shots of Meredith's bedroom that the public had already seen. In those the victim was hidden under the duvet, except for the one foot sticking out. Her brother Lyle Kercher had expressed anger over the use of these photos, pleading with the media to treat his sister's death with dignity.

Now Internet users could see color shots of the murder room after the victim had been removed, revealing everything from the pools of blood by the wardrobe where she had fought for her life, to the tiny bathroom with the bloody footprint on the blue mat. The formerly white bathroom glowed a streaky red in the photos, giving viewers the impression that Amanda Knox had showered in a butcher shop. Instead, the room had been sprayed with luminol, which reacts with many organic substances, not only blood. The list of actual blood evidence in the bathroom mirrored what Amanda had previously described: a blotch on the bathmat, a few drops on the tap. The only thing she hadn't spotted was a narrow ring of blood around the drain in the bidet.

In March 2008, the Sollecito family reportedly leaked crime scene footage to *Telenorba* 7 television. Based in Bari, Raffaele's hometown, the station played the video late at night, after warning viewers that it was disturbing. The goal was to demonstrate the bra clasp's contamination, by showing forensics scientists who scrubbed like cleaning ladies, worked without head coverings, moved mattresses from one room to another, piled up evidence like rubbish heaps, and made irretrievable messes everywhere. But many viewers were appalled at the breach of privacy for Meredith and her family. Workers could be seen, for example, turning the naked victim over to examine her bloodied back. And, inevitably, the video ended up on the Internet.

In Italy's *Panorama* magazine, Francesco Sollecito later

expressed regret over this incident, saying, "We used it wrongly and it boomeranged."

Meanwhile, the case had become so sensational that excerpts from Rudy's interrogation ran as entertainment on *Matrix*, the Italian TV show. The public could listen to an annoyed Judge Matteini drilling Rudy about who had tried to call Meredith's bank shortly after 10 P.M. on the night of the stabbing. As translated by Frank Sfarzo:

> M: So, this message is sent from Meredith's house while the phone was there?
> R: Yes, that wasn't me, madam, I repeat.
> M: There's your hand print on her pillow and you cannot remember even the color of the pillow. But you remember many data and many other details. A call starts from Meredith's cell phone while the phone is in Meredith's house and you are in Meredith's house. Now you must give us a logical explanation for all of this. Do you understand your position?
> R: I understand, madam. I have not sent any message, that's the problem. From no cell phone.
> M: So tell us who sent the message and who was in the house with you. And what really happened in that house in those hours.

Instead of answering the question, Rudy told the judge that if he'd had a phone, then he would've called for an ambulance.

"Do you understand this is not believable?" she asked.

As Frank Sfarzo pointed out, the Kercher case was awash in vexing interrogations:

> We are talking of two boys and a girl here, barely adult. Inexperienced people who should sing like canaries at the first tinkling of the handcuffs. And we are still at this point. The only thing that Rudy confessed to was drinking juice directly from a bottle in the girls' refrigerator.

Except for assistance in nailing the other two suspects, detectives hardly needed Rudy to bare his soul, since he'd left so many traces of himself in the murder room. The wonder was how Amanda and Raffaele could manage to remove all trace of themselves yet leave plenty of invisible reminders of Rudy. As Raffaele's lawyer Giulia Bongiorno would later say, they were college students, not dragonflies flitting in and out of the room on gossamer wings, vanishing without a trace.

Bad news kept piling up for Rudy all month. Coroner Luca Lalli revealed that the DNA that "the Ivorian" left inside the victim came from skin cells, not sperm, evidently from finger cells. Lalli also said Meredith had died of meta-hemorrhagic shock and blood inhalation—and that he couldn't say for sure that she'd been sexually violated. He might have said more, had Mignini not abruptly canned him. Many commenters on the Web assumed Mignini had fired the coroner for not toeing the company line, but Frank Sfarzo on Perugia Shock urged caution:

> The call I had this morning with Dr. Lalli should probably save us from elaborating strange theories about why he got sacked. He talked about the case, which is against the law and he was fired for it. And not just the same old sentences stolen by the newspapers. This time he talked to a "*Studio Aperto*" TV broadcast. Three sentences over the phone, which were recorded. And that was the trouble. A sentence reported in a newspaper is one thing. Your own voice, which everyone can hear on TV, is another.

A panel of professors came to the prison on February 16 to quiz Raffaele for his degree in computer programming. He passed. He had to do without friends and champagne, but his father and a few other family members were allowed to attend. Guards also permitted Francesco to bring in a pin-striped suit and tie for Raffaele to wear during the brief ceremony.

Everyone tried to make as much as they could of this all-important moment in an Italian boy's life, but Raffaele certainly didn't get the graduation party or romantic dinner he'd envisioned with Amanda.

By this time the case was finally catching hold in America, where followers of true crime had had a wealth of criminal investigations to choose from, including the case of Drew Peterson, the Illinois police chief accused of murdering the third of his four wives. Only now did Perugia receive a visit from Joe Tacopina, a showboating New York defense lawyer who lived for the limelight. The Italian-American somehow got investigators to let him look at the evidence and then went on TV to loudly complain that the murder weapon wasn't the murder weapon, the crime theory made no sense, and that police should just admit that Rudy Guede had stabbed Meredith without help from anyone. This heated rhetoric infuriated Rudy's lawyer, Valter Biscotti, so much that he sued Tacopina for slander.

Paul Ciolino, working for the CBS series *48 Hours Mystery*, also popped up in Perugia. He was the first person to cast public doubt on Nara Capezzali, the "ear witness" who'd said she heard a scream on November 1 and the sound of two people running. Ciolino noted that Nara's windows were double-glazed. She didn't live close enough to the cottage to have heard anything important on November 1, he claimed. When *48 Hours Mystery* broadcast his report, it showed Ciolino being snubbed by a frazzled Nara when he knocked on her door and said he was an American investigator. She acted rather daffy, but Frank Sfarzo called her a "fake stupid," meaning she just didn't feel like sharing any knowledge with Ciolino, who had arrived after dark and hadn't been overly polite. So Ciolino was forced to perform a listening test in the apartment above Nara's, which he claimed proved that she couldn't have heard exactly what she said she did when it came to the running. And, in any case, she hadn't seen anything or jotted down the time, and the runners could've been anyone. Like Tacopina, Ciolino was none too popular with Rudy Guede, since Ciolino was more than happy to put the whole blame on him for the murder.

*   *   *

ON March 26, 2008, only four days before the Supreme Court appeal, Rudy's team struck back, saying that Rudy felt he must speak to Mignini. During their three-hour chat, Rudy apparently remembered that Raffaele was the man he'd seen with the knife in hand on the night Meredith died, forgetting that he'd previously "seen" a left-handed man and Raffale was right-handed. Rudy also claimed to have heard Amanda's voice outside the cottage after the stabbing, implying that she was waiting there for her accomplice. Somehow Rudy also claimed to know that Amanda and Meredith quarreled all the time, even though their flatmates said they never fought, and he reasserted his earlier statement that Meredith had suspected Amanda of stealing money from her (even though it was Rudy's DNA that was later found on Meredith's purse). As Frank Sfarzo wrote on Perugia Shock:

> Those who believe this version to be less than credible must bear in mind that Mignini seems quite satisfied with it. We can read this presumed "satisfaction" from the length of the interrogation, about three hours. This relatively short period means that Mignini and his companions didn't really insist upon verifying what was stated via a rigorous cross-examination. Of course, they were satisfied. We can't really say, at this stage, if this is Rudy's slanderous attempt to save himself or if it's the truth. A nice cross-examination question might be, for instance, "Why did you wait so long to tell us this?"

On April 1, the paparazzi set up video cameras outside the Supreme Court in Rome for the closed hearing, which happened to fall, oddly enough, on April Fools' Day. None of the suspects was present, but their lawyers came into the blocky marble building, threw black robes over their suits, and entered the elegant little courtroom, wood-lined like a chapel, with elaborate chandeliers. Six gorgeous brunette *journalistas* from the Italian wire services, clad in couture wool sweaters and skirts, tried to get Amanda's lawyer Luciano Ghirga to talk about her. He laughed and said, to all their questions:

"I don't know."
"Speculation!"
"No comment."
"Nothing."
"Never."
"Stop asking me."
"You're kidding me."
"No."

When the verdict came down late that night, it was a near-perfect victory for Giuliano Mignini's sex game theory. The court threw out Amanda's "confession" from 5:45 A.M., because she hadn't been provided with a lawyer, but they still managed to find enough evidence to rubber-stamp the detention of all three suspects.

Rudy had made a mistake by tinkering with his alibi, according to the judges, for not only did they find his iPod hip-hop-listening story "totally unlikely," but they found his shifting tale suspicious in itself. Not that it mattered, because the judges said he had "grave evidence" against him.

The decision against Raffaele Sollecito and Amanda Knox might have gone differently if the judges hadn't believed the bloody shoe print was Raffaele's, since they cited it as a serious clue against him. The judges were also told that police hadn't found any of Amanda's fingerprints in her own room, which the prosecutor had cited as an example of a cleanup. Yet many people had seen Amanda in that room on the day Meredith's body was found, including Filomena Romanelli and Paola Grande, and that was before the forensic scientists arrived. Later, it would turn out that the forensic scientists simply hadn't tested Amanda's room for fingerprints; and why would they have? She lived there.

So how had this misleading information made its way into the court record? Douglas Preston pointed to the prosecution. "As one distinguished judge said in the *Monster of Florence* case: 'Half a clue plus half a clue does not equal a whole clue: it equals nothing!' "

Indeed, as more reporters gained access to documents, photos, and case videos, they, too, were able to dispute other "half clues," knocking down prosecution arguments that

Mignini would simply delete from his next presentation, as if he had never used them in the first place.

There was, for example, the infamous "wine and mushroom party" scenario that Mignini had used to explain why Coroner Lalli had found a mushroom in Meredith's esophagus, even though she had eaten no mushrooms with her friends at her last dinner. Mignini insisted that "in all probability" Meredith must have eaten mushrooms with Amanda when she got home, since both girls were known to be fond of the fungi. He even managed to find premeditation, noting that "a box of champignon mushrooms," like the one eaten by Meredith, were "filmed by the forensic police in Sollecito's refrigerator." Yet Mignini must have also known that there were mushrooms in the cottage's refrigerator, too, because the same forensic police had also photographed everything there as well. In fact, it looked as if Meredith had simply rolled back the plastic on a package of mushrooms and eaten a few of them raw.

On April 21, 2008, the judges from the Palazzaccio (the sinister name Italians give the Supreme Court) explained why they had upheld the arrests. They said that all three suspects presented flight risks, lacked credibility, were dangerous, and had deviant personalities. Like Mignini, the judges described marijuana as if it were heroin, calling the trio "habitual drug users." Amanda, they said, had "repeatedly contradicted" herself and had "a negative personality." The judges called the *memoriale* scribbled right after her arrest a "self-accusation" that could be used against her in court.

LATER that spring the extended Sollecito family did everything they could to eliminate the bloody shoeprint clue against Raffaele. "We have already demonstrated irrefutably that the bloody footprint near the body was not from his shoe," Francesco Sollecito had announced. For once, he was not bluffing.

The Sollecito family, including Mara, Raffaele's stepmother, his aunt Sara, and his cousin Annamaria, started getting together every Saturday night to strategize their support for Raffaele, whose innocence they'd never doubted. They'd known since November that police didn't find blood on the soles of Raffaele's shoe. Now the twenty-one-year-old Annamaria had come up with the clever idea of counting and measuring the circles on the sole of the bloody footprint, using a compass. The footprint had eleven; Raffaele's Airforce-1 Nikes, only seven.

An expert they'd hired, Francesco Vinci, knew that police had found an empty shoebox in Rudy's apartment that had once contained Nike Outbreak 2s. So Raffaele's uncle, Giuseppe, went out and purchased that shoe model. The family was thrilled to see that the circles on the bottom of that brand matched the famed footprint, meaning Rudy had probably been the person who had hovered over Meredith's bed while she was dying.

"We had to defend the image of a good boy, portrayed as a monster," Raffaele's aunt Sara told *Panorama*, an Italian magazine. They'd rejoiced, she said, when they found the correct shoe. "We thought it was all over. The girls were crying. My husband said, with his eyes to heaven, 'God exists.'"

This new development forced Rudy to come clean on May 15, 2008. In a face-to-face with prosecutor Mignini, he finally admitted, "I wore those shoes. That footprint is probably mine." He also admitted that he'd dumped the bloody shoes in Germany, where he'd earlier admitted to discarding his bloody pants.

If Edda Mellas had ever wondered if her arrival in Perugia on November 6 had had anything to do with the timing of Amanda's all-night interrogation, then Judge Claudia Matteini left her no doubt. On May 16, the merciless judge turned down house arrest for Amanda, who had hoped to live with an order of nuns in Umbria who were allowed to shelter prisoners under supervised care, an option that had been granted other murder suspects.

"Your family lives in the United States, so it would be extremely easy for you to leave the country," Matteini wrote. "The fact that you did not do so before you were arrested is totally irrelevant. We must remind you that your arrest was made very early, and was effected purposely before the arrival of your mother in order to avoid just such a possibility."

The judge also chided Amanda for not showing remorse, for a crime the Seattle girl said she had not committed. Matteini criticized her, as many Italians would, as well, for having taken a shower even after noticing blood on the floor, for hauling a mop to Raffaele's house, and even for eating breakfast before she finally sounded the alarm about the blood.

If by chance Amanda was resting easy in her cell, police also let her know that her footprints had been found in the hallway of the cottage, a natural enough occurrence, except the police gave the press the impression that the footprints were bloody. In court, it would turn out that the scientific police had never tested the footprints for blood, nor had they measured Filomena or Laura's feet to see if the prints could be theirs. It was all meaningless.

At a closed hearing on April 19, the three independent experts appointed by Judge Matteini testified. They confirmed the findings from Coroner Lalli's report, saying they couldn't prove sexual violence, accurately determine time of death, or show that more than one person had been involved in the killing. As for the knife, they said it was "not incompatible," a phrase that in the Italian system means "We don't know."

Peace settled over Perugia for a little while after Giuliano Mignini closed the investigation in June 2008, boasting that he'd assembled a case file more than 10,000 pages long—a total that sounded more impressive than it really was, since it included Raffaele's prosaic blog, Amanda's prison diary, and her MySpace and Facebook pages. Then the court went into recess, as per Italian custom, for the entire month of August, during which the defendants languished in non-air-conditioned prisons until the September pretrial.

Amanda Knox turned twenty-one in prison that summer, which in America would have meant she could have gotten into bars for the first time. She probably would have celebrated by dancing in the discos until dawn, like a typical Seattle girl, with good friends helping her to capture that once-in-lifetime night.

Amanda's mother did wish her "Happy Birthday" in Capanne's visitor's room. Raffaele sent yellow flowers. The press insisted that Amanda had asked for cake and had staged a temper tantrum, but her family said that was ridiculous.

"She already knew that cakes would not be allowed."

CHAPTER SEVENTEEN

PRETRIAL: THE AMANDA SHOW

September 19–October 28, 2008

"To enter by that window does not call for a Spiderman . . . the person needs to be physically agile as Guede surely was and as are thieves that rob from apartments at night. Nor was it necessary to climb up with rock in hand, since it was possible to throw it from that sort of parapet (and not from below, as the prosecutor claimed, with the risk of its falling on the head of the thrower)."

—Judge Paolo Micheli's pretrial report.

"**WELCOME** to the Amanda Show," Italian newspapers proclaimed, when the pretrial hearings into the murder of Meredith Kercher began in Perugia on September 19, 2008. Amanda Knox, Raffaele Sollecito, and Rudy Guede were about to experience a turn of the roulette wheel. After they'd spent nearly a year in prison, a judge would finally tell them whether there was enough evidence to charge them with murder and send them off to trial. The preliminary proceeding would take two months, because it would run only two days, a week at best, sometimes with long intervals in between, as was typical in Italy. But in the end the defendants would finally know their fate.

On Italian TV, the three were already as recognizable as soap opera stars, thanks to the many images lifted from their Facebook and MySpace pages. The fact that Amanda Knox, the "dark angel," hadn't appeared in public for nearly a year only fed the publicity flames. The case had captivated reporters from all over the world and they rushed into Perugia that fall, filling up the pricey Brufani Hotel and Locanda Della

Posta on Piazza Italia and spilling over into the cheaper lodgings farther down the hill. Because the pretrial took place in the Palace of Justice behind closed doors, journalists had to to weave stories from the scraps tossed to them by unnamed BlackBerry-wielding sources within the hearing room or from the lawyers offering sound bites on the courthouse steps. Even the *Times* of London was reduced to quoting "court sources" who fed the prestigious newspaper such insights as "Sollecito exchanged glances with Knox when he entered the courtroom, but they did not speak."

Reporters unable to tap into the police station or the *Procura*, the prosecutor's office, could count on daily comments from Luca Maori, one of Raffaele's lawyers. The powerhouse lawyer Giulia Bongiorno, added to Raffaele's team in May, was also good for a quote. A charismatic member of Parliament, she had defended former Prime Minister Giulo Andreotti against charges of Sicilian mob involvement. Amanda's Roman lawyer, Carla Dalla Vedova, continued to shun reporters, publicly at least, but his Perugia counterpart, Luciano Ghirga, offered daily quips. Rudy's lawyers, Nicodemo Gentile and Valter Biscotti, eagerly sought out reporters, complaining that the other two defendants were trying to blame everything on their client. As for the prosecution, Manuela Comodi kept a low public profile. Prosecutor Mignini would become increasingly media-friendly as the Kercher case wore on, but during the pretrial he was like a football linebacker, hurling himself through the crush of reporters, saying, "No comment, no comment."

Meanwhile, photographers would haunt the doorways and stairwells, hoping to snap the infamous suspects during the brief intervals when prison guards escorted them out of police vans and into the courthouse.

THE Kercher family staged a press conference the day before the pretrial began, managing to temporarily outshine "the Amanda show." They attracted the usual mob scene in the same hotel where they'd greeted the press for the first time. To add to the sense of déjà vu, the same three family members arrived: Stephanie and her parents, Arline and John Kercher.

Stephanie, in a short-sleeved white blouse and dark pants, read a touching statement about how the family missed Meredith and struggled to understand why she had been so brutally taken from them. She could barely be heard over the noise, as cameras clicked, cell phones went off, and chairs scraped against the floor. But still she read on, unflappable. On television, the same scene would look serene and her words would be crisp and clear.

Afterward, Frank Sfarzo shouted out, "Did Meredith get along with Amanda?"

Stephanie demurred; she wouldn't say. Nor would John. Arline looked as if she might like to jump in, but the Kercher lawyer, Francesco Maresca, shook his head and brought the press conference to a close. The press pursued the Kerchers all the way to the entry, a herd of them on both sides. Stephanie put her arm around her mother, smiled sweetly, and disappeared into a conference room to consult with Maresca.

After a while, the lawyer came back out to answer Sfarzo's questions. Maresca, who steadfastly supported the prosecution's talking points, was a middling-tall man with spectacles and curly hair. He usually wore pin-striped suits with white shirts and colorful suspenders.

"No," he told Frank Sfarzo and another reporter, "the two girls did not get along." Why not? "Amanda did not like paying the rent. She did not like to make her bed."

Does anybody like paying rent? By unmade bed, did he mean a general sloppiness or . . . ?

Nobody got a chance to ask these questions. John Kercher emerged from the conference room, and Maresca picked up his briefcase and followed his client out the door and into the parking lot, as video photographers ran alongside. Later, the lawyer would praise the dignified Kerchers for practicing the "elegance of silence." Yet Maresca himself would often speak harshly in their name, especially when it came to Amanda, coming out of the courtroom to speak of her with a tight smile and a shrug of disdain, portraying the UW honor student and Seattle Prep graduate as an immoral, uncouth degenerate whose very presence in the cottage had been an affront to the English girl.

"Is the behavior of Amanda Knox at the police station

logical when Meredith's body was still warm?" was a typical Marcesca comment.

When *La Stampa* asked him why the case had attracted so much attention, he cited the many nations involved: Italy, the United States, England, the Congo, the Ivory Coast. The setting was also important, the beautiful medieval town with the stone staircases, alleyways, and arches.

"One of the features of this crime is that the alleged protagonists could move quickly from one house to another," he said. He complained that the public's fascination with the case was "morbid," yet he freely echoed prosecutor Mignini's drug-fueled sex game theory, the source of the sensationalism. In fact, the Italian news outlet *TamTam* reported that Mignini's indictment claimed that the trio had planned to kill Meredith on Halloween—"the night of the witches" in Italy—and that was why Amanda had sent the messages asking Meredith if she wanted to go out with her. Amanda had literally been setting Meredith up for the kill, in other words, and the English girl had survived only by accident. Just to make things even spicier, Mignini also claimed that drugs, occult rituals, Raffaele's supposedly depraved Manga comic books, the Day of the Dead, and even the start of the Celtic New Year on November 1 may have played roles in the murder.

For Maresca, the case offered a glimpse into a decadent world where drug-addled students "smoked all day long, went to bed at four in the morning and spent hour after hour glued to the Internet with their brains turning to mush." In his estimation, the case was a portrait of "today's burnt-out youth," even though his favorite target, Amanda, was an early riser, an excellent student, and no night owl.

Fiorenza Sarzanini would also link the Seattle girl to degenerate youth in *Amanda e Gli Altri* when she leaked excerpts from Amanda's so-called "green diary," actually just a school notebook that had only about ten pages of personal thoughts amid the Italian grammar lessons.

When they arrested you, in your purse they found three notebooks. I am your diary. Never to be read by anyone. It contains your greatest secrets, your thoughts, your fantasies. An exercise book, light green in color, listed in the police report of seized objects. Dated from August, 6, 2007, before your arrival in Perugia, before those two more months began that now must seem more intense than a lifetime. There are dense pages of notes used to rebuild your complex personality, your desires, and your vices. Alcohol, sex.

THE Amanda show was hyped on every newsstand in Perugia as the biggest thing in town. Yet nobody could get in except the participants. Judge Paolo Micheli lent considerable dignity to the proceedings. He ruled over a small, surprisingly intimate chamber, the white walls set off by a giant crucifix. The defendants sat with their lawyers on long wooden benches in different rows so that Amanda couldn't speak to Raffaele or vice versa, and neither could communicate with Rudy. The two male suspects steadfastly maintained that they'd never met, except now in court, and Amanda's lawyers stressed that she had no desire even to look in Rudy's direction. During the rare times when the Kerchers attended hearings, they sat in the back row, an arrangement designed to help them avoid eye contact with the alleged killers.

During the two-month run of the Amanda show, the press was confined to a sort of glassed-in balcony above the hearing room. Reporters could look down on a corridor, watching the suspects go in and out, but couldn't see into the room itself. And even to observe that much, they had to stand on plastic chairs. Periodically, they would rush out to grab cigarettes, espresso, and panini from the shops on the street and then return to the chairs, hoping they hadn't missed Amanda, Raffaele, or Rudy—in that order of popularity.

The lack of access frustrated even the British tabloid reporters, who took to standing outside the courthouse and yelling out things like "Are you guilty, Amanda?" as she climbed out of the police van. They could then report that the American girl flinched when "somebody" yelled at her from the crowd.

That first morning, before court started, the Kerchers headed into the courtroom looking much more shaky and distraught than they had at the press conference. Stephanie in particular seemed reluctant to go inside. John kept popping in and out, a tall figure in a white turtleneck and black suit, pacing in the hallway, talking to the lawyers, shaking his head.

Meanwhile, the paparazzi, trapped in the glassed-in balcony, were unusually tense. There was a rumor circulating that Amanda had gotten fat in prison, which would greatly reduce the sale price of her photos. In her leaked prison diary, she'd drawn up a list of foods offered to her each day, everything from biscotti and roast pork to sugared breads.

"Do I need all this? No," she had written.

Now videographers grappled for chairs near the viewing window, shoving aside weaker opponents.

"*Bella! Bella!*" a photographer suddenly called out. He captured the first post-arrest photo of Amanda Knox, her face unveiled at last, nearly a year after. This iconic shot of the American college student turned murder suspect would appear on the cover of *Amanda e Gli Altri*, the title printed provocatively across the girl's chest. Amanda looked fit and tan, wearing jeans and an angelic white top with cap sleeves. She wore her hair down, pinned back from her face, and her makeup was tastefully applied.

The mesmerized reporters watched guards sweep Amanda down the hallway and into the hearing room. Pandemonium broke out in the press room. She looked like a fashion model, the reporters said, like she was on the catwalk. She may even have lost a few pounds.

"More beautiful than ever—if that's possible," said one reporter, assured of her guilt. He was ecstatic because, as he pointed out, she sold stories.

Amanda's sizzling reception had its flip side. Italian reporters claimed she'd had a makeover, trying to turn herself in an idealized *raggazza aqua e sapone*, a wholesome "girl of soap and water," yet the only images of her they'd seen before had been swiped from Facebook, and she'd looked neat and clean in every photo there, even when the camera caught her traveling around Europe with a backpack on smoldering summer days.

Amanda's friends said that she'd wanted to look as self-confident as possible. She told them that she'd felt scared, coming into court, but the experience also seemed somewhat unreal, and she tried not to think about the enormity of the

situation, to avoid being overwhelmed, though she knew that
next few months would determine the course of her whole life.

"**THE** photographers were happy because Amanda looked
cute in the pictures," said Mario Spezi, the Italian journalist and the coauthor with Douglas Preston of *The Monster of
Florence*. He smiled, shaking his head, amused. "That's all
they care about."

Although based in Florence, Spezi had taken a keen interest in Amanda's plight because Mignini had thrown him in
the slammer for twenty-three days in 2006, on charges rang-
ing from "criminal libel" to "disturbing an essential public
service" and "obstructing a criminal investigation." Spezi
had spent his imprisonment in Capanne Prison—at first, like
Amanda, in solitary. The experience was so searing that he'd
later had his cell number (3/3b) tattooed on his wrist.

"You are in your cell from morning until night, from night
into morning," he said. "And the worst of it is that you cannot do anything. You are just there. You can't think about the
future. Tomorrow, I will do nothing, you say. Who can live
like that?"

He wasn't sure how prison would change Amanda, but
said that just being driven to court in the grilled police van,
riding in a sort of cage in the middle of it, is a humiliating
experience.

"It depends on the personality of the person, but being in
prison is the kind of experience that you can never forget your
whole life. If you can be strong and true to yourself, then it
will make you grow. If you are not strong enough, then you
will have damage. It's easier if you are older and in your own
country. Who does she talk to? Who are her friends?"

Later, Amanda's priest would answer that very question.
"She has no friends in prison," said Father Saulo Scarabattoli,
adding that she had no real peers there, only fellow inmates.

RAFFAELE Sollecito didn't come into court that first day, it
just dealt "with technicalities," his lawyers said, but reporters wrote dramatic stories about the Kerchers "facing the

accused killers for the first time." Amanda's lawyer Luciano Ghirga assured the press that Amanda had not looked forward to sharing the courtroom with Rudy Guede. In fact, she had scarcely looked at him.

The big news that day was that Rudy had asked for an "abbreviated trial," a fast-track trial that would run simultaneously with Amanda and Raffaele's pretrial, which would determine whether they would be released or charged with murder and sent on to trial. His lawyers insisted he'd chosen the fast-track trial to distance himself from the couple, who they said were trying to pin the murder on Rudy. Typically, suspects who asked for an abbreviated trial hoped to get a reduced sentence. Also, no new elements could be introduced; the judge had to make a decision based on the evidence already gathered. Judge Paolo Micheli, a well-respected jurist, granted Rudy's request.

Amanda and Raffaele's months-long pretrial was most notable for the parade of super-witnesses organized by the prosecution, meaning the witnesses that Mignini considered most important to the case. In addition to Nara Capezzali, the woman who said she had heard Meredith's scream, there was Antonio Curatola, a homeless man who claimed to have seen Amanda and Raffaele hanging around Piazza Grimana on the night of the murder, up to no good. Unfortunately for the prosecutor, Curatola (known locally as "Toto") had mentioned Halloween masks in his first statement, meaning he wasn't sure what night he had seen the two strangers.

After "Toto" testified, Frank Sfarzo went to the piazza that night to talk to him. The bearded, gray-haired hobo, a man of sixty, showed Sfarzo where Amanda and Raffaele had supposedly hovered that night, staring down into the cottage. The theory was that they'd run out of the cottage after Meredith screamed and had waited to make sure the coast was clear before they launched their massive cleanup, the proof for which the prosecutor would never offer. It was enough to bring up mops and bleach now and then, to provide a half clue. As Sfarzo learned from hanging out with Toto in Piazza Grimana:

Actually, you can't see the cottage from the basketball court. In fact, you can't see the house from any point in

Piazza Grimana. The only spot from which you can see just the gate of the cottage is a very small area beneath the trees, which means that from where Amanda and Raffaele supposedly were, they couldn't see the building. So even the testimony itself is not accurate.

The most unusual witness, though, was Hekuran Koko-mani, an Albanian man who said that he had been driving by the "house of horrors" on the night of the murder (or else the night before that), when he'd accidentally knocked over (or merely grazed) a large plastic garbage can. Suddenly a knife-wielding Amanda and Raffaele jumped out from behind the can and confronted him. He claimed that he threw various objects at the two young lovers—black olives, a Nokia cell phone. Then Rudy Guede had stepped out of the shadows. Kokomani, who would soon be hospitalized for problems related to alcohol abuse, claimed to know Rudy slightly, from the latter's gardening days. Rudy supposedly told him that there was a party going on inside the cottage, and also said he needed to rent a car and wondered if Kokomani could help him out.

For reporters, the Albanian was the most eagerly awaited of the super-witnesses, but like most of them, he came to court in disguise, a baseball hat pulled down over his eyes, wearing a hoodie, so that nobody could tell what he looked like.

Since the reporters weren't allowed inside the courtroom for the pretrial, they were never sure of the accuracy of their coverage, especially when it came to the infamous kitchen knife. Prosecutor Manuela Comodi held a mock-up of it in court, marked "evidence handled with care," and this photo was circulated to the press.

Dr. Patrizia Stefanoni, the forensic scientist who had tested the knife and bra clasp, did testify, but reporters were not able to get any details. Nor could defense attorneys, actually, so it was impossible to judge if the DNA evidence implicated the defendants or not. As an "independent expert," Judge Micheli had appointed Renato Biondi, Stefanoni's boss at the crime lab in Rome, who said that she had done a perfect job.

Then prosecutors Mignini and Comodi presented a "recon-struction of the case," the most detailed yet. "They laid out a scenario like from some crime novel," Raffaele's lawyer Luca

Maori told the press. He said the prosecutors "alleged it was some kind of satanic rite, with Amanda allegedly first touching Meredith with the point of a knife, then slitting her throat, while Sollecito held her by the shoulders, from behind, Guede held her by an arm and tried to sexually assault her."

Amanda surprised reporters when she spoke for six minutes near the close of the trial. In a shaky voice, she attempted to explain why she had named Patrick. She described her terror in the *questura* that night, the pressure she'd been under. An enterprising photographer caught a glimpse of her, through slits in the blinds, her arms waving. Even that made the evening news. Amanda cried a little as she described the yelling and the slaps she'd gotten on the back of the head.

"Meredith was my friend and I had no reason to kill her," she said. "I am innocent. I wasn't in the house that night. If I said the opposite before, it was because I was forced to do so because the police pressured me."

ON October 27, 2008, Judge Micheli came out of his chambers at 8 P.M. on a dark, windswept night. A mob had gathered outside the courtroom, from reporters to townspeople. They had been waiting for hours to hear the judge's ruling. Police officers had had to literally pull the Kerchers through the crowd to get into the courthouse. Reporters caught a glimpse of Amanda's parents, Edda Mellas and Curt Knox, hovering near the front door, hoping against hope that the judge would release their daughter to them and they'd all walk out of that courtroom together.

Judge Micheli announced his decision in front of the three suspects, who had been waiting around since the early morning. He condemned Rudy to thirty years in jail and a payment of 2 million euro to each of Meredith's parents and 1.5 million euro to each of her siblings, for a total of 8.5 million euro. He ruled that Amanda and Raffaele would be tried for murder, sexual violence, theft, simulation of a crime, transportation of a weapon, and—just for Amanda—slander.

Later, Judge Micheli delivered a long report in which he stated that he had begun his reasoning with all three suspects in Meredith's room. He conceded that the prosecution had not been able to place them together before the crime, but he said that once they were placed in the cottage, then many things followed. In the Kercher case, more than any other, he argued, you had to look beyond the facts and, instead, make logical leaps in reasoning.

Thus, he wasn't impressed by the defense argument that Amanda and Raffaele would have had no way of contacting Rudy on November 1, since he had no cell phone and they'd never e-mailed him. They could simply have met in the world of Perugia nightlife, the judge said, where nobody needed to make elaborate plans to find another person. He fully agreed with the staged burglary theory, even though he said "any agile person" could have climbed into Filomena's window. It just wasn't the window he would have chosen.

Since the standard of proof at the pretrial level was not "beyond a reasonable doubt," Micheli felt he had enough evidence to send Amanda and Raffaele to trial in January 2009.

As for motive, Micheli did not see premeditation. He bought some version of the sex game gone wrong, albeit without the occult.

Meredith had been murdered that night, the judge said, "because she screamed."

CHAPTER EIGHTEEN

THE PROSECUTION SPEAKS

January–June 2009

"Amanda Knox, a woman who has shocked everyone. Her roommates are shocked, the Italian boys and girls, the English girls, the
police. Nobody who met her on that long day of November 2,
2007, will ever forget her."

—Frank Sfarzo, Perugia Shock

AT the start of the new year, Amanda Knox was voted Italy's
most popular celebrity, overshadowing Carla Bruni, the Italian wife of the French president. People knew everything
about the American girl: that her mother had given her flan-
nel pajamas for Christmas and that Jovanotti was her favorite Italian singer. She had caused enormous controversy by
appearing in a walk-on role in a film shot over three months
at Capanne Prison, in which she recited Shakespeare's "To be
or not to be" speech from *Hamlet*. Called *The Last City*, the
fifty-five-minute film featured eleven inmates and explored
the common prison fantasy of escape. "Knox recites in Italian
and English and, like all the actresses, was committed and
enthusiastic," director Claudio Carini told the *Guardian*. "I
would give her ten out of ten for her performance."

Pundits argued furiously on national TV about whether
an accused murderer should be allowed to appear in a film,
even a work whose stated goal was rehabilitation. Many com-
mentators felt Amanda's participation was an affront to the
Kercher family. Others wondered what the fuss was all about.

Should the American girl just sit in her jail cell and rot? Eventually, the film's sponsors had to pull it from the Perugia Film Festival because of all the criticism.

Meanwhile, Italians eagerly anticipated the day when Amanda and Raffaele would appear in court, kicking off what the press called "the trial of the century." And yet the world did not lack for murder mysteries. So why had this one become an international obsession?

"It has a cast of characters that Patricia Highsmith couldn't make up," said Richard Owen of the *Times* of London. He described the lovebirds as "children of privilege, that's what they look like, really him more than her. She's probably more middle-class. He's got flashy cars, all kinds of gadgets—a wealthy, indulgent father. With Amanda, it's more her looks that attract, I think. That's a big part of it. The pretty, all-American girl. And Italy has a long-standing fascination with America, anyway, much more so than with England. Perhaps because Italians immigrated there, America has become a symbol of prosperity and opportunity. And then there's Meredith, a girl of English and Indian background, typical of modern England. Then you have Rudy, the street-wise Italian of African origin who's the link between the student world and what you might have to call the lowlifes."

SITTING in front of a giant crucifix, Judge Carlo Massei kicked off the long-awaited proceedings in Perugia on January 14, 2009, in the Hall of Frescoes, a small rectangular room with arched windows, twin Madonnas who peeked from an ancient wall painting, and a large metal cage that stood ready to house violent prisoners. Amanda Knox and Raffaele Sollecito sat with their lawyers at long wooden tables. They faced Judge Massei, a patient, middle-aged man with spectacles and thinning brown hair, who looked like the comedian Woody Allen. His partner on the bench, Judge Beatrice Cristiani, was a plain-looking woman with curly brown hair who skillfully stayed in the background, scarcely speaking during the entire proceedings. Six citizen jurors of varying ages and occupations sat on either side of the judges, having been chosen at random from a computer. They would not be sequestered. They could read whatever they liked about the case, watch the TV coverage, and discuss the details freely with one another.

Although Raffaele's defense team seldom missed a chance to work Rudy Guede into the conversation, he would make only one appearance during the trial. Summoned by prosecutor Giuliano Mignini, Rudy showed up in handcuffs one morning, fresh from prison, neatly dressed in a sweater and slacks. He sat on a chair in the front of the courtroom for a few minutes. Mignini had hoped that Rudy would give his latest alibi, in which he claimed that he had overheard Amanda fighting with Meredith about money on the night of the murder, but it was not to be. Rudy exercised his right to remain silent. Then guards led him away.

The relatives and friends of the family could sit near the accused each day in the courtroom, but were forbidden to speak to them. Amanda was allowed to hug her father, Curt Knox, when he was in attendance, but only for sixty seconds. The court had barred her mother, Edda Mellas, until June 2009, because she'd been called as a witness by lawyers for Patrick Lumumba, who was suing Amanda for defamation. Patrick came to court each day, a curiously diminished figure who sat quietly next his beefy lawyer, Carlo Pacelli, the most belligerent of all the lawyers.

The Kerchers and the owner of the cottage were also continuing their civil suits. The civil cases would be tried simultaneously with the criminal trial—unlike the procedure in the United States, where the two are separated. Because the civil suits ran concurrently with the criminal action, each witness had to run a gauntlet of lawyers. All of which added to the length of the trial, which would ultimately last almost a year, from January to December of 2009. As with the pretrial, the hearings would run only two days a week for the most part, and the court would take long breaks and close down entirely for the month of August.

In addition, the trial had two criminal prosecutors, Giuliano Mignini and Manuela Comodi, a petite brunette with a peculiar voice, like a thousand pigeons cooing. Just to complicate matters, Mignini commuted from Perugia to Florence during this time period for his own abuse of office trial, but continued to prosecute the Kercher case.

The parade of witnesses began on February 7, 2009, after Judge Massei made a flurry of announcements. He declined to toss the two *memoriale* that Amanda had written just before and after her arrest, meaning that jurors would be allowed to read the handwritten documents that expressed her confusion over Patrick and her own alibi. Amanda's 1:45 A.M. witness statement and her lawyer-less 5:45 A.M. statement (which had been tossed by the Supreme Court) could be used against her in Patrick's slander suit, since she'd named him as the murderer in both of them.

Massei also denied a request by Francesco Maresca, representing the Kerchers, to bar cameras from the proceedings. Instead, the judge worked out a compromise. He allowed photos to be taken only before and after the sessions and during breaks. Thus, each morning would begin with the defendants suddenly popping out, like movie stars, from behind a big bronze door. Guards in blue uniforms and berets would march them past the cameras, escort them to their seats, and stand behind them during the proceedings. Both Amanda and Raffaele often turned to acknowledge friends, family members, and lawyers during these brief times when court wasn't in session, resulting in photos of Amanda smiling and seemingly having a marvelous time in court, which would appear each day in the tabloids, to much criticism.

On the first day of the trial, Raffaele asked to speak to the court, a privilege allowed defendants in Italian courts. Ashen, nearly in tears, he held the microphone and assured the court that he would never hurt a fly. "I am the victim of a judicial error," he said. "I barely knew Meredith. Rudy? I never met the guy. Amanda, yes, but I'd only known her since October 25. We had just started our romance."

"Some of the female jurors actually cringed" at the sight of Raffaele, said Zach Nowak, who worked for various media outlets during the trial. "It was like he was this horrible person who was up there in front of them." Later in the proceedings, Raffaele would spring to life, frequently rising to defend himself. Once he even assisted prosecutor Comodi, when she couldn't get her computer to work properly during a presentation.

Next, the cell phone family—Elisabetta Lana and her son and daughter, Alessandro and Fiametta Biscarini—took the stand looking posh, upper-class. Elisabetta described how they had discovered Meredith's cell phones in the garden after the murder and called the Postal Police. She had given the phones to an officer named Mauro Bartolozzi, who also testified. He was supposed to help shed light on the ever-growing controversy over whether Raffaele had called the Carabinieri before or after the arrival of the postal officers. But like nearly everyone involved in the case, the officer told a baffling story. First, he said that he'd sent a squad car to the cottage around 12 P.M., which would have meant that it arrived around 12:30 P.M., definitely before Raffaele called the Carabinieri. But in his police log, Bartolozzi had jotted down 12:46 P.M. for the receipt of the second phone, meaning that he had probably not sent the squad car yet. So which was it? Bartolozzi claimed that he'd just goofed when he wrote 12:46 P.M. How had he gauged the time? Oh, he'd just looked at his watch. So how did he know when the unit arrived, if he'd never left the station? Don't ask.

As Frank Sfarzo wrote on Perugia Shock:

[The Postal Police] found Amanda and Raffaele sitting and hugging in the garden, in a narrow sun spot, right in front of the window. Only Raffaele had a jacket on. We are waiting for the Carabinieri, they simply said. So, we have two possibilities: Amanda and Raffaele may be lying about their call time or the police may be mistaken about their arrival time. We have the police word against the behavior of Amanda and Raffaele. The only proof that the police have provided in favor of their version is because I looked at my watch. Amanda and Raffaele's behavior, instead, seems to support their version perfectly. The police didn't say they looked surprised or they stuttered out a sudden excuse. You wait outside to make it easy to the Carabinieri to find you, and while waiting you sit back and take care of your tan. Something that looks credible.

*   *   *

NEXT up was Paola Grande, a young woman with a cool head. She was Amanda's roommate Filomena Romanelli's friend, the one who'd been with Filomena at the Fair of the Dead on the morning that Amanda called to say something seemed strange in the cottage.

Yes, Paola said, Filomena had been upset, and she'd told Amanda to check the house, but Paola hadn't heard her tell the American girl to call the police. She said they'd walked around the fair, weaving their way through the booths, and then Filomena decided to call Meredith, but couldn't reach her. Then she got very upset. She called Amanda back. The American said something about thieves in the house, but Filomena couldn't understand her very well, because the girl had spoken in English.

Filomena became very agitated at that point, said Paola, and she couldn't remember where she'd parked the car. So they moved away from the booths and called their boyfriends, Luca Altieri and Marco Zaroli, who promised to hurry over to the cottage and check out the scene.

The picture Paola drew of her friend was quite different from the cool, take-charge Filomena described in the judge's report, the one who had known for sure that the glass from the window had fallen on top of her clothes, allowing investigators to refute the crime scene photos and claim that Amanda and Raffaele had staged a burglary.

Paola described instead a wrecked Filomena, a woman who needed her friend, Paola, to stay with her and make sure she was all right. When they reached the cottage, postal cop Michele Battistelli was already there. The first thing Filomena did was rush into her own bedroom to see if anything was missing. Even when she saw that she'd been spared, she had remained extremely agitated.

To calm her down, Battistelli then made a clumsy joke: "*Ma sta tranquilla, mica c'è il morto sotto il divano.*" Don't worry, it's not like there's a body under the sofa.

Paola proved to be an important witness for the defense, because she was the first to say that, yes, the American girl had a heart. She'd seen her break down over Meredith's death. She also explained how Amanda could know details "only the killer would know." Paola had been the first of the young people to learn how the British girl died. She'd seen Battistelli come out of the cottage and say to another officer, "Her throat was slit."

"I read his lips," she told the court.

Paola said she also told Filomena this. Then, in the car on the way to the *questura*, she and Luca gave Raffaele the same information, which Raffaele passed along to Amanda.

In court, Paola told Mignini that the American girl had sobbed when she heard the news.

"What do you mean sob? Are you talking about tears? What kind of tears?" Mignini inquired. Questions he had not asked about Filomena.

"I heard Amanda cry," Paola said. "I turned around to ask her if she wanted a bit of water, but her head was down and I didn't see the tears."

THE next day, the bespectacled Filomena Romanelli took the stand, sitting about twenty feet from her former roommate, but occupying an altogether loftier plane. "She was twenty-nine going on forty-two," one of the reporters said. In fact, the legal trainee managed to annoy lawyers on both sides of the case by injecting her own opinions into every argument.

"By studying as a lawyer, Filomena apparently learned that witnesses are called to give their opinions rather than facts," Frank Sfarzo wrote on Perugia Shock.

> She took today's testimony as a personal show, she looked very pleased with her performance. She wanted it to go on and on, even until night, she recommended. . . . She didn't notice the rebukes from Maresca and the others to stick to the facts. Up to the point that Carlo Dalla Vedova, representing Amanda, couldn't avoid remarking: "She's ready to represent us in Supreme Court. . . ." That didn't make her laugh. But she got a clue, finally, and things turned better.

Although Filomena was a prosecution witness, her testimony helped the defense by establishing that the two foreign girls had gotten along just fine. There had been no melodrama between them in the cottage. Sure, Filomena would have appreciated a little help around the house and Amanda's yoga was annoying, but she always paid her rent.

Filomena was also useful to defenders because she was the second witness to testify that the supposedly dry-eyed Amanda had shed real tears for Meredith. In fact, by the end of the trial, Amanda seemed to have racked up a considerable amount of weeping. As one online commenter catalogued:

> She cried at the start, per Raffaele. She cried in the car, per Paola. She gave a little sob in the *questura*, per Filomena (grudgingly dragged out of Filomena by defense). She cried with the knives. She cried Nov. 5th in front of Mignini. She cried when she said Patrick's name. She cried when arrested on the morning of Nov. 6. When she saw Edda, she cried and cried. She cried in prison.

Predictably for an Italian, Filomena harped on the shower that Amanda had taken, after she'd seen the blood in the bathroom. "I thought that was strange," she said, again and again. This was an argument that resonated with the judges, who would later ask Amanda questions like "Wasn't it cold that morning?" "Why did you shower when you'd already showered the night before?" "Why did you wash your hair?" Amanda would repeatedly explain that she was in the habit of showering every morning, that Americans liked to shower and wash their hair daily. Indeed, she could not win on this issue. Later, Patrick's attorney would conversely accuse her of poor hygiene, along with venal attitudes and promiscuity.

Filomena did not escape the stand without the usual questions about drug use.

"Yes," Filomena admitted, she did smoke hashish, but she claimed she'd only done it once.

"I have sinned," she told Judge Massei, describing the very drug that supposedly drove three people into a murderous rage.

"We all have," he said.

*   *   *

PAOLA'S boyfriend, Luca Altieri, also testified, sowing yet more controversy. He'd been the one to knock down Meredith's door, because postal officer Battistelli said he didn't have the authority. Now the two men were involved in a war of words in court. The Italian system had a mechanism for working out disputes—when witnesses disagreed on an important point, they were brought together for a face-to-face.

The next day Officer Battistelli and Luca returned to the chamber, where they sat across from each other and thrashed it out in front of everyone. Had there been one cell phone or two? The point being that if Battistelli had arrived with both of Meredith's phones, then he couldn't have arrived before Raffaele called the cops, because of the time that Elisabetta delivered the second phone to the *questura*.

During a thrilling exchange, Battistelli managed to win Luca over on the two cell phone issue. Luca had seen two cell phones on the kitchen counter and assumed that both had belonged to Meredith, meaning that the officers had not headed for the cottage until they received the second one from Elisabetta. So Luca said, "Okay, maybe I'm wrong about that one. Maybe the two phones I saw weren't both Meredith's." But he was unmovable on another crucial point. He was certain that he'd seen Battistelli enter Meredith's bedroom after the door came down, and that the officer had lifted the duvet and checked to see if the girl was alive, actions that Battistelli now hotly denied. He claimed that he'd merely stood in the doorway and observed the scene, which was enough to tell him that the girl's throat had been slit. Frank Sfarzo found the officer an unpleasant witness.

> Battistelli was already nervous when he was right, about the cell phones. Now he's agitated, he loses his temper all the time, shaking his head and body as if he was trying to escape from a nightmare, interrupting the questions with excuses for not answering, saying loudly, Counselor, it's stuff of one year and a half ago! Trying to kill the interrogation with a series of I don't knows. . . . He even doesn't remember if there were two cell phones anymore.

He can't help anymore or he doesn't want to help. He doesn't remember anything.

Luca calmly fought Battistelli on this point about entering the crime scene, certain that he was right. And as the defense pointed out, even the investigators seemed to feel that Battistelli wasn't telling the truth. That's why they'd insisted he give them his shoe size, so they could be sure he hadn't made the bloody footprint by the bed himself.

If he would lie about this, the defense asked the court, then why believe him when he says he arrived at 12:30 P.M.? Our client, Raffaele, has cell phone records that can tell you exactly what time he called the Carabinieri. Are we supposed to believe this man when he says that Amanda and Raffaele were whispering together "like two accomplices"? How about when he says the famous broken glass in Filomena's room was on top of the clothes?

THE international press corps came out in full force the next weekend for the eagerly awaited testimony of Meredith's English friends, seven in all, flown in at public expense to dish one last time about Amanda Knox.

A reporter spotted Natalie Hayward, one of the British girls, at breakfast time with her parents at the Fortuna Hotel on Piazza Italia on February 13, 2009, the day of their testimony.

Natalie was a tall girl with dark blond hair, wearing a sweater with a long skirt and high boots. Her mother had brought dried cereal, evidently from the UK, in a plastic bag, and begged her daughter to eat some before her testimony, to keep up her strength. Natalie shook her head.

"Yogurt then. Something to settle your stomach."

"No, no."

The mother waited for a while. "You know, dear, maybe you should come back with your father and me and not stay on here with the other girls."

It was *Carnivale* time in Perugia. The bakeries made special treats; the merchants put up decorations. The bars filled up. A lovely time to be there, if one wasn't in court.

Natalie got up from the table and became rather charming, pouring tea for her mother, smiling, chatting with her father.

Later that morning, a photographer snapped Natalie with the other girls, their wool coats buttoned against the cold, scarves wound around their necks, as they approached the courthouse. He took one perfect shot of the group as snowflakes started to fall. Then the girls started running. They raced uphill to Café Perugia and disappeared inside.

ROBYN Butterworth was the first of Meredith's British friends to take the stand. She was a tall, brown-haired girl, who posed with Meredith and Sophie, both petite, in many of the Facebook photos. In real life, her features were much softer and prettier than they appeared in the snapshots.

The rumor was that the girls were going to "nail" Amanda, even though none of them had described her as alarming in their first witness reports. She was just "Meredith's friend Amanda," identified as a flatmate who used to go out for dinner with Meredith. But Robyn and Amy in particular had become very suspicious of Amanda after her arrest.

The "nailing" talk had begun when Mignini traveled to Bergamo, in northern Italy, to interview Amy and Robyn there in the spring of 2008. He had managed to assemble six girls, although in court at least one claimed they'd arrived in Bergamo coincidentally, somehow all deciding to visit Italy and stop off to see their good friends at the exact same time.

In court, prosecutor Giuliano Mignini encouraged each girl to gossip freely about Amanda, to chronicle her every fault, to repeat every bit of hearsay, to cast suspicions, to give opinions—even though Meredith wasn't there to correct a misimpression. She couldn't say, as roommates typically do, Oh, I was just venting that day; it wasn't a big deal.

Under Mignini's guidance, Robyn brought up Meredith's complaint about the unflushed toilet, which the prosecutor morphed into an accusation of general piggishness. Robyn delivered this revelation in a somber, shocked tone, with "the earnestness of English girls," as Frank Sfarzo put it.

The prosecutor's theory—as he would explain in closing arguments—was that Amanda hated Meredith because the British girl had criticized her. So, on November 1, when Amanda discovered that she didn't have to go to work, she decided to take her revenge. At 8:45 P.M., after talking to Jovanna Popovic (who said that the American girl appeared completely normal, not drunk or angry, as Mignini would contend), Amanda somehow went into a drug-fueled rage. She insisted Raffaele go to the cottage with her and wreak havoc on Meredith (despite not knowing where the British girl was at the time or when she'd get home).

Amanda grabbed a large kitchen knife from the cutlery drawer, according to this theory, and stashed it in her purse (right after she'd finished watching the whimsical *Amélie* with Raffaele on DVD). Somehow, on the five-minute walk over to the cottage, they encountered Rudy, who didn't have a cell phone, whose e-mail address they didn't have, who had never met Raffaele. The couple immediately decided to stage an orgy with him, even though they'd never expressed any interest in group sex before and had known each other only six days. When they got to the cottage, Meredith was either already there or came in shortly afterward. Amanda, Mignini declared, told her that she was sick of the criticisms, accused her roommate of being prissy, and said, "You're going to have sex with us." Meredith refused, and the knives came out. Not just the kitchen knife, but also one that Raffaele supposedly brought with him. Rudy sexually violated her, and then Amanda slashed her throat, assisted in some way by Raffaele.

For the prosecution, the problem with this story was that after 8:45 P.M., it was pure invention. Mignini didn't pretend otherwise. "We can hypothesize," the prosecutor liked to say. "We can imagine. We can make the supposition that . . ." etc.

Now Robyn had accidently undermined his case, by saying Meredith had been too classy and reserved to discuss her issues with Amanda directly, who could hardly be expected then to kill her over them, if she wasn't aware of Meredith's complaints in the first place.

So Mignini switched gears. Although all four flatmates were sexually active and smoked marijuana, he now portrayed Amanda as the depraved girl in an otherwise conventlike household who had exposed her British roommate to sexually explicit materials. The shocking news was that Amanda had kept a clear plastic bag on the floor under the sink (since there was no other place to store it in the tiny room), filled with her own personal toiletries. Some of the investigators had evidently poked through it after Amanda's arrest, and Meredith had once shown it to Robyn.

"What were the contents?" Mignini asked her.

"Meredith pointed out a beauty case with condoms and I think a *vibrator*," Robyn said as she described visiting the cottage for what seemed to be the only time. Amanda was out that day; in fact, she and Robyn had scarcely ever been in the same room.

So why were the two British girls checking out Amanda's toiletries, stored in a clear plastic bag in the American's own bathroom? Robyn didn't want to explain.

"Did you see the condoms? Did you see the vibrator?" Mignini kept pressuring her.

"I did not look inside the bag," Robyn finally said, adding that she was only in the bathroom to brush her hair. While bent over this task, she spotted the bag on the floor, after Meredith had showed it to her.

No, she finally admitted, she could not see the objects inside. Nor did Mignini explain why seeing a condom would shock anyone since condoms with devilish names were displayed in Italian drugstores and could be purchased on street corner machines, even right across from the University for Foreigners.

Nevertheless, Amanda's condoms and vibrator lit up that day's coverage. Mignini had a genius for inserting these spicy nuggets into the morning testimony, ensuring that the sexy stuff would always make it into the newspapers, unlike the later cross-examination by the defense.

Amanda's attorney Luciano Ghirga would criticize several Perugia police officers—referring to them as the "women of the Perugia Flying Squad"—for "clashing" with his client, saying they had disliked Amanda right away because they found condoms and a vibrator while exploring her private beauty case. He said Amanda had "suffered as a result of this antagonism."

Next, Mignini asked Robyn about Halloween, that last dinner party with Meredith, and the night at the *questura* when Amanda had upset the English girls by not crying when they cried, responding stiffly to Sophie Purton's hug, talking loudly to her Seattle friends on the phone and, well, being insensitive to the needs of others.

"Why did you tell police that Amanda was proud of finding the body?" Mignini asked.

"Because she kept saying, 'I found her. I found her, and it could have been me.'"

"You told British authorities that Amanda was proud of finding the body?"

"Yes, that was the absolute truth, because I thought that she was proud."

To many reporters, the British girls' testimony sounded numbingly rehearsed. Somehow every girl, while emotionally distraught, had heard Amanda make the same remarks in the *questura*, no matter where she was sitting or at what time. They had all listened in on her private phone calls. They had all watched her interact with her boyfriend. As Frank Sfarzo wrote on Perugia Shock:

> The versions the English girls provided were almost identical and perfectly coherent to each other, just if they were one person. Many elements were passed from one of them to the others, but at the police station they were all common eyewitnesses of what was going on, even if someone heard something the others couldn't hear. The only notable difference, for what it may count, was that for some of them Amanda referred to having seen the blood and then taking the shower, for others of them it was the opposite.

Not all of the girls ripped into Amanda, however. Helen Powell said she thought the American was just upset and "trying to put a good face on things." Jade Bidwell and Samantha Rodenhurst admitted that they hadn't cried either. They'd all felt terribly sad and upset, of course, but tears hadn't flowed. Some girls had hugged Meredith's other roommates, Laura

Mezzetti and Filomena Romanelli, but nobody saw them sobbing either.

Jade Bidwell said the American girl wasn't the only person saying strange things that night.

"Amanda said she was in the wardrobe, but somebody else said Meredith was on the bed or on the floor, so everybody had their own version."

In any case, Rudy came off worst in all of this because none of the girls had seen him talking to Meredith on Halloween, as he'd claimed, nor had she ever mentioned him. They actually helped Amanda a bit, because it turned out the details she'd given them about the murder were wrong, therefore she didn't know things "only the killer would know." During all this testimony, Amanda sat quietly, rubbing her eyes, looking tired. When it was finally over, she rose slowly from her chair. She smiled and fidgeted. The vibrator was just a toy, she finally said, a little pink rabbit. A gag gift that a friend had given her before she left for Europe. She spread her fingers about an inch apart, demonstrating how small it was.

"Why I had Rabbit Toy at Murder House" was one of many headlines sparked by this revelation. Which was a pity because a brokenhearted Sophie Purton spoke beautifully about her friend Meredith, and so did the other girls. They all sat with their parents in the courtroom afterward. Sophie cried. Robyn was visibly shaking.

For Mignini, though, it had all been a triumph. He would continue to argue that Amanda had killed Meredith over the complaints, even though his own witness, Robyn, had said Meredith never shared her complaints with Amanda.

After court, Curt Knox, Amanda's father, spoke to reporters, making his usual attempt at damage control. "You have seven young ladies and it appears they have amazingly consistent points of view," he said. "They made virtually the same set of comments. That raises a question."

As for Amanda's behavior at the *questura*: "She was the only person who spoke English, so she was asked to speak to others who spoke English. Furthermore, everybody reacts differently to stress. You go through many different moods when something terrible happens. Anger, sadness, even giddiness.

"Amanda had been dealing with the death for many hours when she met the English girls. She had been thrown out of her home. She had nowhere to live. Was her behavior right for her? Probably yes. Was it right for the people around her? Maybe not."

THE next day in court, Amanda created a spectacle by show-ing up casually dressed in jeans and a long white T-shirt with "All You Need Is Love," emblazoned in pink, a tribute to her favorite Beatles song. Although some of the male reporters took this as Amanda flaunting her sexuality, her friend DJ Johnsrud said she was simply reacting to the criticism heaped on her from the day before. She believed in the message of the song and thought that if people would be kind to one another, many problems could be solved.

Laura Mezzetti, one of Amanda's Italian roommates and a newly crowned lawyer herself, smiled and smiled all through her testimony that same morning. One of her roommates had been murdered, the other sat in front of her facing thirty years in prison (life imprisonment in Italy), yet the only time Laura stopped smiling was when Amanda's attorneys asked her questions.

"Amanda will not idolize Laura any more, it seems," Frank Sfarzo said, calling Laura the "Queen of Smiles."

Laura had come with an agenda, too, and it was not a pretty one. She spoke of a mysterious mark on Amanda's neck, which she said she had noticed at the *questura* that first night. The implication was that this mark, clearly visible in photos of Amanda standing with Raffaele outside the cottage right after the body was found, was a cut or bruise sustained during a vicious fight with Meredith. Indeed, in the blogosphere this small red mark had also been noticed, and it had grown larger and larger until it became a gaping sore and "wound."

Laura said she'd noticed the mark only out of concern for her roommate. She'd wanted to make sure Amanda was all right. Yet she had told Mignini about it only recently, in one of her many witness statements. When Amanda's law-yers told her that it was a hickey, a love bite, Laura insisted that, no, it was a scratch. Later, Amanda would testify that it was a hickey and her father would point out that Amanda had been photographed when she was arrested, and the mark had already faded by then.

Laura did help the defense by saying that nobody in the house drank much. They might have a glass of wine at dinner, but that was all. That would prove useful when prosecutor Mignini threw alcohol into the "drug-fueled" mix that had supposedly fed the sex game. Laura also admitted that she smoked hashish at times, as did Meredith and Meredith's boyfriend, Giacomo Silenzi, but none of them appeared to be more than casual users.

Next up were two of the boys from the downstairs apartment—Giacomo and Stefano Bonazzi. The normally deadpan jurors smiled when Giacomo admitted that he'd been growing marijuana in a special locked room. He also testified that Amanda got along just fine with Meredith.

The prosecutor wanted both boys to say that Rudy had a tremendous crush on Amanda, but all he wedged out of them was the "Is she available?" remark he'd made the first time he met her. Rudy, they said, "was a basketball guy, who socialized easily when he was drunk."

That day Raffaele sprang to life, when the court played the recording of his 112 call to the Carabinieri on November 2, 2007. He swiveled around in his chair and smiled at friends, looking proud. As his lawyers pointed out, his voice was loud and clear in the recording, as if he weren't concerned about the Postal Police overhearing him make the call. As if, in other words, the Postal Police weren't there yet.

At the end of the day, Amanda again exercised her right under the law to speak, which she did in Italian, as always. She said she was saddened to hear about the complaints from her roommates after all this time. "This business of the cleaning was extremely exaggerated," she said, and "I always had good relationships with those girls. It really wasn't like that."

NOW began a long parade of police officers, describing the investigation. More days were also devoted to the Postal Police controversy, not to mention blood spatters, fingerprints, and DNA, with no one agreeing on anything. And it all awaited a re-airing when the defense took the stand. As for Amanda's interrogation, each officer said that she had been treated perfectly, given every legal right, offered espresso and brioche. And, anyway, look how the girl acts . . . the cartwheels, the disrespect . . .

"There are no words anymore for describing this unbelievable character of our time," wrote Frank Sfarzo on Perugia Shock. "Actress, lovebird, bad girl, and now even dancer and gymnast at the police station." In fact, the cartwheels came up so often that he did an inventory:

NAPOLEONI: Amanda was doing cartwheels and splits.
ZUGARINI: Amanda was doing the cartwheel.
FICARRA: I came out of the elevator and I saw Amanda doing the cartwheel and the splits.

When Amanda's team protested that she'd done only yoga poses, the officers took offense. As Frank Sfarzo wrote:

"I can tell the difference between yoga and dancing," the policewoman reacts. "I've seen her doing a real cartwheel, turning upside down on her hands and then landing on her feet. In another moment I saw her doing a split. All my colleagues have seen it. Why should we lie about that? You just look at the way she acts in the courtroom . . ."

Actually, as he pointed out, Amanda didn't do anything strange in the courtroom, "except maybe the time of the T-shirt, a really unforgivable eccentricity. Anyway, clearly we have a sporty girl and a free spirit, now let's go back to the case."

After days and days of police testimony about her interrogation, Amanda finally rose to protest.

"I just wanted to insist that witnesses are not saying the truth about the night between the 5th and 6th of November. I wanted to clarify some events that for me are very important. There are hours and hours . . . before Raffaele ever said that I wasn't with him. They were very, very aggressive on this story of the messages. They called me a liar. . . . Then there are these *scappellotti* [little slaps] that I really received on my head."

Raffaele, too, got up to protest that things hadn't been handled as they were being described.

"I just wish to respond to what I've heard today, that I stayed a very short time barefoot at the police station and that I was asked if I wanted to call a lawyer—that is absolutely not true. I couldn't call a lawyer and not even my father."

THE prosecution brought in a long string of witnesses, with mixed success.

Nara Capezzali, the witness who'd heard the scream on the night Meredith was murdered, got confused toward the end of her testimony and couldn't be sure if she'd heard the scream that night or the day before.

Curatolo (aka "Toto"), the homeless man who'd testified at the pretrial that he'd seen Amanda and Raffaele on the basketball court in Piazza Grimana on November 1, casing out the cottage, also became confused. When he'd first told his story to investigators, he'd appeared to be describing Halloween night since he remembered masks and witches. But under skillful guidance, he'd settled firmly on November 1. The problem for this witness was that now he was a little too firm about having seen Raffaele and Amanda on the fateful night. Now he thought he'd seen them casing the house all evening—up to 11 P.M.—giving the two students alibis, as the press was quick to point out.

For this reason, Mignini had to move the time of death to 11:30 in his closing arguments, even though the coroner had said that Meredith had died within two or three hours of her last meal, which had been around 6:30 P.M.

Then there was the infamous Albanian witness who'd claimed he'd had an altercation with all three suspects the night before the crime. Not only was he arrested for possessing cocaine shortly before his court appearance, but his testimony was so riddled with falsehoods that it evoked laughter. He claimed that Amanda had an Italian uncle and that he'd met the two suspects in August, before they'd even met each other. He also said that Amanda had large gaps in her teeth. In the end he came across as delusional.

Another witness who claimed that he'd seen all three defendants coming out of the cottage with Meredith on October 30 looked foolish when Raffaele proved he was at a party near that time. The witness had insisted that Amanda wore a red coat, although she didn't own one. Likewise, a storeowner who testified that Amanda had come into his Conad store the day after the murder and hovered near the cleaning supplies was contradicted by his own employees, who saw no such thing.

Meanwhile Coroner Luca Lalli had come into the courtroom to present his original findings, saying that he had not been able to prove whether the victim was sexually violated, nor had he ever asserted that she'd died a long, lingering death. Instead, he said, the victim had probably died within ten minutes of that last, terrible blow, a crucial point in establishing alibis for the defendants.

However, Lalli's testimony went virtually unreported. DNA was the real star of the show, as it was on *CSI*, and there the prosecutors shone, if only in terms of presentation. They'd boasted of "unassailable evidence," while managing not to reveal, for many months, exactly how Patrizia Stefanoni, who'd handled all of the DNA, had conducted her tests in the (unaccredited) Rome crime lab.

The kitchen knife would prove to be most controversial for the way the DNA results on the blade had been analyzed and reported by Dr. Stefanoni. The knife blade sample that showed the DNA of Meredith Kercher was a LCN (low copy number) DNA sample (now also referred to as LC-DNA or low template DNA) and may have yielded results not relevant to the case. It's possible for scientists to extract a DNA profile from minute bits of matter, even from a few cells, but following more cautious data interpretation rules, low copy samples should be run several times for a consensus profile to develop. A very sterile environment is necessary, as the chances for contamination are higher in low copy work.

But while the Rome lab had processed abundant DNA from Meredith Kercher, Stefanoni hadn't even been able to get enough DNA from the blade for a second test, having used up part of the sample in running a test that actually gave a negative result for blood. Also, as was revealed much later, the machine she had used to detect Meredith's DNA had repeatedly warned her that the sample readings were "too low," yet she'd plunged ahead regardless. The Rome police forensic lab also did not provide complete information to the defense on the testing.

In the end, Mignini and Comodi put on a largely circumstantial case built around the eccentricities of one defendant, Amanda Knox. As Frank Sfarzo pointed out, "There was no end to the crazy things the Seattle actress, gymnast, bad-girl and comedian allegedly did in those days after the crime," but that wasn't the same as evidence.

Reporters were still waiting for the smoking gun.

CHAPTER NINETEEN

THE DEFENSE SPEAKS

June–November 2009

"You keep a girl of twenty up all night without a lawyer and take advantage of her naiveté and you can get her to tell the Patrick story."

—Giulia Bongiorno, attorney for Raffaele Sollecito

"I read, study, write, paint, and play soccer. But there is no entertainment that can bring peace. In this nightmarish situation you find yourself in pitch-black darkness and the only light that gives you hope of moving forward is your consciousness, which seeks the help of God."

—Raffaele Sollecito, from a letter to an Italian journalist

IF accused murderer Amanda Knox testified in court, would anybody believe a word she said? That was the question her defense team faced in early June 2009 after the prosecution finally rested. Amanda had been devastated when Judge Paolo Micheli had ended the pretrial by charging her and Raffaele Sollecito with murder and sexual assault. A few days later, Micheli had delivered another stinging blow. He denied them house arrest, a right he'd freely granted to other murder suspects. Amanda and Raffaele were too dangerous, Judge Micheli said, they were "ready to kill again."

"We are not like that," Amanda had protested. She'd thought things were looking better. The court had finally accepted that when she told her parents "I was there," she meant "I was at Raffaele's when Meredith's throat was slit." The prosecution had stopped forgetting that she'd said, "good evening," after "see you later." Rudy had told Mignini in May that he'd made the bloody shoe print by the bed. Police had admitted that Amanda had never called, e-mailed, or been over to Rudy's place.

She'd listened to her defense team tear into the prosecution's scientific witnesses and rejoiced when they exposed the Albanian "super-witness" as a liar and a clown. Except for that one day of rebellion, when she'd worn the Beatles T-shirt, she'd done her best to act appropriately in court. She stood up every time the judge and jurors entered the room, nodding at every single one of them, even though they never looked her in the eyes or in any way acknowledged her.

Yet here she was still in a prison cell, unable to escape the constant noise or the horror of being locked in. She did her best to establish a healthy routine. She wrote poetry, read books, and tried to avoid news reports on TV. She kept up her guitar lessons, took specially designed UW correspondence courses, and studied Chinese and German. She counted the days between family visits, which took place twice a week. She waited for the ten-minute phone call that she was allowed to make to the Mellas home in Seattle each week. Her college friends stayed overnight at her mother's house, so they could speak with her during that precious time. She'd written a mountain of letters, more than six hundred since her imprisonment, managing not to release a single detail that could be spun against her. The girl who'd once told the world everything had learned how to mask her thoughts.

But Amanda was lonely. Though she now had three cellmates, none wanted to talk to her, she confided to her mother, because they'd read in an Italian magazine that she complained about them. All she'd said was that they were "awesome," a typical American expression taken as an insult. The girl whom the prison guards had taken to calling "Bambi" couldn't seem to say anything right.

In fact, prosecutor Giuliano Mignini had put Amanda under investigation for slander after she'd stood up in court to directly contradict the account Monica Napoleoni and other officers gave of the bed-and-breakfast treatment they claimed to have shown her at the *questura*. Meanwhile, a parallel investigation into whether police actually did hit her was going nowhere. And Mignini would wait until Amanda's parents showed up for closing arguments to smack them with a defamation suit as well, because they'd told the *Times* of London that Amanda said she was hit.

Now their daughter had a decision to make. Should she follow Raffaele's lead and remain silent? Or should she speak out? Her lawyers and family members encouraged her to take the stand, believing she'd be her own best witness. They said she would have the chance to tell her story to a worldwide audience, because her testimony would be videotaped and posted on the Web in perpetuity. So her answer was yes. Then she decided to tell her tale in Italian, because she'd suffered from clumsy translations, most spectacularly with the transformation of Foxy Knoxy into "Evil Fox" and "Okay see you later good evening!" into "See you really soon."

AMANDA Knox took the stand on June 12, 2009, a balmy summer day in Perugia. All around the Palace of Justice, the media had set up radio vans. Photographers huddled by the front door, lined up in the hallways, spilled down the dusty staircases, and stood on plastic chairs in the frescoed courtroom, making sure they got the best camera angles for the big event. As usual, many journalists showed up an hour early, leaned across the wooden rails, and talked to the family members and lawyers. Even prosecutor Giuliano Mignini had started coming out to talk to reporters during the breaks.

"Amanda's not going to change up there on the stand," her aunt Christina Hagge told journalists right before Amanda's testimony started. "She likes her personality. She doesn't feel she has to change herself and become a different person in court."

Several days before this court appearance, Christina had visited Amanda in jail and marveled at her self-control. "I thought I was going to see her fall apart when I said good-bye to her, but I felt good about it. She seemed very confident."

After a rocky beginning, the Knox family had learned how to handle the press, mainly by making themselves accessible and freely giving out quotes. Curt Knox in particular felt it was important to have somebody in court each day to combat whatever negative talking point the prosecution was putting out. And Italians noticed that the Knoxes never missed a visitor's day at Capanne and never left Amanda alone in court. They found that touching—and only right—no matter what their daughter may have done.

"We sent our daughter to study abroad. And now we're trying to bring her home. That's all we care about," Curt would tell the press. He'd traveled six thousand miles simply to hear Amanda testify, as had his wife, Cassandra, a pleasant-faced blond woman with blue eyes who reeled at the media onslaught, a new experience for her.

"I'm just going to stay as close to my husband as I can and help out wherever I can," she said, adding that their two young daughters had trouble with the long separations from their father. He was one of the family members who rotated in and out of Italy for a month at a time. Amanda's relatives took turns living in a drab apartment outside Perugia so that Amanda would never be alone. It wasn't easy, dealing with the enormous legal bills that now plagued them, which they estimated at $1 million and climbing. They had mortgaged both their houses to pay for Amanda's defense, but Cassandra said it was a team effort.

"My girls are Amanda's sisters. We're doing this for her and they know that. They are very close and always have been. The family's goal is to prop up Amanda, to keep her optimistic."

Although Giuliano Mignini referred to the Knoxes as a "clan," Curt said he wasn't interested in carrying out a vendetta. "If Amanda can get her story across this time, then things will look up for her. If people can just go by what they hear in the courtroom and not by what they get elsewhere, then she has a chance at freedom."

Although nobody knew what judges or jurors were thinking, Curt insisted that the defense was in a good position. They'd knocked down "a lot of evidence" on cross-examination, even though the newspapers had not reported it. Instead, their stories had focused on Amanda's looks and behavior, Curt complained, calling her "gleeful in court" if she smiled during those few minutes when she was allowed to greet her family. And in his opinion, the prosecution's reliance on "character assassination" showed how weak the case was. He noted that not a single expert had ever been able to place Amanda in the murder room.

"No DNA, no blood, no skin cells of any type in the room where the murder occurred. Tell me how that's possible. You can't clean up just your own evidence. It just can't be done."

Raffaele's father, Francesco Sollecito, also came to court nearly every day, often accompanied by the most charismatic of the lawyers, Giulia Bongiorno, a member of Parliament whose frenetic speech and constantly waving hands had a calming effect on the shy Raffaele. Like Amanda, she was the bubbly type.

THE now twenty-two-year-old Amanda had learned how to cut a *bella figura*. In fact, Meo Ponte, a well-known Italian reporter, sometimes referred to as "Amanda's third lawyer," would begin his coverage of her testimony with a fashion review: "White blouse, beige trousers, flat shoes, a blue ribbon tied charmingly around her blond pony tail. Amanda Knox comes dressed as a graduate student, for what surely is the most awaited hearing in the trial."

Ponte also reported that Amanda had put on a little weight, unlike Raffaele, implying that she was the stronger of the two, able even to thrive on prison grub.

Amanda faced an intimidating group of questioners, two judges, two prosecutors, Patrick Lumumba's bulldog lawyer, as well as the Kercher lawyers. In the stands were Monica Napoleoni, Rita Ficarra, and other officers who'd orchestrated her lawyer-free, all-night interrogation. These officers came in and out continuously during Amanda's entire testimony, opening and closing the bronze door, sitting at a table near the door, whispering to one another, making angry gestures. The brown-haired Ficarra was the angriest, frowning and muttering under her breath when Amanda described being hit at the *questura*.

Judge Massei seemed to tip his hand toward the prosecution by announcing that Patrick Lumumba's very intimidating lawyer, Carlo Pacelli, would go first; a decision that caused a lot of chatter among the journalists. Pacelli, a beefy man with thick glasses and a tendency to smirk, had made no bones about detesting Amanda. As he stood outside the courthouse each day, talking to the media on the steps, he was more than happy to portray her as a promiscuous young woman who enjoyed telling lies.

Amanda faced Pacelli at a two-person podium, with an interpreter sitting next to her. She looked both tense and self-confident, like a college student prepped for finals. Although well groomed, she did have dark circles under her eyes and a cold sore on her lip. The reporters focused on the blemish, which they took as a sign of her indulgence in sex.

Pacelli smiled and wished *la signorina* Knox a good morning. He first questioned her about whether she'd known Rudy, and Amanda replied "vaguely," then told the now familiar story of how she'd been strolling in the old town when she saw Rudy with the boys from the downstairs flat. They all walked back to the cottage together. She spent most of that night with Meredith, but they were in the downstairs flat at some point.

"Was that the only time you saw Rudy?"

"I think he might have come into Le Chic one time," she said indifferently. Pacelli then switched to the night when she named Patrick, demanding to know why she did that. Unflappable, she simply took this as her cue to tell her story.

"When I went to the *questura* that night, I didn't expect to be questioned," she said, beginning in English, but "after a while they took me into another interrogation room." She described the lengthy and intimidating questioning.

"*Mama mia,*" she said later, when she switched into Italian. Then she demonstrated the raps she'd gotten on the back of the head. Who had done this to her? An officer with "long chestnut hair."

Amanda spoke for five hours, without tears or drama. But was she telling the truth? As Meo Ponte pointed out, that depended upon whether you thought she was innocent, like her father ("I have never been more proud of her") or whether you were her former roommate Filomena Romanelli, sitting unrecognized in the front row. She told Meo, "She's inconsistent; she continues to change her story; that is not how it went."

Meo Ponte also pointed out, however, that the same story Amanda told in court could be found in a letter she sent to her lawyer Luciano Ghirga on November 9, 2007. A letter whose existence was a surprise to many reporters. Even more than Amanda's testimony, it filled in the dead air between 10:30 P.M. on November 5, 2007—when the Seattle girl was just a twenty-year-old college student doing her Italian language homework—to 5:45 A.M. on November 6, when she was a murder suspect carted off to prison with her alleged accomplice Raffaele and Patrick Lumumba.

"They told me that they had already arrested the murderer," Amanda wrote in English, "and that they only wanted me to say his name, but I knew nothing. An officer hit me twice in the head. My mind was searching for answers. I was really confused. I thought that I'd been at home with my boyfriend, but what if that wasn't true. I tried and tried but I could not remember anything until all of the officers had left the room except one. She told me there was only one means of avoiding spending the next thirty years in jail. . . . I imagined that I'd met Patrick near the basketball courts. I imagined that I must have covered my ears so I wouldn't hear the screams of Meredith and I named Patrick and I totally regret it now because I know that what I said has hurt him."

As Douglas Preston commented later in the *Observer*, her original statements were written in Italian police parlance. "There was no way that an American girl who'd been in Italy less than two months could possibly understand them." He contended that Italian interrogators were extremely skilled, trained to deal with the Mafia, and a young foreign girl would be helpless against them.

Amanda took the stand again the next day, facing down prosecutors Mignini and Comodi. Again, she managed to get through without breaking down. She did seem to forget one phone call that she made to her mother on November 2, 2007, right before Meredith's body was uncovered. The prosecution made much of this nonexistent phone call, despite the long parade of police officers who hadn't been able to remember what time they'd gotten to the cottage that same day, who'd kept insisting that they hadn't looked at their watches or logged down the time and therefore couldn't be expected to be exact. Lawyers also questioned why Amanda had called her mother at such an early hour in Seattle. Why wake somebody up at 4 A.M. for a few drops of blood, if you didn't know that there'd been a murder? "Because I was worried," Amanda said. Conversely, she was also criticized for not having reacted quickly enough, for callously blow-drying her hair after seeing blood on the floor.

The next week Amanda's mother, Edda Mellas, took the stand, and Patrick's lawyer grilled her about the early calls. "She's my daughter," Edda explained. "Of course I want her to call me in time of trouble. She can call me anytime." Pacelli also questioned her about her first visit with Amanda on November 10. Why didn't she tell the world that her daughter thought Patrick was innocent? Edda shook her head, looking bewildered. She'd been in a foreign country, trying to deal with a daughter who'd been thrown in prison.

"I don't speak Italian," she finally said.

After this testimony, Pacelli picked up his big black briefcase and stormed out of court.

Andrew Seliber, who called himself Amanda's "best friend," also testified on her behalf, having paid his own way from Seattle for this purpose.

"Can you tell us about Amanda's sex life in Seattle?" asked Francesco Maresca, the lawyer for the Kerchers.

"No."

Maresca then introduced into the court record, as a sign of Amanda's debauchery, the noise violation ticket she'd gotten for hosting a loud going-away party in Seattle. Surprisingly, Judge Massei even allowed Maresca to introduce into evidence a baseless story that had run in the *Daily Mail* that erroneously described the party as a street riot and portrayed Amanda as a girl gone wild.

The defense objected strenuously. While lawyers yelled all around him, Andrew waited patiently and then explained that the citation was similar to a traffic ticket and, in fact, logged on the same form. It was just a party, the leaf-thin Andrew said gently. A college party. He explained he'd been at fault because he and his band had performed at the house. Amanda had gone to the door when the police arrived because she was the most sober person there.

THE *Daily Mail* provided a rare moment of unconscious humor when the notorious tabloid shamelessly took Amanda's younger sister, Deanna Knox, to task for wearing a shorts-and-T-shirt ensemble in the colors of the American flag on the Fourth of July. She'd just been trying to cheer Amanda up, Deanna said. And it wasn't like anyone was going to let Amanda out to celebrate American's liberation from the British, never more desirable than when the *Daily Mail* went after a family member. The tabloid had managed to steeplechase over the competition when it came to raunchy stories about the Kercher case, including:

> "Meredith: Two Month Relationship with 'Secret Boy-friend' "
> "Strands of Hair in Hands of Murdered Meredith 'Could Belong to Her Killer' "
> "Amanda Knox: Behind the Hollywood Smile, a Liar, a Narcissist, and a Killer"
> "The Wild, Raunchy Past of Foxy Knoxy"
> "Flatmate: Inside the Twisted World of Flatmate Suspected of Meredith's Murder"
> " 'I'm Confused About Who Cut Meredith's Throat,' Says Foxy Knoxy in New Plea"

The *Daily Mail* also scolded Deanna and her sister Ashley in the same melodramatic story—"Revealed: Foxy Knoxy's sisters posing happily for 'macabre' photos in house where Kercher died"—for posing in front of the house of horrors, again in shorts, for the far more respectable *Gente*, the Italian version of *People* magazine. Far from looking happy, the girls appeared tense and miserable in the photos, their arms wound around each other for comfort. Moreover, the *Daily Mail* hadn't been shocked when the jurors in the Kercher case had smiled and chatted on the very threshold of the house of horrors during an official visit on April 18, 2009. The jurors weren't just standing on the road, like the Knox girls, but actually preparing to go inside and see the room where Meredith's throat was cut.

Police had done a poor job of safeguarding the premises during the two years that the cottage had been roped off as a crime scene. In fact, that year vandals had burglarized it several times, each time breaching the windows. And as if to taunt a prosecutor known for his satanic murder theories, the intruders had created a sort of shrine in one room, lighting candles and arranging knives all around to suggest some sort of occult ritual. On the most recent visit, the intruders had even stolen Meredith Kercher's mattress, the one on which her purse had rested on the night of the crime.

On August 27, 2009, the court unsealed the house of horrors. It was no longer a crime scene. The owner installed new locks on every door, put grilles over the windows, and renovated it from top to bottom. In the fall, she would rent it out to a new batch of foreigners.

LIKE the prosecution, the defense presented many experts, but without the timing and stagecraft for which Mignini was known. As one family member said, they had to present experts when they were available, not when it made thematic sense. Some hearings were jammed, such as those featuring the famous forensics expert Carlo Torre and Dr. Sarah Gino, a DNA expert who annoyed prosecutor Manuela Comodi by attacking the scanty DNA samples used to implicate the suspects. Other hearings were nearly empty.

And the jurors openly suffered from what journalists call MEGO (My Eyes Glaze Over). One gray-haired juror, wearing an Italian tricolor sash, napped through many afternoons. Prosecutor Mignini also slumbered occasionally, although his abuse of office trial in Florence had wrapped and he was now awaiting the verdict. It kept getting pushed back.

The jurors did seem to enjoy anyone who came with exhibits, such as the distinguished forensics expert Francesco Intorno, who brought in a blond mannequin's head into which he inserted a Swiss knife, to demonstrate that the kitchen knife was too large to be the murder weapon. He believed that Meredith died around 9:30 P.M. As Frank Sfarzo described Intorno's theory of the crime:

> A hostile presence in the house, a lonely presence. Meredith is naked from the waist down. He reaches her at the end of her room, he grabs her from behind. He lifts the T-shirt she wears. Then he blocks her mouth and nose. A gesture that wants to mean "don't worry, do what I want and I won't do anything to you." He grabs her bra and cuts it off with a knife. He pushes her down on her knees in order to rape her. But here something happens. And the will of possession becomes the will of killing. Staying still behind her he puts the blade on her face. Then he grabs her at the jaw and he sticks the blade completely into her throat. One time and a second time right after. Meredith falls over on her back. He gets on top of her. While she lies bleeding and trying to breathe, he takes her bra away. She will bleed to death in 10 minutes, suffocated by her own blood.

Although this scenario was certainly a common one, when Intorno brought in two women to act out the murder, a juror to the left of the judge burst out laughing.

The famous forensic expert Carlo Torre, a professorial type with unruly silver hair, also testified for Amanda's team. He scoffed at the two knife theory, saying it would be the first time in history that a murder was carried out that way. He used a Styrofoam head to demonstrate that the kitchen knife was too large to have made the two smaller wounds.

"Everything leads me to believe that it is not the murder weapon," he said.

Raffaele's team, meanwhile, tried to shore up his computer alibi, with assistance from Raffaele himself, who followed the court case carefully. His team also went after Rudy Guede as the lone killer, while the prosecution, now that he was safely serving a life sentence, all of a sudden made him sound like a mere spectator.

Raffaele's team did all they could to show that Rudy had a criminal past. They brought in witnesses who described his arrest in the nursery school in Milan and the alleged second-story window break-in at a lawyer's office in Perugia. They also had a deposition from a bartender at Merlin's who claimed Rudy Guede had climbed through the window of his apartment one night, armed with a knife, and stole credit cards and cash before the bartender chased him out the front door.

The defense never let the jurors forget Rudy's modus operandi. It was a textbook reflection of the Kercher case they claimed: He entered though windows. He carried a knife. He allegedly stole cell phones.

The problem for the defense, which had managed to get Rudy's alibi testimony kept out of court, was that the prosecution suddenly benefited from a judicial sleight of hand. Rudy Guede's appeal was supposed to begin in November and last only a few days, since he had chosen the fast-track (abbreviated) trial. These trials were never open to the public—except in this case. The trial judge granted Rudy's unprecedented permission to let the public and the cameras in, meaning that the unsequestered jury would now hear him claim that Amanda and Merdith fought all the time and that the American girl had been at the crime scene.

But there was cause for hope. Certainly the prosecution would have a hard time hanging the theft charge on the couple, since it turned out neither had been caught with the money. Rudy had been acquitted for a similar reason, even though, as Mignini finally admitted in *Oggi*: "Rudy rummaged through the purse. But Judge Paolo Micheli has absolved him of theft."

But the greatest drama circled around the DNA on the bra clasp and the knife. When Patrizia Stefanoni, the previously unflappable scientist who'd performed the DNA test, couldn't say exactly how much DNA she'd found on either item, the judge closed down the the proceedings. He ordered that she produce all of the paperwork concerning the DNA results to the defense by July. Then the court went into recess until September.

* * *

WHEN the trial resumed in the fall, Manuela Comodi brought in the knife that had been taken from Raffaele's kitchen, the one with the disputed DNA evidence on it. The defense experts hadn't even been allowed to handle it, only look at the knife from afar. It arrived with its own armed guard, wrapped in plastic like a rose and displayed in a cardboard pizzalike box stamped "Handle With Care" in English. But, the defense claimed, the proper paperwork still hadn't materialized.

The defense side nearly ended in triumph when it brought in the three neutral witnesses that Judge Claudia Matteini had chosen long ago to take a second look at the Lalli autopsy report. They agreed with Lalli's conclusions, it turned out. They were not able to prove that the victim was raped, nor did they see signs of a group attack. Nor did they contend that she died a long, lingering death (which would have been useful for the prosecution because it would have meant that alibis had to be lengthened). In fact they said that Meredith had probably died within ten minutes of the attack—and judging by the mysterious cell phone call to her bank, they would place the time of the attack at around 10 P.M., or, going by her stomach contents, they could conclude that it happened before 11 P.M.

The defense then asked Judge Massei to appoint neutral experts, common in Italian trials, to look at the disputed evidence, including Raffaele's computer and the DNA.

In another ongoing murder trial at the same time, Alberto Stasi, accused of murdering his girlfriend Chiara Poggi in a sensational case, had been saved at the last minute from sure defeat by a judge who said he didn't buy the computer and footprint evidence.

Like Giuliano Mignini, the prosecutor in that case had based his argument on a quarrel which no one else had witnessed. Stasi had been looking at pornography on his computer, the prosecutor declared, and Poggi had caught him at it and threatened to expose him.

The judge scoffed. "Pure invention," he said. Then he set Stasi free.

In contrast, on October 9, 2009, Judge Massei delivered a hard blow to Amanda and Raffaele. He refused to appoint neutral experts to view any of the evidence. "We have all the evidence we need," he said, even though the only expert who had ever reviewed Stefanoni's use of low copy DNA was her own boss, called to court during the pretrial to say that everything was perfect.

Amanda put her head down when she heard this news; Raffaele appeared shaken. The defense teams tried, in vain, to spin this refusal as a positive development. The neutral experts had now testified, the defense lawyers reminded the press, the ones appointed by Judge Matteini. And they'd cast doubt on the six-and-a-half-inch kitchen knife supposedly used to murder Meredith. Forensic expert Mariano Cingolani said it was too large to have caused one of the smaller wounds, and that many knives were more "compatible with that kind of wound."

So there was hope. Soon an international group of top-flight scientists would meet in Las Vegas and devote an entire session to the use of controversial DNA on the knife and bra clasp in the Kercher murder case. Later, after several scientists reviewed the procedures used to identify the DNA, they drafted a letter of concern and released it to the media on November 19, 2009. It was signed by two very well-respected scientists: Elizabeth A. Johnson, Ph.D., and Greg Hampikian, Ph.D., from the Idaho Innocence Project.

The DNA on the knife, they pointed out, had tested negatively for blood. Amanda's DNA on the handle was of no consequence, because she cooked in Raffaele's kitchen. Since the knife was tested in a lab where numerous samples of Meredith's DNA had been taken, "There exists the real possibility that the low-level partial profile attributed to the knife blade is a result of unintended transfer in the laboratory during sample handling." In short, they said that no "credible scientific evidence" had been presented to link the knife to Meredith's murder.

Then the same scientists looked at the bra clasp. They noted that it had been found under a "disheveled" rug, forty-seven days after the murder, not in its original place under the victim. They pointed out that no DNA of Raffaele's appeared on the actual bra (which did bear traces of Rudy Guede's). Moreover, there was no way to date the DNA, and since Raffaele was a visitor to the house, he could have left his traces from before the crime; there was no way to tell.

Their deduction: "the DNA testing results described above could have been obtained even if no crime had occurred. As such, they do not constitute credible evidence that linked Amanda Knox and Raffaele Sollecito to the murder of Meredith Kercher."

CHAPTER TWENTY

CLOSING ARGUMENTS AND VERDICT

A VERY PUBLIC STONING

November 20–December 4, 2009

"The lack of evidence is both compelling and profound."
　　　—Criminal lawyer Theodore Simon, on *Good Morning America*

"Amanda is the *'Amélie'* of Seattle, a girl who looks at people through the eyes of a child, bursting with energy and has a spontaneous, reckless approach to life."

　　　　　—Giulia Bongiorno, attorney for Raffaele Sollecito

CLOSING arguments in the Hall of Frescoes had a grandeur that the rest of the trial had lacked, for all its Kafkaesque turns and twists. After eleven months and 140 witnesses, it all came down to this. Daily hearings at last, from November 20 to December 4, skipping only one Sunday. After which Judge Giancarlo Massei would come out of his chambers, face the defendants, and read the verdict. Judgment day seemed very real, everything racing swiftly toward the final words.

Had police officers really come to court to complain about Amanda's splits and cartwheels? Did she really wear the "All You Need Is Love" T-shirt on Valentine's Day? All that seemed long ago and far away, like the time that prosecutor Manuela Comodi couldn't get a crime scene video to run on her laptop. Murder suspect Raffaele had jumped up to help her, even though she was trying to convince the jurors that forensic police had carefully handled the bra clasp that allegedly tied him to the crime.

In the courtroom now, even a moment like that seemed

impossibly playful. The mood was somber, as judges and jurors faced the grand finale.

Amanda often showed up in a light pink cardigan with a Beatles insignia on the back, but her smiles came less frequently and she often turned her face to the side to hide tears. Raffaele looked paler and thinner by the day. Their relatives weren't allowed to speak to them, but they were never alone in court. Amanda's relatives had arrived en masse: Edda and Chris Mellas, Curt and Cassandra Knox, aunt Christina, and sister Deanna. Her two younger sisters, Delaney and Ashley, were too young to get into the hearings, but were permitted to wait in an antechamber behind the big bronze doors to the left of the room, where they could shout out greetings to Amanda as the guards escorted her in and out. Raffaele Sollecito's sister Vanessa, father Francesco, and stepmother Mara also came to court. Reporters knew the names and faces of all the relatives by now. In fact the whole courtroom was like a big dysfunctional family, brought together for the finish.

Amanda's family had bought her a plane ticket to Seattle, hoping she'd get to use it, a move that certain members of the Fourth Estate found presumptuous. Raffaele's family scarcely needed such elaborate plans, but they also dreamed of taking him home. Often Vanessa and Francesco would sit in the row behind him, peeking at him over their computers, hoping they could at least look him in the eyes when he turned around. Now and then he would turn to look at Amanda or smile at the Knoxes. His stepmother, Mara, came less frequently, and when she did, she seemed agitated, unable to listen anymore, reluctant to sit down. Vanessa, too, had her difficulties; she said that she was no longer in the Carabinieri because the name Sollecito had won her no friends.

PROSECUTOR Giuliano Mignini's closing argument would be remembered for its brutality. He was the first to speak on November 20, 2009, and he harangued the defendants for eight hours.

Amanda Knox, he kept saying. Amanda Knox! She did everything. Rudy Guede wanted to please Amanda. So did Raffaele Sollecito. They would have done anything for her.

It turned out the prosecutor had not changed his vision of the crime—Meredith was killed while resisting an orgy—since November 2007, even though Coroner Luca Lalli and the three independent, court-appointed experts had all said that they could not prove sexual assault or a group attack. Nor did they buy into the prosecutor's two-knife theory. It wasn't them that Mignini had to convince, though, but the two judges and the jurors.

He told them that Amanda had been in the center when Patrick texted her on November 1 and told her not to come to work. She was maybe looking around for a bit of fun, because Raffaele was busy, having promised to drive Jovanna Popovic to the bus station at midnight. By chance Amanda saw Rudy, on his way to meet Meredith, and Amanda made some kind of appointment with him for later. Then she decided to go see Raffaele, conveniently arriving just in time to speak to Jovanna at 8:45 P.M. Learning that Raffaele no longer needed to drive Jovanna to the station, Amanda convinced him to come with her on the Rudy date—or whatever it was. They headed for Piazza Grimana, where Toto saw them. Finally, Rudy showed up and they all went into the cottage together—Raffaele with some reluctance.

When Amanda let the two men in, Meredith was already there, probably, and a savage quarrel broke out. Maybe over the missing rent money or the toilet flushing or Rudy's presence in the house. Amanda hated Meredith. Probably she had meant to kill her on Halloween, hence the seemingly innocent text messages saying "Do you have a costume?" and "Do you want to meet up later?"

Amanda was tired of the British girl's complaints, Mignini said, his voice rising and falling, becoming thunderous. He claimed that Amanda and the two men were in a drugged-up rage and eager for a four-way sex scene. Only Meredith thought that was a bad idea. Amanda had brought a knife along from Raffaele's apartment, just in case her roommate resisted.

"After a heated discussion the three, under the influence of the drugs, and probably alcohol as well, decided to put into action the plan they'd had to involve her in an extreme sex game," Mignini told the court. He even provided dialogue for Amanda.

You little saint, I'm going to teach you a lesson. You're going to have sex with us.

Mignini described an overwrought Amanda, one who bore little resemblance to the laid-back, neo-hippie from Seattle, a place where people prided themselves on their tolerance and calm.

The three accused killers were like "unleashed furies," Mignini said. Raffaele flashed the small knife; Amanda, the great big one. Raffaele tried to force off Meredith's bra, somehow touching only the tiny metal clasp, while Rudy tried to rape Meredith as she screamed. Amanda slashed her roommate's throat. Then they all fled; Rudy going one way, Raffaele and Amanda the other. Rudy went dancing at the Domus, while the couple waited until they could be sure nobody had called the cops and then they returned to break the window, simulating a robbery, and cleaned up all traces of themselves.

AFTER hours of enduring the prosecutor's wrath, Amanda Knox collapsed in her lawyer's arms and had to be taken out of the courtroom. Frank Sfarzo captured the ordeal on Perugia Shock:

> The voice is harsh, the voice is loud and keeps on accusing her while the thousand eyes study all her reactions, like a guinea pig in a cage. That voice full of hate continues to yell, ruthless, and it seems to convince everybody, it seems to convince those six strangers who stare at her, silent, the jury that will have to decide her life.
>
> If she smiles it's wrong, if she cries it's wrong, if she moves it's wrong, if she's still it's wrong, if she watches it's wrong, if she doesn't watch it's wrong.

When Amanda returned, Mignini continued—and continued. For proof that all of the above had occurred, Mignini cited the broken window, which he insisted was a staging. For proof of that, he made the old claim that a burglar would have to scale twenty feet to get inside (instead of climbing up the little grate below the window or using the planter box near the front door as a ledge). He also claimed that the rock would have to be thrown from a great distance, instead of from the parapet, a claim that Judge Micheli had chided him for in the pretrial.

The next day co-prosecutor Manuela Comodi went over the DNA, with the jurors looking nearly as bored as the reporters. But then Mignini, with his usual sense of timing, sprung the surprise he'd been promising.

The prosecution showed a twenty-five-minute video re-imagining of the crime, using cartoon characters as stand-ins for the three suspects (the three pigs, prosecutor Comodi called them) with the suspects' real faces stuck on the bodies. The video showed Rudy, Raffaele, and Amanda arriving together at the cottage, pictured them teasing and taunting Meredith with the kitchen knife, and ended in a sea of red, when Amanda struck the final blow. Most disturbingly, the film used real crime scene footage and graphic images of Meredith's body to tell the tale, even though reporters had previously been forced to leave the courtroom whenever such images were introduced into court.

The real Amanda turned her head. She could not look at the video.

The film was based on little more than theory, with almost no forensic evidence to support it, but more than one observer said it had a hypnotic effect.

The video was aimed, reporters believed, not at the judges, but at the bored lay jurors, such as the silver-haired man who had continued his habit of sleeping through the defense testimony.

ONCE the prosecutor finished, the civil plaintiffs took their turn. Francesco Maresca, the Kercher lawyer, used his time to contrast the reserved Kerchers with the in-your-face Knoxes, although their situations, and thus tactics, could not have been more different. He called the prosecution case "*logico*" and then hammered Raffaele in particular for inconsistencies in his stories.

Patrick Lumumba's pit bull lawyer Carlo Pacelli, was just as brutal as Mignini. A balding, overweight man, tall and intimidating, he delighted in showing Amanda's "confession," thrown out by the Supreme Court but brought into court via Patrick's civil suit. He kept putting it up on a screen, the key sections outlined with Magic Marker. He yelled at Amanda for several hours, angering many females in the courtroom by calling her a "typical woman": depraved, scheming, murderous. "She lies in a blatant and shameless manner," he said. He claimed that Amanda had named Patrick in her "confession" because she thought his bar was closed that night and he would not have an alibi. He also berated the American girl—who showered and washed her hair far too often for the two judges—for poor hygiene.

For Vanna Ugolini of *Il Messaggero*, that was finally too much. She pointed out that Pacelli had exaggerated when he called Amanda a "shameless liar" and wondered aloud why so many people felt they could pass judgment on private matters unrelated to the crime.

"'In her beauty case she had condoms.' Something that is [hardly] a crime; in fact is in line with Ministry of Health directives. Just as it is not a crime to have romantic or even purely sexual involvements. This doesn't make Amanda an 'explosive mix of sex, drugs, and bad hygiene,' when the 'bad hygiene' the lawyer was probably referring to was her roommates' complaints that Amanda left the bathroom messy."

Ugolini also objected to the stereotypes on which the entire case was framed. "Give me a break," she wrote. "Saint or prostitute, witch or Snow White, Cinderella or stepmother: for women, no third possibility seems to have yet been invented." Where was the in-between? Where was normal life?

NO one could blame jurors for nodding off when Raffaele's lawyer Luca Maori got up to read, and read, and read. He droned on for more than 250 pages of testimony. Even the Italian reporters found his words hard to follow, just a constant drip, drip, drip of convoluted phrases. Rudy Guede was the name most often on Maori's tongue. His presentation came alive only when he played recorded intercepts from the convicted murderer, whose thick Umbrian accent was startling. As other defense lawyers pointed out, Rudy Guede had had knife cuts on his hands, he'd left his DNA inside the victim, on her purse, on her jacket, in the larger bathroom, on the toilet paper, on the floor, everywhere. Yet the prosecution was now presenting him as a mere spectator, yet another pawn in Amanda's game.

Amanda's lawyer Carlo Dalla Vedova complained that the police had questioned his client for more than forty hours before her arrest and said that "since November 6 two years ago, a huge wave, a tsunami, has swept up Amanda Knox, a girl of soap and water," i.e., an innocent. Her other lawyer, Luciano Ghirga, who'd been lackluster in cross-examination, suddenly sparkled. As for the controversial lack of tears, why was only Amanda required to cry publicly? What was wrong with her eating pizza, or kissing her boyfriend? What did any of that have to do with murder?

The fiery Giulia Bongiorno, one of Raffaele's lawyers, mesmerized the courtroom with a spirited, arm-waving defense of both defendants. "I'm here to impress you, not the other lawyers," she told judges and jurors. Clad in a black robe and running shoes, she said Amanda was like the "*Amélie* of Seattle," a reference to the doe-eyed heroine of Amanda's favorite film, the one she and Raffaele said they watched the night of the murder.

"Amanda's friends think she is like Amélie, because she likes the little things, like birds singing," said Bongiorno. "I agree with Amanda's friends, Amanda looks at the world through Amelia's eyes. She is spontaneous, immediate."

But Bongiorno also called Amanda "fragile and weak" and "a little bizarre and naïve," as a way to explain behavior the prosecution had called cold and uncaring—cartwheels in the police station, for instance. "She's extravagant, and unusual, full of contradictions."

Amanda's third lawyer, Maria del Grosso, took Giuliano Mignini to task for his ideas about women, their supposedly manipulative nature, their presumed power over men. She criticized the prosecution for working sex into everything, falsely portraying Amanda as a promiscuous young woman who endangered Meredith by bringing home strange men, when in fact she'd had a lover in her bedroom only once—and Meredith had been in Giacomo's room that night.

* * *

THE testimony ended with a day of rebuttals, in which the lawyers simply repeated their former arguments, with less heat and at far shorter length. Manuela Comodi played solitaire on her computer and stared at her frosted nails when she wasn't on the podium. She made a valiant attempt to prove that Raffaele couldn't possibly have called the cops before the Postal Police arrived, using long dull lists of numbers put up on a screen. But in the end, the trial of the century was like a police property room, where everyone could rummage through the contents, picking out what they needed to prove any theory. PowerPoint presentations, blood samples, telephone records—it all became a blur.

Meanwhile, the reporters noticed that as the trial wound down, Amanda looked more and more upset, but also more pulled together in appearance. She wore her hair up in a French braid and showed up each day in a green wool jacket over a pretty blouse and slacks.

"She's dressing now as she should have dressed in the beginning," said Richard Owen of the *Times*.

The last day of court, Raffaele Sollecito faced the judges and jurors. Looking fragile in a white turtleneck and khaki pants, he nevertheless rose from his chair and spoke to them in a soft, firm voice, pleading his case. As Frank Sfarzo wrote on Perugia Shock:

> Raffaele, with big emotion, took the stand, he maintained his innocence, he even defended his image. Me, dependent on Amanda? Me, on the leash? If someone asks me to do something and I don't want to do it I say no. Imagine if they told me to kill a girl, said the Puglian boy, adding that he would never do it. As for Amanda killing Meredith over complaints about impure hygiene, he called it "an absurd story."

Amanda also spoke to the court in Italian. Her voice shook so badly that the judge interrupted her, asking if she wanted to switch to English. She said no. "In these situations, I breathe and try to find the positive," she said.

Then she rambled, saying that people had been asking her how she could stay so calm, that in her situation they would have torn their hair out or destroyed the jail cell, but Amanda insisted that she didn't feel calm; she felt scared, especially of being labeled something she was not. "I am afraid to have the mask of a murderer forced upon my skin."

"Now the decision will be made," she told the court. "In front of you I feel vulnerable."

She thanked her friends and family for support, her lawyers, and, bizarrely, even the prosecutors, "for doing their jobs, even if they don't understand. They are trying to bring justice to a person who has been taken from the world."

Then she put her head down and rushed out of the courtroom, accompanied by two guards.

"She had tears running down her face," said her sister Deanna Knox, who'd mouthed "I love you" as Amanda walked by. "I knew she was horribly upset. She doesn't like it, sitting there and hearing terrible things about herself. She keeps it all inside, but I can tell."

Caroline Kelly, a tall American college student with long hair parted down the middle, was staring at Deanna, who was visibly shaking.

"I'm trying to send a nod of encouragement to her," said Caroline. She and another girl named Caroline Doyle, a small blonde who was also hoping to give Amanda's family some encouragement, had come to court with a small group of American female students from the American-run Umbra Institute, which had only about eighty students enrolled in Perugia that fall.

They were very different from the other American college students who had shown up occasionally during the trial. The girls who'd come earlier, especially, had been proud to say that they didn't empathize with Amanda, even though they were the same age and nationality. Maybe she did it, they said, we don't know. They refused to identify with her. They were not like that.

"That's because everyone thought Amanda did it," said Caroline Doyle, when asked why the American students had been so unsympathetic. The other Caroline, the small blonde, said she was writing a paper on the case and had gradually become convinced of the UW student's innocence. "The proof isn't there. There's no way you can look at the facts and come to any other conclusion."

Prosecutor Giuliano Mignini hurriedly left the room, right after Amanda. Delaney Knox, Amanda's eleven-year-old sister, was standing on the other side of the bronze door when he came through it and went down the hall.

He was crying, she said.

The next day, Mignini let it be known that he had *not* wept after seeing Amanda Knox plead for her freedom. Absolutely not, he insisted, it wasn't true. He'd merely felt hot and gone into the bathroom to dab water on his face. That accounted for the moisture, he said.

If Mignini wept for Amanda, then he must have cried crocodile tears. He and Manuela Comodi ended the prosecution case that same day. They asked the court for the highest possible penalty, life imprisonment, based on counts of murder and sexual violence. Life meant thirty years, the same sentence given to Rudy Guede, but Mignini felt Amanda deserved more. He also wanted the twenty-two-year-old American to endure nine months of solitary confinement.

Oggi magazine saw Mignini's final argument as high performance art:

A little Mr. Hyde and a little Dr. Jekyll, Giuliano Mignini is a character sometimes disturbing, sometimes very pleasant. A good conversationalist, a man of great culture, fond of jokes, good Umbrian cuisine and beautiful things in general, he is what is known as a "nice guy." [But] in the courtroom, with his gown over his shoulders, before the bench, his features almost change, his words become stones thrown with violence. His toughness borders on fury: "Amanda is a witch. She hated Meredith, prissy, as she hated anyone who wanted to steal her limelight. When she killed, she was a compressed spring ready to explode," he said with a voice vibrating with disdain. "The lawyer takes over from the man [in me]," he explains. Therefore, he did not consider life imprisonment sufficient, and also asked for solitary confinement.

* * *

THE jury deliberated for twelve hours the next day. It was just after midnight when they announced their decision on December 4, 2009. Reporters had to fight through the darkness while throngs of young people created a mob scene around the front door. Even the families of the suspects had to fight their way in, with the Knoxes being forced to go around the building and find a back entrance.

It was packed, hot, and dark in the courtroom, and the air seemed to give off sparks. So many people had crowded in that it was difficult to see all the jurors.

Amanda was the easiest to spot, because she wore the bright green jacket. As Judge Massei announced the verdict, her shoulders slumped. She leaned against her attorney and sobbed, "No, no." Raffaele's stepmother screamed and screamed, shouting "*Forza!*" strength. He didn't react; he was numb, disbelieving, he later said. The Knox women started to sob.

"Condemned!" Frank Sfarzo said, shaking his head. "How can you condemn somebody without proof? There's no proof."

It was startling to see the one juror, the silver-haired man who was always asleep, up on his feet, staring in Amanda's direction, alert for once. Judge Massei never looked up. He kept reading in an expressionless way, in hypnotic rhythm, like a Gregorian chant.

Amanda, central to the crime, got twenty-six years, Raffaele twenty-five, for murder and sexual assault. They were convicted of every charge except theft, which the court hadn't been able to pin on Rudy Guede either. The pair was also told to pay a total of $7.4 million to the Kercher family. Amanda, in addition, had to pay $60,000 to Patrick Lumumba.

Raffaele stayed stoic. Amanda continued to lean against her lawyer and sob. "No, no," she said. Deanna Knox burst into tears. So did other women, like Raffaele's stepmother.

"We bought her a plane ticket, do you understand? She was going to come home with us," Cassandra Knox said in the courtroom, after Judge Massei finished reading the verdict in a monotone. "Don't ask me what I think of it. You don't want to know. Devastated, is that the right word? I can think of a lot stronger words, but I don't want to say them."

"There will be an appeal," a British journalist told her. "She has a good chance of getting out."

"An appeal, are you kidding?" Cassandra said. "Here in Perugia? It will be the same thing all over again. They're never going to give her a chance."

Then, as quickly as it began, the drama was over. Guards rushed the defendants out of the courtroom, their family members hurrying behind, although they could only shout out "I love you." They weren't allowed to speak to the convicted murderers.

On the other side of the door stood brown-haired Rita Ficarra and Lorena Zugarini, the two officers who'd interrogated Amanda all night on November 5/6, 2007.

"In for the kill," as one reporter put it.

The Kerchers waited there, too, in that little antechamber. As Frank Sfarzo wrote shortly after he left the courtroom that painful night:

> It was their revenge on those they think killed their angel: looking at them in the moment of their desperation, while they were being brought to jail, now officially murderers. The moment long awaited, since the day the Kerchers must have asked their lawyer, Did they really do it? And he must have answered, Yes.
>
> Revenge past the door, satisfaction in the courtroom too, with Mignini seeming to enjoy the view of the relatives. Piety takes possession of the proceedings, while Amanda and Raffaele disappear in the darkness.

OUTSIDE, an actual merry-go-round had been set up, for some unrelated celebration, adding to the carnival atmosphere. Italian students, with beers in their hands, hovered by the TV vans, watching reporters do their setups. Silver Christmas tree lights glowed over the alleyways all across town.

A much larger group of young Italians had gathered on the cobblestones slightly uphill from the courthouse and right outside Bubble. They applauded the verdict, bursting into cheers. They watched Curt Knox fight his way out of the courthouse, pulling his little blond daughters through the crowd.

"Assassin! Assassin!" shouted a drunk.

Curt picked up his pace. Photographers chased him and the girls across the Corso, all the way to the Brufani Hotel on Piazza l'Italia, past which Perugia ends in a steep cliff that drops down into the valley.

Inside the posh Brufani, the rest of the family had gathered. All of the women were crying. Curt Knox and Chris Mellas drove the others back to their apartments outside town and dropped them off, but the men found themselves restless, unable to sleep. So they returned to the Brufani, where ABC and other networks had set up their cameras. Chris and Curt gave countless interviews, tapping into TV networks all over the world, staying in the hotel until dawn.

News reports were beamed back to Seattle, where DJ Johnsrud and other friends of Amanda had gathered around a TV in her grandmother's house. When the verdict hit the airwaves, they covered their faces, sobbed, or shook their heads in disbelief. Later, they said they felt shock, nausea, disbelief.

Madison Paxton told the *Today* show that she was stunned, because she'd believed the court would make its decision based on the forensic evidence, not on psychoanalysis of Amanda's character, especially her so-called "promiscuity."

"Whether she's had no sex or a lot of sex is completely irrelevant. It's basically a witch hunt, where they're taking this woman—and she's a young educated woman having sex—and it's, oh, my goodness, that better not be my daughter doing this, so we're going to make an example of her."

Curt Knox and Edda Mellas released a statement saying, "While we always knew this was a possibility, we find it difficult to accept this verdict when we know that she is innocent.

"The prosecution has failed to explain why there is no evidence of Amanda in the room where Meredith was so horribly and tragically murdered."

They blamed the press: "It appears clear to us that the

attacks on Amanda's character in much of the media and by the prosecution had a significant impact on the judges and jurors and apparently overshadowed the lack of evidence in the prosecution's case against her."

PHOTOGRAPHERS had captured one last iconic image of Amanda Knox that dark December night. She was being held in a police van outside the courthouse, waiting for guards to take her inside, where a black-robed judge would read her fate. The camera caught her in that last moment of innocence. An American college student, gazing through the barred window of an Italian police van, before she knew the verdict would go against her, before she heard the word "condemned."

Amanda had a sweet face, dominated by powerful blue eyes. It was the kind of face upon which many stories could be written.

That was her fate.

BUYERS' REMORSE, WORLDWIDE

December 2009

"They convicted 'Foxy Knoxy.' That's not Amanda."
—Madison Paxton to the Associated Press

"I should be trusting, but it is very difficult. My world collapsed around me with that verdict. It collapsed around me and Amanda."
—Raffaele Sollecito to *Il Messaggero*

PRISON guards, carrying bronze keys on a big ring, locked Amanda and Raffaele into their cells. Then they put them on suicide watch. The Italian boy vanished into a world of his own, frightened, confused, and fragile. In the days leading up to the verdict, he'd expressed a longing to be anonymous. He said if police had caught Rudy Guede before he'd fled to Germany, then the world never would have heard of Amanda Knox or Raffaele Sollecito.

Amanda felt "horrendous" after the verdict, but her cellmates waited up for her, gave her warm milk, and sat with her while she sobbed through the night.

"*Non fare cosi, Bambi*," a prison official reportedly said to her. Don't carry on like that. Reverend Saulo Scarabattoli told reporters that the Seattle girl had maintained a positive attitude throughout the trial, but as the verdict neared, she'd acted like a person awaiting the axe. Still, she'd never wavered on one point: She was innocent.

"I believe she had nothing to do with what happened but what went on that day, I really don't know," he said, adding that he'd met Amanda in prison two years before "and I can tell you that she is not a witch."

The morning after the verdict, prison guards allowed the Knox family a quick visit with Amanda. Afterward, Edda, Curt, and Amanda's three sisters faced the TV cameras in the Capanne parking lot, looking chilled and exhausted. Ashley and Delaney clung to Deanna, the older sister, a tall girl in a black down jacket who had dropped out of college because she was having trouble coping with her sister's incarceration. Even before the closing arguments began, Deanna said her hair had starting falling out.

Amanda, the oldest sister, was the only one missing from the picture frame. The Knoxes had planned to celebrate her release by taking a photo of the four girls together. They'd wanted to bring Amanda back to the United States for Christmas, everybody on the same plane flight, sitting side by side. They'd all tried to believe in that fantasy during the trial, with varying degrees of success.

"You bet there's going to be an appeal," Curt now told the reporters. Indeed, appeals were automatic in the Italian court system. If Amanda failed to win that first appeal, then she could take her case to the Supreme Court of Italy, the highest in the land.

"We told our daughter to be strong," Edda said, wrapping her bright blue coat around her. "We said, 'Don't give up. It's just going to take a little longer, but you're going to get out of here.'"

She and Curt praised the guards for helping their daughter deal with the verdict. Edda insisted that many people at the prison thought Amanda was innocent, hence the nickname "Bambi."

Before an appeal could be launched, the Knoxes would need to wait for the judge's report, due to come about three months later, which would outline the reasoning behind the verdict.

In the meantime, American journalist Judy Bacharach—a contributing editor for *Vanity Fair* who'd written one of the first Amanda Knox stories—was cautiously optimistic. "There is a possibility if Italy is ashamed enough, she might win on appeal, but it will take a lot of influence and a lot of clout, a lot of work, I'm afraid," she told *Good Morning America*. She also said several jurors had decided to vote guilty—two weeks before the verdict. Other reporters had talked to a juror who'd complained about how hard it was for the jurors to have the defendants in front of them all those months, "knowing what had been done to Meredith."

In fact, it turned out the jurors had considered only two options: life imprisonment (thirty years) or a lesser sentence that took into account the young age of the defendants.

An unnamed juror told ABC News that even that was "an agonizing decision" and that they'd all had trouble sleeping the night before. This juror had then provided a new standard for "beyond a reasonable doubt": "It's possible."

"It is hard to envision Knox doing this. But it is possible. We can all drink too much, then get into a car and drive."

That statement stunned a Seattle lawyer: "The fallacy is that driving is something that you do on a normal basis and, sure, it's dangerous while you're drunk. You might hurt somebody. But you would never kill anybody, even while drunk, unless you are a depraved person."

And who'd said the suspects were drunk? Only Mignini, tossing in that new unsubstantiated charge during the final arguments. Jovanna Popovic had talked to Amanda at 8:45 P.M., not long before Meredith was attacked, and she'd been polite, rational, and willing to have Raffaele drive Jovanna to the bus station if she so desired at midnight.

Amanda's friend Madison Paxton also told CNN that she saw jurors sleeping every day that she went to trial. "The prosecutor sleeps. The juries sleep. I have seen people on the podium, the president [Judge Massei] even, answering his cell phone while the trial is going on. But every time the prosecutor spoke, the jury was wide awake."

Douglas Preston, also on CNN, asked what had happened to recordings that could clear up many questions about Amanda's "confession." Police had bugged private conversations between Amanda and Raffaele at the station, even when they were talking about where to order out for pizza. Why wouldn't they have taped her questioning?

"The police first claimed that they had lost the videotape or the audiotape of the interrogation," he said, "then they claimed that they never made one to begin with. And then they claimed that they don't even have a transcript of this interrogation."

Prosecutors Giuliano Mignini and Manuela Comodi, meanwhile, celebrated the verdict, regretting only that the defendants didn't get life sentences.

Mignini himself, however, still faced possible prison time as a result of his abuse of office trial in Florence. Now dubbed the "Foxy Knoxy prosecutor" by the *Daily Mail*, he would learn his own fate on January 22, 2010, when he was not only convicted but also received a sixteen-month suspended sentence. He said he was surprised by the verdict. "My conscience is clear, I know I did nothing wrong."

THE morning after the Knox-Sollecito verdict, a worldwide backlash began, kicked off by a fiery statement from Maria Cantwell, a senator from Washington State, home of the Knox/Mellas families.

"I am saddened by the verdict and I have serious questions about the Italian justice system and whether anti-Americanism tainted this trial," she wrote. "The prosecution did not present enough evidence for an impartial jury to conclude beyond a reasonable doubt that Ms. Knox was guilty. Italian jurors were not sequestered and were allowed to view highly negative news coverage about Ms. Knox. Other flaws in the Italian justice system on display in this case included the harsh treatment of Ms. Knox following her arrest; negligent handling of evidence by investigators; and pending charges of misconduct against one of the prosecutors stemming from another murder trial."

Cantwell had already taken her concerns to Secretary of State Hillary Clinton, who said on national television that she was busy with a crisis in the Afghan war, but would be happy to listen to anyone who had information on the matter. Highly placed Italian officials complained of interference, echoing the very anti-Americanism of which Cantwell had complained. How many times had Italian judges said that Amanda couldn't have house arrest, that she couldn't be trusted to stay in Italy, because she was American? Raffaele could not be let out either, because his American girl could "easily free him." Guantánamo Bay, which came up every time Amanda testified to being hit, once again floated through the coverage—its connection to the brutal slashing of Meredith Kercher as tenuous as ever. One Italian official said he was surprised that Americans had time for Perugia, when the detention center at Guantánamo was still open. Douglas Preston and other insiders blamed the verdict on *la faccia*, the need for Italian leaders to look good in the eyes of their citizens.

The backlash wasn't hard to pin down. Where was the unassailable proof that the prosecutor had been promising for two years? He hadn't even nailed down a motive, resorting to "poor hygiene" in the end. As *Il Messaggero* pointed out, women don't kill over messy bathrooms. Crime reporter Meo Ponte of *La Repubblica*, puffing on an unlit pipe in court, had complained about the trial's sideshow ambience ever since the English girls testified. That's your motive, he'd asked, housework? Toilet flushing? Now he was "somewhat surprised" at the verdict because of the inconsistency. Thirty years for Rudy Guede; only twenty-six for Amanda Knox, supposedly the stabber?

"It is like Pontius Pilate washing his hands," Meo told *Time* magazine.

Mignini spoke of Amanda's supposed hatred for Meredith, but those who actually lived with the two girls had never seen a moment of tension between them, nor heard Amanda utter a word of complaint about anything.

"*Tranquilla*," the flatmates had called the relationship between the two foreign girls. "*Normale*." And they were testifying for the prosecution.

Mignini had wrapped up his case by asking the court to imagine a quarrel between the two girls, putting his words into Amanda's mouth. When had the American ever called Meredith "prissy" or "a little saint"? When had the gracious Meredith ever presented herself in such a smug, unappealing way?

Amanda had also helped herself considerably by testifying for two days, producing TV footage available to anybody on the Web. Viewers saw a typical-looking American college student, bright, self-confident. She never lost her temper, despite considerable prodding from Mignini, Pacelli, and Maresca. She neither cried nor went into hysterics. She seemed plausible. In fact, she looked like the girl next door, which was Mignini's first impression of her, before he visualized group sex.

Yet everything paled beside the discovery that the DNA results weren't reliable. When the top-flight American scientists had examined the LCN DNA testing for the knife and bra clasp, they'd cast great doubt on the results, released a letter of protest, and watched it pop up all over the Internet. The Kercher jurors could even have read it, had they been so inclined.

Frank Sfarzo had studied the black mood in the courtroom while Judge Massei read the verdict. Where was the jubilation on the part of the jurors, he wondered, the pride in justice done? Judge Massei never glanced up from his papers; the other judge never gazed at him. The jurors just stood there. Curt Knox made a point of looking at each of them, individually, but none met his eyes. As Sfarzo wrote on Perugia Shock directly afterward:

> Suddenly people realized there wasn't any motive. There wasn't any blood on "The Knife," there was no trace of Amanda and Raffaele in Meredith's room. That drama played out in the courtroom, that's where people suddenly understood that there was no proof, no way to convict Amanda and Raffaele, that we can't be certain beyond a reasonable doubt. Call it buyer's remorse, worldwide.

ONLY a few reporters showed up for Patrick Lumumba's press conference the day after the verdict, while the Kerchers drew a standing-room-only crowd in the hotel hearing room where they'd first met the press on November 6, 2007. Then Stephanie had worn her black hair in a short bob, falling over one eye, but now it reached her shoulders, a reminder of how much time had passed since her sister's murder. She entered the room first, accompanied by her father, John, and brothers Lyle and John Jr. Then Arline straggled in, looking exhausted, her flushed face overshadowed by big thick glasses. She'd been confined to bed, getting up only long enough for the press conference, it turned out.

The Kerchers exhibited their usual grace, patiently enduring the constant background noise and intrusion of the video cameras. Francesco Maresca, their lawyer, sat to the far right of the rectangular table, beaming as he started things off. He didn't seem to realize that he faced a changed world. This was nothing like the mood among the reporters after the conviction of Rudy Guede. Investigators held "grave evidence" against Rudy, as the Supreme Court of Italy had said in 2008.

So when Maresca once again praised the Kerchers for the "elegance of silence," it felt like a silencing technique. Certainly, a case could be made for reasonable doubt. And it wasn't as if the prosecution had been classy.

"There's a girl killed and they fantasize about orgies," Amanda's Perugiano lawyer Luciano Ghirga had complained during his heated closing argument. "They should be ashamed of that. They should be ashamed to have asked Giacomo Silenzi about the sex. We refused to disrespect Meredith; we refused to ask about sex; we didn't even bring in the statements he'd made about it."

Moreover, the press had spent two years in close contact with the Knox/Mellas and Sollecito families. Whether the children were guilty or not, many reporters had found it hard to listen to the parents' reactions while Judge Massei read the verdict in a monotone. Now two British reporters stood up at the press conference and asked the Kerchers if they really thought the two college students killed Meredith, and whether it worried them when their lawyer basically mimicked everything the prosecution said.

Stephanie wouldn't say. She held back. So did her father, but it was hard to miss his tight little smile, because reporters had never seen him smile before. Lyle and John Jr. tossed a ball back and forth. The thing was, they insisted, you had to trust your lawyer.

Arline had the final word that day. "You have to go by the evidence; there's nothing else."

Later, she would blame the murder on "Amanda's excesses" and John Kercher would tell the *Daily Mail* that charges of anti-Americanism were "ludicrous." "I believe the verdict was based entirely on the evidence," he said.

"I have to accept many things that I do not accept and I do not think are fair," Amanda said, when a delegation of Italian politicians visited her in prison within weeks of her condemnation. She added that she felt sad and frightened at the thought of spending twenty-six years behind bars.

The visitors found her in a new jail cell, about ten feet square, that she shared with a fifty-one-year-old prisoner, also American. Some reporters would linger over the fact that this cell had its own bathroom, complete with a toilet and bidet, as if it were a luxury spa room at the Brufani Hotel. Others noted that Amanda was locked in twenty-three hours a day, that she saw visitors for only a few hours a week, and that she was doing her best to stay busy, working in the prison laundry and exploring the library's selection of English books. She was also writing poetry and continuing with her UW courses.

"I was certain that the verdict would put an end to a nightmare; instead, it didn't," Raffaele said in a prison interview with *Il Messaggero*, given through his lawyer. He, too, planned to appeal the verdict. "When the sentencing was read, I didn't understand what was happening and even now it seems impossible and I still don't understand why I was convicted." He said Amanda was a "very sweet girl," incapable of murder, and even though he was no longer in love with her, he still felt close.

"She is also in a nightmare and a harrowing situation like mine."

Meanwhile, Rudy Guede's thirty-year prison sentence was nearly cut in half on appeal. On December 22, 2009, his lawyers argued, successfully, that it didn't make sense for him to get life imprisonment, when his alleged co-conspirators got less. Rudy said he wasn't happy about the reduction "because I'm not guilty," and his lawyers vowed to appeal to the Supreme Court for a full acquittal.

AS for what the locals thought of the trial of the century, some saw Mignini as a beleaguered visionary, and they pointed to the DNA evidence as proof of certain guilt. Others said the prosecutor was a strange man, not a typical Perugino, and that he'd helped police make a mess of things. It was a disgrace, they said, and nobody knew how to put it right.

"We are tired of *parlare, parlare, parlare*," a local named "Marilla" insisted the morning after the verdict, complaining of the talk, talk, talk of the lawyers, the print reporters with their tiny tape recorders, the TV anchors setting up in the Brufani, the armchair detectives on Italian television, and the shrill voices raised on the Internet, calling for blood.

Even the bar chatter . . . it was all too much.

"Marilla" wasn't about to give her theory of the crime. Nor would she stone the convicted couple. What she wanted was for every single journalist to shut up and go home.

"We are not stupid here in Perugia. We already know what we think about this matter."

The hilltop town's cozy sister-city relationship with Seattle took a blow on January 1, 2010, when officials there scrapped the name "Perugia" for a new park, citing local outrage over the Amanda Knox verdict. Perugia's mayor, Wladimiro Boccali, didn't help matters by insisting the UW honor student had received perfect treatment, but he vowed to repair Perugia's new and probably temporary rift with the Emerald City.

FRANK Sfarzo had been pretty certain that Amanda and Raffaele were mixed up in murder when he began covering the Meredith mystery on Perugia Shock. Then Patrick, their supposed co-conspirator, turned out to be innocent. Police found Rudy Guede's DNA everywhere. Giuliano Mignini never altered his crime theory, simply subbing in Rudy for Patrick and assigning the same motives and certainties to this much younger and entirely different suspect. Maybe, just maybe, Sfarzo thought, no orgy took place that night. Eventually, he was able to study the experts' reports, pore over the interrogation documents, evaluate the autopsy results, view the crime scene video, and finally hear witnesses speak in open court. Where he'd hoped to find concrete evidence, he discovered only speculation.

"A conviction with no proof: that is the darkness of the

mind," he said after the verdict. "Twenty-six years in a cell: that is the horror. When you are innocent: that is the nightmare."

But Frank Sfarzo believed the two college students would be freed upon their first appeal "or in the worst hypothesis, the penalty would be reduced to about fifteen years and then the Supreme Court will cancel the conviction. And everything will end up with a toast of *tarallucci e vino*, as always.

"*Tarallucci e vino* [cookies and wine], that's the expression we use when there is an insolvable problem, when an irremediable conflict suddenly ends up with a good laugh, and everyone goes home as it nothing had ever happened."

Not even in the beautiful Umbrian hills could a murder mystery reach a happy ending. But one could still raise a glass to the dead.

"On December 28th we will celebrate Meredith's birthday just as we did in 2008," Stephanie Kercher told reporters. "We will toast to Mez."

AMANDA AND RAFFAELE FIGHT FOR FREEDOM

December 5, 2009–October 4, 2011

"I am not the person they say I am—the perversion, the violence, the disrespect for life and for people. I've always been the same. And I did not do what they said I did. I did not kill, I did not rape, I did not steal. I was not there. I was not present at this crime."

—Amanda Knox

"I never hurt anyone, never in my whole life. [My arrest] was so outlandish that I thought it would disappear, that at least in a month it would all get clarified, but this didn't happen. And so I had to endure, go on living day by day—and I've been living a nightmare."

—Raffaele Sollecito

WHEN Amanda Knox's mother, Edda Mellas, stood outside the concrete walls of Capanne Prison the morning after the verdict on December 5, 2009, and predicted that her young daughter's conviction would not hold, the Seattle math teacher seemed crazily optimistic. Who knew how the dice would roll in the next phase?

Nearly a year went by before the appeal trial began. For Amanda Knox and Raffaele Sollecito, time crawled on the calendar.

"Every day in jail, at the end of every day, is already a death," Raffaele said, although he continued his computer studies and still dreamed of working in the video game industry. He fantasized about sleeping in his father's house and strolling with friends along the Adriatic Sea.

Amanda likewise longed to walk on green grass, to climb mountains, and see the evening stars. She found jail time "frustrating and mentally exhausting," but tried to keep to a schedule, rising early and doing yoga, answering mail, studying, painting, listening to music, reading, and attending Mass. No matter how mundane her activities, though, the press continued to report on them—she created worldwide headlines in June 2010 when she debuted a cropped haircut.

Both Amanda and Raffaele also wrote warmhearted letters to an ever-growing army of supporters, many of whom had legal and scientific degrees and were appalled by the scanty evidence used to convict the two students. Prosecutor Mignini complained that these unpaid supporters, who waged war on Facebook and sites like Injustice in Perugia and Friends of Amanda, were part of a million-dollar public relations campaign. No such thing existed. The only P.R. campaign came from the tiny office of Gogerty Marriott Inc. in Seattle, hired after tabloids demonized Amanda.

Amanda's and Raffaele's families filed appeals documents and shored up morale for their children, who were more fragile, sad, and terrified than the press had been told. Penned up in their respective jail cells—Amanda in Capanne, Raffaele in Terni Prison—the former lovers were spared much of the media wars raging outside.

"Amanda doesn't know about the craziness," said her sister Deanna Knox. "She has no idea." Deanna said she got dirty looks or worse from some people who recognized her from television. But other Italians would offer encouraging words and express belief in Amanda's innocence. *Gente* and *Oggi*, two of Italy's largest magazines, published long investigative pieces that zoned in on Rudy Guede as the lone killer.

Amanda's stepfather, Chris Mellas, moved to Perugia after the verdict so Amanda would never be alone on visiting days. Locals would often see him in the town center, wearing a fleece jacket, jeans, and a baseball cap. He also cooked meals, such as tacos, for Amanda, and delivered them during visiting hours.

Even Amanda's friend Madison Paxton moved to Perugia for the appeal, braving the many prison checkpoints to visit Amanda. The two still dreamed of one day sharing an apartment and finishing college together at the U.W., and Madison encouraged Amanda to speak up for herself at the appeal, to let jurors see who she really was.

"A trial is supposed to be about the evidence," Madison told the press. "She's not supposed to have to prove her innocence. . . . If you're in that defendant chair, then you're guilty until you can prove you're innocent."

AMANDA found little peace in the run-up to her appeal. Not only were her parents ordered to stand trial for slander after telling the *Times* of London that she'd been hit during her lawyer-less interrogation, but local police also filed a slander suit against Amanda, because she'd said they'd pressured her to name Patrick Lumumba. Twelve officers signed on to the suit, revealing just how many cops had tag-teamed the Seattle girl that night in 2007.

The Knox family also filed a lawsuit of their own against Lifetime Television for airing *Amanda Knox: Murder On Trial In Italy,* a steamy docudrama starring Hayden Panettiere as the U.W. honor student. Amanda's lawyers said the film caused their client "irreversible damage."

"I'm devastated by this invasion into my life and the way I'm being exploited," Amanda said. "I consider it the pinnacle of the repeated violations by the media against my person, my personality, and my story."

In Perugia, covering the case had become more difficult. The prestigious Committee to Protect Journalists (CPJ) posted an open letter, outlining prosecutor Mignini's attempts to muzzle the press in the Monster of Florence and Amanda Knox cases. CPJ reported that blogger Frank Sfarzo of Perugia Shock, the only Italian reporter who covered the hearings in English, had been beaten by five local police officers. Mignini also accused Sfarzo of "defamation by blog" and got Google to shut it down (though U.S. fans immediately rebuilt it).

* * *

THE appeal trial began on a chilly morning in late 2010. That day, November 24, Raffaele and Amanda faced two judges and six jurors in the jewel-like courtroom in the Hall of Frescoes. More than four hundred reporters showed up throughout the ten-month trial, including superstars from Italy, the UK, and every major U.S. network.

This marked the first time that Amanda and Raffaele had seen each other since their conviction nearly a year earlier, although they had kept in touch by mail. The two college students looked less like children and more like adults now, especially Raffaele, who'd bulked up in prison, shed his thick Harry Potter spectacles, and chopped off his hair. Amanda looked thinner and frailer than before, but more sophisticated. Gone were the Beatles sweatshirts and blue jeans. She wore silk blouses over long flowing skirts—and seldom smiled or moved around. A deliberate strategy, her family said, knowing that her every twitch would be psychoanalyzed.

Prosecutor Giancarlo Costagliola was supposed to be in charge, but prosecutors Manuela Comodi and Giuliano Mignini had inserted themselves into the case as "technical consultants." The two students also faced the same lawyers for the civil plaintiffs—Patrick Lumumba and the Kercher family. All of these lawyers seemed allergic to Rudy Guede's name. They seldom mentioned the supposed cohort, who'd already been convicted for Meredith Kercher's murder and sexual assault. To many crime-scene experts, Meredith's bedroom told an everyday tale: A man breaks in, looking for money, credit cards, and other things that he can quickly grab. He finds a woman alone. He sexually assaults, then kills her.

Hard evidence pointed to Rudy as the sole killer, an argument the defense had been making since 2007. It was Rudy's DNA found on Meredith's jacket, on her purse, on the straps of her bra. It was Rudy's bloody shoeprint by the bed; his bloody handprint on the pillow found under Meredith's body. It was his Y chromosome found inside her.

No evidence placed Amanda at the crime scene; the only evidence tying Raffaele was the contested speck of DNA on Meredith's bra clasp, which had rusted in police custody.

Although the prosecution would continue to insist on a staged burglary theory, no proof other than the glass supposedly found atop Filomena's clothes (something no photo showed) was ever offered. Moreover, breaking in through windows armed with a knife was Rudy's M.O. The judge's report condemning Rudy listed many incidents leading up to the murder, from the bartender who said Rudy had broken into his flat through a window, flashing a knife; to Rudy's arrest in the Milan nursery school, armed with a knife; to the computer and cell phone found in Rudy's backpack, stolen from a lawyer's office via a second-story window.

Rudy Guede did come to court to accuse Amanda and Raffaele as the real killers, but offered no proof. He presented a letter of accusations, but faltered while trying to read it, and had to hand that task off to Mignini. He left court before the former lovers could refute his statements.

"THE ONLY thing we know for sure is that Meredith Kercher is dead," Judge Claudio Pratillo Hellmann, a tall, silver-haired man born in Padova, said when he opened the appeal. Lateral judge Massimo Zanetti nodded his head. The six jurors kept their faces carefully neutral.

Italian appeals are supposed to be do-overs, but reporters were astonished by Hellmann's openness. When he ruled on the case, his reasoning would replace that of the Massei Report, which the previous trial judge had issued postconviction—and which plainly showed his dismissal of forensic evidence in favor of the group sex game theory featuring three alleged conspirators never seen together.

The defense hoped that Hellmann would be more of a scientist. They made many requests, most of which he denied. Still, the few he granted proved disastrous for the prosecution.

Prosecutor Mignini's star witness, the homeless Antonio Curatola, returned to court as a convicted heroin dealer and testified that he'd observed Amanda and Raffaele near the crime scene on Halloween—not on the night of the murder. He ranted about having seen students dressed as witches, and disco buses that didn't run on November 1. Hellmann ordered Curatola to leave the stand after he admitted that he'd been high on heroin both nights but insisted that it was not "a hallucinogen."

Most important, Judge Hellmann ordered independent review of the DNA on the murder weapon and bra clasp for the first time. His court-ordered forensics experts, Carla Vecchiotti and Stefano Conti of La Sapienza University, delivered a scathing report. They called the DNA "unreliable" on both objects, and listed more than fifty police errors in gathering and testing evidence. They evoked laughter when they said the speck of matter on the murder weapon—which had previously been attributed as Meredith Kercher's DNA—was probably only rye bread. They showed crime-scene footage of Italian police finding the bra clasp, handling it with dirty gloves, passing it back and forth, throwing it on the ground to photograph—and only then packing it off to the lab for testing. The police had also tossed the victim's bloody jacket into her laundry basket with other clothes.

Patrizia Stefanoni did come to court to defend her tests, unsuccessfully. She revealed that she'd inserted key evidence into plastic bags, not paper envelopes, and had stored evidence in the packed freezer shared by all four cottage roommates.

DESPITE these forensic victories, on October 3, 2011, the last day of the appeal, Raffaele Sollecito's and Amanda Knox's supporters were still afraid to hope, though Amanda's family had again bought her a plane ticket, praying that she would use it this time.

Without a murder weapon, motive, or any way to place the two college students at the crime scene, the prosecution resorted to name-calling and dubious science in final arguments. Mignini once again cast himself as the victim of a supposedly massive public relations campaign by the Americans. Comodi made a valiant attempt to pin Raffaele to the squishy, half-missing footprint on the bathmat. Carlo Pacelli, Patrick Lumumba's lawyer, delivered another rant about Amanda, "a diabolical, Satanic, demonic she-devil," so over-the-top that two of the male jurors burst into laugher.

On the final day, Amanda and Raffaele both spoke. Raffaele seemed shaky, his lawyers calling for water, but

Amanda—her Italian much improved by her imprisonment—rose to eloquence.

"Meredith was killed and I have always wanted justice done for her," she said. "I do not run from the truth and have never run. I insist on the truth. I insist, after four desperate years, on my . . . on our innocence, because it is true and it deserves to be defended and acknowledged."

Both defendants expressed a simple desire: to go home. After the closing statements, the Knox family waited in a little salon at the Brufani Palace Hotel; Edda reading a book, Deanna chatting with her two younger sisters, everybody trying to keep up their spirits. Finally, they got the call that the verdict was ready, and raced back to the courtroom.

A long line of Perugia police officers made a show of force that night, and only about thirty reporters were allowed in court. Stephanie, Lyle, and Arline Kercher, in their first and only appearance in the appeal, sat at the prosecution table. Nobody spoke as the two judges and the jurors filed in and took their seats. Several of the jurors looked at Amanda, a departure from the last trial, when no one would meet her eyes.

Then the judge started reading the verdict at 9:48 P.M. "*Confirma*," he began, upheld—meaning the slander conviction against Amanda regarding Patrick Lumumba, for which Hellmann ordered her to pay legal expenses and serve a three-year sentence (a moot point, as she'd already served four).

Then came another long silence, before Hellmann said the magic word: *Freedom*. Immediate freedom, for both defendants. He cited Article 533 of the Italian criminal code, meaning that they were not freed just on insufficient evidence, but innocent of the charges. They had not committed the murder.

Wild cheering broke out in the courtroom among the defendants' families, while the Kerchers sat quietly, waiting to file out when all the happiness was over. Amanda and Raffaele were whisked away in a black sedan instead of a police van, Amanda sobbing, Raffaele reminding her that "We are free. We are free." Back at Capanne, the inmates cheered Amanda's exoneration, and after collecting her things, she was spirited away to a secret location in Rome.

*   *   *

AMANDA Knox left Italy the next day for Seattle, that mystical city of deep water and mountain light, large enough to fit Perugia into a single neighborhood. The Emerald City welcomed her back joyously. Raffaele's father had already brought him home to Bari.

In the following weeks, Amanda would be chased by paparazzi, cope with TV reporters camped outside her home, and weigh lucrative book deals and interview requests. John Kercher would criticize her "cult of celebrity," while conceding she hadn't created it. The tabloids would insist that Amanda was about to get rich on Meredith's murder; unlikely, as her family had racked up more than $1 million in legal bills and had remortgaged their homes, borrowed against their credit cards, and emptied retirement accounts to pay for them.

The prosecution announced that it planned to appeal the acquittals to the Supreme Court of Italy, but legal experts called extradition a pipe dream. Meanwhile, the Knox family saw an opening to attack the slander suits still pending against Amanda and her parents. According to their lawyers, Mignini had said during closing arguments that Amanda might have been "elbowed" by police during her interrogation. If coercion were proved, then that could pave the way to have the slander suits tossed.

When Amanda's plane touched down in America, the land of the second chance, she gave a short press conference to more than a hundred reporters, her voice breaking, fighting back tears. She thanked "everybody who has believed in me." Then she took her mother's hand and leaned against her sister, Deanna.

After 1,450 days in jail, Amanda Knox was finally home.

FOR the Kerchers, the acquittals brought no relief. They gave a press conference the day after the verdict, wondering how convictions that had seemed so "certain" had been overturned. They still did not know who killed Meredith, they said. They could not accept Rudy as the lone killer. They described themselves as being back at square one.

"As a father, I have a real feeling for the Kerchers' pain," Fabio Angeletti, one of the jurors, told the *Guardian*. "But you need conclusive motives to condemn, as well as conclusive evidence. There were lots of mistakes by the forensic investigators that robbed the case of any certainty."

"I saw the faces of these two kids, and they couldn't bluff," juror Mauro Chialli told the same reporters. "They didn't bluff. My point of view is that these kids weren't guilty. They weren't there . . . What didn't convince me was that in the end, it was an accusation based on so many conjectures. 'It could have been this way; it could have been another way.' "

"We've said all along that we don't want the wrong people put away for a crime they didn't commit," said Meredith's sister, Stephanie. Her mother, Arline, added that "What happened was every parent's nightmare. Meredith was at home, in the very safest place."

Then the Kerchers slipped out of the spotlight—forced one more time to leave Perugia without their beautiful daughter Meredith.

TIMELINE

2007

End of August. Meredith Kercher arrives in Perugia. Rudy Guede booted from his adopted family.

September 10. Meredith moves into cottage.

September 20. Amanda Knox moves into cottage.

End of September. A Merlin's bartender alleges that Rudy broke into his flat through a window and tried to rob him at knife-point.

October 13. Raffaele blogs that he's "tired of the usual evenings."

October 13/14. Rudy allegedly breaks into a Perugia lawyer's office through a second-story window.

October 15. Amanda's last blog entry. Rudy meets Amanda and Meredith around this time in the boys' flat downstairs.

October 20. Giacomo Silenzi, Amanda, Meredith and Daniel de Luna go to the Red Zone.

October 25. Amanda meets Raffaele at a classical music concert.

October 27. Rudy is arrested for breaking into a Milan nursery school. He is carrying a stolen computer and cell phone from the Perugia lawyer's break-in, and a large knife taken from the nursery school.

October 31. Everybody celebrates "Crawloween."

November 1. Meredith Kercher is murdered.

November 2. Meredith's body is found. Friends and flatmates go to the *questura*.

November 3. Amanda questioned and taken to cottage.

November 4. Amanda questioned, taken to cottage, and shown knives. Coroner Luca Lalli completes autopsy and says he can't prove sexual assault.

November 5. Meredith's candlelight vigil in Perugia. Amanda and
  Raffaele at *questura*.
November 6. At 1:45 and 5:45 A.M., Amanda names Patrick Lumumba
  as Meredith's killer. Amanda, Raffaele, and Patrick arrested.
November 9. Judge Claudia Matteini rules that the three suspects
  can be held for a year.
November 15. Police announce new murder weapon, allegedly with
  Meredith's DNA on tip and Amanda's DNA on handle. It tests
  negatively for blood.
November 19. Rudy identified as the "fourth man."
November 20. Rudy arrested in Mainz. Patrick released.
November 30. Amanda and Raffaele in court. Detentions approved.
December 6. Rudy extradited to Italy.
December 14. Meredith buried in Coulsdon, South London.
December 17. Amanda interrogated by prosecutor Giuliano Mignini.

2008

April 1. Supreme Court of Italy upholds the detentions of Rudy,
  Amanda, and Raffaele.
April 16. Three independent, court-appointment experts affirm
  Lalli autopsy report, saying they can't verify sexual assault or a
  group attack.
May 15. Rudy admits the bloody shoeprint is his in a face-to-face
  with prosecutor Mignini.
July 9. Amanda turns 21 in jail.
July 11. Prosecutor Mignini closes the investigation and asks to
  have all three suspects charged with murder, sexual assault and
  theft. For Amanda, also slander of Patrick.
August. Court takes the traditional summer break.
September 19. Pretrial hearings begin. Judge grants Rudy's request
  for an abbreviated trial.
October 28. Rudy sentenced to thirty years. Amanda and Raffaele
  charged with murder and sexual assault and sent to trial.

2009

January 16. "Trial of the Century" begins.
February 6. Prosecutors Giuliano Mignini and Manuela Comodi
  present witnesses to testify about the early stages of the

investigation, including those present when the body was discovered. Raffaele gives a statement, saying he wouldn't hurt a fly.

February 7. Cottage tenant Filomena Romanelli testifies.

February 13. Seven of Meredith Kercher's British friends testify against Amanda Knox.

February 14. Three cottage tenants testify: Laura Mezzetti, Giacomo Silenzi, Stefano Bonassi. So does the officer who took Raffaele's 112 call. Amanda shows up in a Beatles T-shirt.

February 17. Perugia Flying Squad officers testify.

March 16. State of Italy awards Patrick Lumumba 8,000 euros for false imprisonment.

May 22–23. Patrizia Stefanoni testifies about DNA evidence.

June 12–13. Amanda testifies.

June 19. Edda Mellas, Francesco Sollecito testify.

July 6. Famous forensic expert Carlo Torre says only one small knife used in crime, and there was only one assailant.

July 18. Trial suspended. Court takes a two-month vacation.

September 14. Trial resumes.

October 9. Judge Massei refuses defense request to appoint neutral experts.

November 18. Rudy Guede's appeal begins.

November 20. Prosecution closing arguments begin.

November 21. Comodi wraps up for prosecutors. They ask for life imprisonment for both defendants, plus nine months of solitary confinement for Knox.

November 27. Civil plaintiffs present case.

November 30. Raffaele's lawyers finish their arguments.

December 1. Amanda's lawyer Carlo Dalla Vedova gives summation for the defense.

December 2. Amanda's other lawyers, Luciano Ghirga and Maria del Grosso, give summations.

December 3. Rebuttals, prosecution and defense.

December 4. Verdict. Amanda Knox and Raffaele Sollecito are convicted of murder and sexual assault, but absolved of theft. She gets twenty-six years in prison; he gets twenty-five. She's also convicted of slandering Patrick.

December 22. Second day of Rudy Guede's appeal. A judge reduces his sentence from thirty to sixteen years.

2010

January 22. Prosecutor Giuliano Mignini convicted of abuse of office and given a sixteen-month suspended sentence for his role in the Monster of Florence investigation.

March 4. The Massei Report released, expressing judge's motivations for Amanda and Raffaele's convictions.

November 8. An Italian court orders Amanda to stand trial for slandering police officers.

November 24. Amanda Knox and Raffaele Sollecito's appeal begins.

December 16. Rudy Guede's conviction upheld by Italian Supreme Court.

December 18. Judge Pratillo Hellmann orders independent review of DNA used to convict Amanda and Raffaele.

2011

February 11. Lifetime Movie *Amanda Knox: Murder on Trial in Italy* airs and Knox family announces intention to sue.

February 24. Curt Knox and Edda Mellas charged with slander for saying to the *Sunday Times* that the police hit Amanda.

March 11. Giuliano Mignini accuses Frank Sfarzo of "defamation by blogging" and gets Google to shut down Perugia Shock. Committee to Protect Journalists protests.

March 25. Leaked court report shows experts have rejected DNA on knife and bra clasp as "insufficient to convict."

March 28. Superstar prosecution witness Antonio Curatola's claim to have seen Amanda and Raffaele at murder scene is destroyed in court.

May 17. Amanda in court on slander charges for seventeen minutes. Adjourned to November 15, 2011.

June 27. Rudy Guede comes to court and presents a letter, which he cannot read himself, blaming the murder on Amanda and Raffaele.

June 29. Independent court-ordered forensics experts Carla Vecchiotti and Stefano Conti call DNA "unreliable" and list more than fifty police errors in gathering and testing evidence.

July 4. Edda Mellas and Curt Knox's slander trial begins, as does Amanda's lawyers' defamation lawsuit against Lifetime.

July 25. Vecchiotti and Conti testify that they found no blood or
    trace of Meredith Kercher's DNA on alleged murder weapon.
    Bra clasp has DNA from at least four people, probably from
    contamination.

September 23–29. Closing arguments.

October 3. Verdict. Meredith's family makes their only appearance
    in appeals court. After ten hours of deliberation, Amanda Knox
    and Raffaele Sollecito acquitted, and declared innocent of
    murder charges.

October 4. Amanda returns to Seattle. Raffaele returns to Bari.
    Prosecution announces that it will appeal to Italian Supreme
    Court.

ACKNOWLEDGMENTS

I wish to thank the following: my very talented editor, Shannon Jamieson Vazquez at Berkley Books, and my hardworking agent, Andrew Stuart of the Stuart Agency; investigative journalist Frank Sfarzo, creator of the Perugia Shock blog, for his sparkling prose and good company; Douglas Preston and Mario Spezi, coauthors of *The Monster of Florence*, for their insights and quotes; the Knox/Mellas families; lawyer Anne Bremner; Zachary Nowak, author of *Peril in Perugia*; Richard Owen, correspondent for the *Times*; Daniela Querci and Elio Bertoldi, reporters for *Corriere dell'Umbria*; Italian crime reporter Roberto Fiasconaro, author of two books about the Monster of Florence; lawyers Francesco Maresca, Nicodemo Gentile, and Marco Brusco; prosecutor Giuliano Mignini; my many sources in Perugia, including Esteban Garcia Pascual, Lucy Rigby, and Pasquale "Pisco" Alessi; authors William Dietrich and Erik Larson, for encouraging me to write this book, at the Whidbey Island Writers' Conference; my longtime writing coach, Waverly Fitzgerald, for her careful eye and calm manner; the Seattleites who shared their memories of Amanda Knox, especially Madison Paxton and DJ Johnsrud; Mike and Donna James, of the Seattle-Perugia Sister City Association; producer Garfield Kennedy and the Eye Film documentary crew, for letting me hang out with them; Washington Lawyers for the Arts, for contract assistance; Dorine Kunst at the Locanda della Posta for the wireless; and my Italian teacher, Sasha Cruciani de Montoya.

I'd also like to thank Funny Cat, my Italian angel Anna, Cool Cat, Joe Bishop, Jim Lovering, Mary H. Bob, Tufa, Ferdi, Palmetto, Show Me Your Sources, Someone Who Knows, Edwardo, Dan Anthony, and others who contributed to my Let's Talk About

True Crime blog during the four stormy years it covered the Meredith mystery. Special thanks to Vanessa Sollecito, Kay Taylor, Ray Turner, Collin Tong, Linda Byron, Nina Burleigh, Mark Waterbury, Eve Applebaum-Dominick, Karen Parker Pruett, Noel Temple Dalberth, Joe Starr, David Anderson, Bruce Fisher, Patrick King, Chris Halkides, Steve Shay, Sarah Snyder, Jodie Leach, Frédéric Charles Schultz, Andrew Lowery, Dana Howard Neuts, Jason Leznek, P. Segal, Paul Smyth, Jake Holmes, Dave Piedrahita, Don Smith, Keren Brown, MaryElizabeth Williams, Susan Lange, Ron Hendry, Tim Appelo, Tom Wright, Michelle Fabio, Steve and Michelle Moore, Sisters in Crime, Michael Charles Becker, David Kamanski, Anna Gilmour, Jim and Carol Brooks, William Ryan, Daraious Billimoria, Rick Bonin, Heather Coy, and Lisa Rieger. Many thanks to my husband, son, mother, brothers, sisters, nieces, nephews, and cousins in the U.S.; my cousins in Bologna, Rome, and Calabria, who've endured my bad Italian for years; writers Amanda Castleman, Judy Witts, for your comments; Doris and Pearl, for the dinners and the fun; Grim Bjercke; and my writing buddy Nick Gallo, R.I.P.

Grazie to the people of Perugia for the espresso, truffles, gelato—and many kindnesses.

Finally, and most importantly, my profound condolences to Meredith Kercher's family: Arline, John, Stephanie, John Jr., and Lyle Kercher.

* * *

Candace Dempsey is an award-winning Italian-American journalist, true crime blogger and travel writer based in Seattle. Her blog, Let's Talk About True Crime, is hosted by the *Seattle Post-Intelligencer*. Dempsey's coverage of the Meredith Kercher case has been featured alongside the *Times* of London, the Associated Press, NBC and other giant media outlets. She appeared on CNN, CNN International, CNN *Headline News*, BBC-TV, MSNBC, *Anderson Cooper 360*, and Italian television to discuss the trial. She has decades of writing experience in newspapers, magazines, and on the Web. She has also been a magazine editor and a producer, editor, and writer for MSN. Her homepage can be found at www.candacedempsey.com and her blog at http://blog.seattlepi.com/dempsey.